THE
SUCCESSION (SCOTLAND) ACT 1964

THE SUCCESSION (SCOTLAND) ACT 1964

Fourth Edition

By

Michael C. Meston

M.A., LL.B.(Aberd.), J.D.(Chicago)

W. GREEN/Sweet & Maxwell
EDINBURGH
1993

First published	. . .	1964
Reprinted	. . .	1967
Second edition	. . .	1969
Reprinted	. . .	1976
Third edition	. . .	1982
Reprinted	. . .	1988
Fourth edition	. . .	1993

ISBN 0 414 01048 5

Typeset by LBJ Enterprises Ltd. of
Chilcompton and Aldermaston.
Printed in Great Britain

To Doris

PREFACE

Anyone who thinks that the law of succession is an unchanging backwater rapidly discovers that new problems crop up with considerable regularity even in areas which seem to have been settled for years. In addition, the importance of the subject is being recognised more widely, especially as a result of the increase in personal assets brought about by the inflation of house prices.

Major changes in the law of succession have been recommended by the Scottish Law Commission in its *Report on Succession* (Scot. Law Com. No. 124) but there is as yet no indication of whether or when the Government will find time for the necessary legislation. It seems probable that it will take several years before the changes come into force and this new edition is now necessary to take account of the multiple changes since the appearance of the last edition in 1982. The law is stated as at January 1993.

Among the important changes in the law noted in this edition there is the effect of the Age of Legal Capacity (Scotland) Act 1991, which leaves open a number of questions about its precise effect in the case of beneficiaries aged 16 to 18, and which has also created a uniform minimum age of testamentary capacity at the age of 12, instead of the previous 12 for girls and 14 for boys. The substantial progress made by the Law Reform (Parent and Child) (Scotland) Act 1986 towards abolishing the status of illegitimacy is taken into account. There is also a first attempt to analyse the consequences if the proposed reforms were to be enacted by Parliament in the form of the draft Bill attached to the Scottish Law Commission's report, but there has been no attempt at a detailed commentary, given that the Act which may eventually result will contain alterations.

The disqualification of persons who killed the deceased and the effects of the Forfeiture Act 1982 have given rise to several reported cases. There has also been some tension between the strength of the original rule (partly based on the Parricide Act 1594) and the discretionary power to "modify" it now conferred on the courts.

My thanks are due to reviewers of previous editions for their helpful comments. I am particularly grateful to Dr James Blaikie of Aberdeen University for reading the chapter on Private International Law and Mrs Evelyn Laing, Deputy Sheriff Clerk of Chancery, for her assistance. As ever, my wife has displayed great patience as the papers spread.

M. C. MESTON

Department of Private Law,
University of Aberdeen.

ADDENDUM

As this edition goes to press, it seems likely that the statutory limits on the value of prior rights will shortly be increased to

section 8(1)—House—£110,000
section 8(3)—Furniture, etc.—£15,000
section 9 —£29,000 or £48,000.

M.C.M.

PREFACE TO FIRST EDITION

The purpose of this work is to state and to explain the substantial changes in Scots law made by the Succession (Scotland) Act 1964. The main effects of the Act are in the law of intestate succession, but there are very important provisions making completely new arrangements for the property consequences of divorce and a number of provisions affecting testate succession and *inter vivos* deeds. Taken together, these changes amount to the most important reform of Scottish private law in recent years.

It is hoped that this book will provide a guide through the provisions of the Act which will be of assistance to practitioners and to students and others concerned with the law of succession. An attempt has been made to present a complete picture of the law of intestate succession in Scotland, with a new Table of Heirs and some illustrations of particular situations in the Appendices. Those parts of the previous law left in existence, *e.g.*, in the field of legal rights, are considered, albeit briefly, along with the changes made by the Act. In relation to the other topics dealt with by the Act, comment has been limited to the specific changes made. Any suggestions for improvement will be gratefully received.

Although the Act will not come into force until September 10, 1964, the text has been written as if this had already happened.

My thanks are due to my colleagues for the willingness to act as guineapigs on whom ideas could be tried out, and in particular to Professor D. M. Walker and Professor J. Bennett Miller who suggested valuable improvements.

M. C. MESTON

Faculty of Law,
University of Glasgow,
July, 1964.

CONTENTS

TABLE OF CASES

TABLE OF STATUTES

1964 Succession (Scotland) Act—*cont.*

1973 Conveyancing and Feudal Reform (Scotland) Act (c.52)

Administration of Estates Act

Succession (Scotland) Act

Prescription and Limitation (Scotland) Act (c.52)

Rent (Scotland) Act

Family Law Reform Act

1972 Presumption of Death (Scotland) Act

1978 Adoption (Scotland) Act

1980 Law Reform (Miscellaneous Provisions) (Scotland) Act

1981 Matrimonial Homes (Family Protection) (Scotland) Act

1985 Family Law (Scotland) Act

1986 Legal Capacity (Scotland) Act

Law Reform (Miscellaneous Provisions) (Scotland) Act

[illegible]

Chapter 1

INTESTATE SUCCESSION IN SCOTLAND BEFORE SEPTEMBER 10, 1964

The Succession (Scotland) Act 1964[1] came into force on September 10, 1964. It does not purport to be a code in itself, for it adopts the device of requiring succession to be regulated by the provisions of the Act and by "any enactment or rule of law in force immediately before the commencement of this Act which is not inconsistent with those provisions and which, apart from this section, would apply to that person's moveable intestate estate, if any."[2] Nonetheless, when read with the subsequent amending legislation, it does in fact state most of the law relating to intestate succession in Scotland (together with various other topics) and it was certainly the first attempt to set out intestate succession as a coherent body of rules.

Despite the passing of nearly 30 years since the Act came into force on September 10, 1964, it remains necessary to understand the previous law. This is particularly true for succession to heritage, for a very large, and apparently never-ending, series of cases still arises in which the title to land was not completed on a death prior to 1964. It seems to have been very common for a member of the family of a deceased houseowner to continue to live in the "family" house whether or not a will had been made and without any attempt to make up title. Sharply increased house values mean that disputes, and Inheritance Tax, have become significant in many estates which would previously have been too small, so that title to the house now becomes vital on the death of the occupier. The older law is necessary to guide one through possibly several generations of inheritances in order to provide a good title to a purchaser.

The system of intestate succession in Scotland prior to the passing of the Succession (Scotland) Act 1964 was one based on common law (which itself derived partly from feudal law and partly from canon law) with a succession of piecemeal amendments contained in a variety of statutes. The general principles were tolerably well known, but the exceptions and special statutory provisions were such that difficulties could be experienced in applying them to practical situations.

For example, the Intestate Moveable Succession (Scotland) Act 1855[3] gave the deceased's father in certain circumstances a right to one-half of the intestate's "moveable estate." That phrase was defined by section 9 as

[1] 1964, c. 41.
[2] s. 1 (1).
[3] 18 & 19 Vict., c. 23, s. 3.

"the whole free moveable estate on which the deceased . . . might have tested, undisposed of by will." The Intestate Husband's Estate (Scotland) Act 1911 gave to the widow of a man who died intestate and without lawful issue a prior right to the first £500 out of his estate. The deceased might clearly have tested on this £500. Thus it was difficult to establish that the £500 was meant to be deducted before the father took one-half of the balance under the 1855 Act, although that was the only sensible course. The difficulty was not resolved until the passing of the Intestate Moveable Succession (Scotland) Act 1919[4] which deemed any sums due from an intestate's estate to the surviving spouse not to be estate on which the intestate might have tested.

Similarly, when the 1855 Act first introduced the concept of representation in intestate moveable succession[5] it did so in the broad general form that "the lawful child or children of such person so predeceasing shall come in the place of such person, and the issue of any such child or children, who may in like manner have predeceased the intestate, shall come in the place of his or their parent predeceasing, and shall respectively have right to the share of the moveable estate of the intestate to which the parent of such child or children, or of such issue, if he had survived the intestate, would have been entitled." This broad assertion of the principle of infinite representation among descendants did however use the term "next of kin" to describe the person predeceasing the intestate and this use of a technical term led to the remarkable decision by the Court of Session in *Turner* v. *Couper*[6] that representation was not in fact complete among descendants, and commenced only at the nearest class of descendants in which there were any surviving members. This peculiarity still bedevils our law.

Proof of death and of survivorship

The law of succession prior to the Succession (Scotland) Act 1964 began with the usual problems of establishing that the deceased had in fact died and that potential beneficiaries had survived. Then, as now, the rules of succession depended on proof of the death of the person whose estate was being divided. In most cases this prerequisite is so obviously satisfied that it is seldom considered beyond the steps necessary to obtain a death certificate, but in cases of disappearance proof of the fact of death and of the date of death can become matters of considerable difficulty.

Actions were available, both at common law and under the Presumption of Life Limitation (Scotland) Act 1891[7] for settling the question of death and the date on which it occurred. The common law action was based on a general presumption of the law that human life, once shown to

---

[4] 9 & 10 Geo. 5, c. 61, s. 4 (1).
[5] s. 1.
[6] (1869) 8 M. 222.
[7] 54 & 55 Vict., c. 29.

have been in existence, continued until the extreme limits of human age. It was never completely clear what those limits were, but they seem to have meant that life was presumed to continue until the missing person would have been between 80 and 100 years old.[8] The effect of this was that the onus of proving an earlier date of death fell upon the persons propounding it, and if no clear evidence of earlier death could be produced, the result was that 40 or 50 years might have to elapse before the missing person's property could safely be distributed.

The statutory action under the 1891 Act solved some of the problems by introducing the seven-year rule. It came to be widely used and the result usually was that in the absence of fairly cogent evidence pointing to an earlier date of death, a missing person was presumed to have died exactly seven years after he was last known to be alive.[9] However, the Act dealt only with property, and did not affect other issues such as the continued existence of the missing person's marriage. Conversely, dissolution of marriage on the ground of presumed death under the Divorce (Scotland) Act 1938[10] had no effect on the succession to the missing person's property, and in theory it was necessary for the representatives of the missing person to raise a number of separate actions to establish death for different purposes.[11]

Closely linked with the question of establishing the death of the owner of the property in question is the problem of establishing that the beneficiary survived the date of the previous owner's death. Again this requirement is so obviously met in most cases that it is not considered, but problem situations can arise in which the issue is by no means clear. The approach taken is that unless a potential beneficiary can be affirmatively proved to have survived the deceased, he has no claim on the succession.[12] The problem which caused the greatest difficulty was that arising out of the common calamity. There was, until the passing of the 1964 Act, no presumption of survivorship in such cases. Thus if, for example, a husband and wife died intestate in a common calamity without proof that one survived the other, the result was that neither set of representatives could claim their predecessor's share of the estate of the other. The practical result was much the same as if the husband had predeceased his wife and the wife had predeceased the husband, but in fact predecease was not established either. All that was established was that neither had been *proved* to have survived the other. Thus if two

---

[8] Stair, IV, xlv, 17, nineteenthly; Bankton, *Inst.*, II, vi, 31; *Secretary of State for Scotland* v. *Sutherland*, 1944 S.C. 79.

[9] *Ibid.*, s. 3. If he reappeared, the missing person had a right to recover his property for a period of 13 years from the registration of title to it or the transfer of possession, as appropriate—ss. 6 & 7.

[10] 1 & 2 Geo. 6, c. 50.

[11] *Report on Presumption of Death* (Scot. Law Com. No. 34, 1974).

[12] "Survivance is in every case a matter of proof, and . . . when a claimant whose claim depends upon proof of survivorship is unable to establish the fact of survivance, his claim necessarily fails." *Drummond's J.F.* v. *Lord Advocate*, 1944 S.C. 298, *per* Lord President Cooper, p. 302.

persons, whether or not they were spouses, died in a common calamity leaving wills in each other's favour, neither could be proved to qualify as a beneficiary in the other's estate. Equally, however, neither could be proved to have precedeased the other, so that even if the wills provided for an alternative disposal in the event of the "predecease" of the other, the alternative could not be used either and the result would be intestacy.[13] Under section 31 of the 1964 Act this is still the case when the common calamity involves husband and wife, but there is now a presumption of survivorship for other cases.

Once these preliminary questions of death and survivance had been considered, the rules of division came into play.

Fragmentation of approach

The pattern of the 1964 Act in having several different sets of rules, with different characteristics, any or all of which might be applicable in a given case, was also evident before it. Three different sets of rules had to be considered before the precise division of a particular estate could be established. These were first, the preferable right to the first £5,000 of a deceased's estate given in certain circumstances to the surviving spouse, secondly, the legal rights of spouses and children, and thirdly, the ordinary law of intestate succession. These three sets of rules had to be considered in that order, and if all were applicable, the preferable right would first be deducted from the estate to which legal rights applied. Then the entitlement to legal rights would be applied and deducted, leaving the balance subject to the ordinary law of succession.

Statutory preference of the surviving spouse

This right was created by the Intestate Husband's Estate (Scotland) Acts 1911 to 1959.[14] Despite the title of the Acts, the right applied in favour of a husband in his wife's estate as well as vice versa. Where one spouse died intestate and without lawful issue, the surviving spouse had an absolute right to the first £5,000 of the free estate, with interest at 4 per cent. from the date of death until payment, taken rateably from heritage and moveables belonging to the intestate. If the intestate's total estate was less than £5,000, and the conditions were satisfied, the surviving spouse took the whole estate. If the deceased's intestacy was only partial, the surviving spouse had this right in the estate undisposed of but had to deduct from the £5,000 any legacy left to him or her.

Legal rights of spouses and children

As a result of the feudal relic expressed in the differentiation between heritage and moveables, these rights were divided into rights in heritage and those in moveables.

---

[13] *Ross's J.F.* v. *Martin*, 1955 S.C. (H.L.) 56.

[14] 1 & 2 Geo. 5, c. 10; 9 & 10 Geo. 5, c. 9; 3 & 4 Geo. 6, c. 42, s. 5; 7 & 8 Eliz. 2, c. 21. The figure was raised from £500 by the 1959 Act.

(1) The rights exigible from heritage existed only in favour of a surviving spouse of the deceased, and were of an income nature. A widow's right was known as terce and gave her a liferent of one-third of the heritage owned by her husband at the date of his death. (Note the important difference from the Anglo-American concept of dower which could apply to land owned by the husband at any time during the marriage.) Even after the removal of some peculiarities deriving from a rule that terce existed only in heritage in which the husband was infeft,[15] certain items of heritage were still not subject to terce, *e.g.* the principal mansion house, feuduties[16] and minerals.[17] The practical value of the right was usually negligible, being to one-third of the net income after payment of local rates, interest on heritable debt, etc. The corresponding right of a widower was known as courtesy, but it was a liferent of the whole of the heritage belonging to the wife at her death. It has been said that it was awarded to the husband more as father of an heir than as husband of an heiress, for it applied only if a live child had been born of the marriage, and that child was at some time the wife's heir.

(2) The rights exigible from moveable estate were full rights of fee, and were available to both surviving spouse and to children. There were three possible units of division, namely *jus relictae* (widow) or *jus relicti* (widower), being the surviving spouse's share; legitim, being the surviving children's share; and dead's part, which fell to be regulated by the ordinary law of intestate succession (or of which the deceased was completely free to dispose if he left a will). If there was a surviving spouse and also surviving children, the moveables were split into three for the purposes of legal rights, one share going to each of the units above. If there was a surviving spouse, but no surviving children, the moveables were split into two shares, the spouse taking one share as *jus relictae* or *relicti* as the case might be, and the other share going to dead's part. Similarly, if there were surviving children, but no surviving spouse, the children shared one-half of the moveables as legitim and the other half as dead's part. In the division of the legitim fund so arrived at, the doctrine of collation *inter liberos* was applied to preserve equality. Any child claiming legitim who had received an advance, *e.g.* for setting him up in life, could be required by other children claiming legitim to collate that advance by adding it to the legitim fund and taking his rateable share of the total fund.[18]

For the purposes of legal rights "surviving children" had to be literally interpreted. There was no representation in legitim, and thus only those of the immediate children of the deceased who survived him were entitled to it. Grandchildren could not in any circumstances represent their parents in claims for legitim, nor could they have independent claims in their own right.

---

[15] Conveyancing (Scotland) Act 1924 (14 & 15 Geo. 5, c. 27), s. 21 (4).
[16] *Nisbett* v. *Nisbett* (1835) 13 S. 517.
[17] *Grosset* v. *Grosset*, 1959 S.L.T. 334.
[18] *Coats's Trs.* v. *Coats*, 1914 S.C. 744.

The best known feature of legal rights was, as it still is, that they were indefeasible, apart from certain exceptions, and operated as a bar to capricious disinheritance by a testator. The origin of legal rights in moveables in Scotland seems to have been in a germanic system of common family ownership of property[19] and in theory a testator had no power to deal with any part of his estate other than the one-third or one-half included in the dead's part. Legal rights could of course be evaded by transactions during the deceased's own lifetime, *e.g.* by making a gift of the fee of his whole estate *inter vivos* and reserving only a liferent, which left nothing at his death on which legal rights could operate.[20]

Of more importance from the point of view of intestate succession was the fact that legal rights might be excluded, either by an express discharge granted by the party prospectively entitled,[21] or by exclusion in the deceased's ante-nuptial marriage contract.[22]

The ordinary rules of intestate succession

These rules applied to the estate left after any statutory preference and legal rights had been deducted. For historical reasons, there were entirely separate bodies of rules applying to the succession to heritage and to the succession to moveables respectively. They were similar to the extent that both employed the same general notions of propinquity in seeking heirs. Instead of using either the civil law or the canon law system of computation of degrees of relationship through a common ancestor, Scots law used (and to some extent still uses) a modified version of the parentelic system. This system employs the principle of lines of succession, so that the whole of the first line must be exhausted without finding a surviving heir before any member of the second line can take. Thus the claim of any member of the second line, however close by a system of degrees, is postponed to that of any member of the first line, however remote. Within a particular line, the order of priority is determined by the number of steps from the head of the line.

In the version employed in Scotland the first line consisted of the children and other more remote lineal descendants of the deceased. In the absence of such descendants, the succession opened to the second line, consisting of the collaterals of the deceased and their descendants. Failing successors in these categories, the succession opened to ascendants. But although both used these basic principles, intestate heritable and moveable succession were very different in detail.

A. Intestate heritable succession operated on the principle of picking out the one individual who would succeed as heir at law to all the heritage of the deceased. This was based on the necessity under the feudal system of

---

[19] J. C. Gardner, *Origin and Nature of Legal Rights in Scotland*.
[20] *Campbell* v. *Campbell's Trs.*, 1967 S.L.T (Notes) 30.
[21] *Melville's Trs.* v. *Melville's Trs.*, 1964 S.C. 105.
[22] *Panmure* v. *Crokat* (1856) 18 D. 703; *Dunbar's Trs.* v. *Dunbar* (1902) 5 F. 191; *Galloway's Trs.* v. *Galloway*, 1943 S.C. 339.

preserving the unity of landed estates so that the appropriate military services might be rendered, but in certain circumstances in which the succession opened to females, a group of females might be regarded as a collective heir and were known as "heirs portioners." The principles on which the heir at law was selected were as follows:

(1) The succession opened first to lineal descendants of the deceased.

(2) In the absence of descendants, the succession opened to collaterals of the deceased and their descendants.

(3) In the absence of descendants or collaterals, the succession opened to ascendants of the deceased. Emphasising the importance of direct blood relationship in this system, and also the feudal preference for males to perform military services, this meant that the mother and maternal relations were excluded and ascendants meant the father, whom failing the father's collaterals or their descendants, whom failing the paternal grandfather or his collaterals or their descendants, and remoter ascendants *ad infinitum* on the same principles.

(4) Preference of males applied in any given category. If there were one son and several daughters, the one son took the whole of the heritage. Only if there were no males in that category did females succeed. Thus, if the deceased left only daughters, they could inherit the heritage, but they took it as heirs portioners, which meant that they were a kind of collective heir at law. Heirs portioners shared the heritage equally, except that any indivisible items of heritage went to the eldest daughter as her *praecipuum*. The main examples were titles of honour and the principal mansion house of a landed estate with its garden and ornamental policies.

(5) Primogeniture was used as the principle to select the one male descendant of a given category to succeed as heir at law, *i.e.* the eldest son had this position. Primogeniture did not apply among collaterals, so that the selection of the one brother of the deceased (or the brother of his lineal paternal ascendant) in cases in which the succession opened to such collaterals was not carried out by primogeniture. It also did not apply to succession by females, except to the extent that items regarded as indivisible fell to the eldest heir portioner.

(6) Representation was unlimited in every degree of intestate succession to heritage (entirely different from the position in moveables). Any descendant, however remote, and whether male or female, of someone who would have been entitled to inherit if he or she had survived could stand in that ancestor's shoes. It did not matter if the whole of an intervening generation had died. Thus if the eldest son predeceased the intestate, his issue, however remote, could represent him and take in preference to the second son of the intestate. Primogeniture and preference of males operated to select the person to act as representative, but even if the representatives were a class of females, they were still preferred to the second son of the intestate. If sisters would have inherited as heirs portioners, their children took their respective shares. It did not matter if *all* the sisters had predeceased the intestate. The issue of each still took the share which their mother would have taken, and did not divide the estate *per capita* among all the grandchildren.

(7) Exclusion of the mother and all maternal relatives was complete in heritable succession. While the child was heir to its mother, the mother and anyone tracing relationship through her could *never* be the heir at law of the child.

(8) The full blood excluded the half blood in all degrees of succession. This meant that any collateral who shared both parents with the deceased took in preference to any collateral sharing only one parent with the deceased. However, if there were no collaterals of the full blood, or their issue representing them, the half blood consanguinean could inherit. This meant that collaterals sharing the same father with the deceased could inherit in these circumstances. The complete exclusion of the mother and maternal relations in heritable succession had the consequence that collaterals of the half blood uterine (sharing the same mother with the deceased) were completely excluded from the succession.

(9) The rule that heritage descends was applied in cases where the succession opened to brothers of the intestate or of his lineal paternal ascendants, but was not applied where sisters succeeded collectively. Although the intestate might have had elder brothers, the rule of descent pointed out the next younger brother to the deceased as his heir at law. Failing that brother (or his issue by representation) the next brother down the line was entitled. Failing younger brothers, or their representatives, or if the intestate was himself the youngest of three or more brothers the succession opened to the immediate elder brother in preference to the eldest.

(10) The Crown, as *ultimus haeres*, was entitled to the heritage of anyone dying intestate without other lawful heirs entitled to the succession. The Crown's interests were, and still are, represented by the Queen's and Lord Treasurer's Remembrancer, a position which is now part of the functions of the Crown Office.

The process by which the heir at law proved that he was the heir at law and obtained a judicial declaration to that effect was Service of Heirs. Until 1964 all sheriff courts had jurisdiction in services. For the continuing flow of cases in which it is necessary to obtain a service in respect of deaths prior to 1964, the process has been centralised with the Sheriff of Chancery in Edinburgh.[23]

B. Intestate moveable succession operated on the different principle that all surviving members of the class nearest in degree to the intestate should share equally in his moveables, as next of kin. This at least was the common law principle, although it was subject to various statutory modifications. The general rules of propinquity to the intestate were the same as in intestate heritable succession, but the special rules of primogeniture and preference of males applied to heritable succession in order to select the one member of the class to take the whole did not apply to

[23] For procedure, see Act of Sederunt (Edictal Citations, Commissary Petitions and Petitions of Service) 1971 (S.I. 1971 No. 1165). A new Act of Sederunt, together with guidelines issued by the Sheriff of Chancery, is expected early in 1993.

moveables. Further, since the principle at common law was that only the next of kin, *i.e.* the *surviving* members of the class nearest in degree to the intestate, could succeed, there was at common law no representation in intestate moveable succession. Thus at common law the next of kin, even if the class consisted of only one person, took the entire moveable succession in preference to any number of people in the next or remoter degrees of propinquity.[24]

The various statutory amendments to the common law of moveable succession had the effect of creating a dichotomy between the next of kin identified on the common law principles and the heirs *in mobilibus*, *i.e.* the persons who actually took the moveable estate. As a result of the changes, the heirs *in mobilibus* became a class including the next of kin, but not limited to the next of kin. The three major statutory changes were the introduction of representation in moveables to a limited extent, improvements in the position of the parents of the intestate, and the grant of limited rights in favour of collaterals of the half blood uterine.

Representation in succession to the free moveable estate was introduced by section 1 of the Intestate Moveable Succession (Scotland) Act 1855.[25] Apparently copying a provision of the English Statute of Distribution of 1670, the 1855 Act limited the principle of representation to descendants and collaterals of the deceased. The moveable estate in which representation became possible was defined as "the whole free moveable estate on which the deceased . . . might have tested."[26] As it was well established that a testator had power to test only on the dead's part, and not on the part of his estate subject to legal rights, the result of this definition was that there was no representation in legitim. When the succession opened to ascendants and their collaterals, representation was no longer applicable. Thus, even after the introduction of representation, grandchildren could not share in legitim along with surviving children, but could share with them in the dead's part by representation. Nephews and nieces could share by representation along with surviving brothers and sisters, but one survivor of the class of uncles and aunts would take the whole free moveable estate in preference to cousins by virtue of his position as next of kin at common law.

The improvements in the position of the parents of an intestate were effected by the 1855 Act and by the Intestate Moveable Succession (Scotland) Act 1919.[27] At common law the father of an intestate ranked next after the intestate's collaterals and before his own collaterals, forming in effect a special class of next of kin. The mother of the intestate had no rights as such. Section 3 of the 1855 Act gave the father an extra right to share in moveables in a situation where the succession would not have opened to him at all by providing that he was to have one-half of the

---

[24] *Ormiston* v. *Broad* (1862) 1 M. 10.
[25] 18 & 19 Vict., c. 23.
[26] *Ibid.*, s. 9.
[27] 9 & 10 Geo.5, c. 61.

moveable estate in preference to brothers and sisters of the deceased or their descendants. The mother's position, finally contained in section 1 of the 1919 Act, was effectively a right to represent the predeceasing father, so that if the father had predeceased the intestate, the mother took over his right to one-half of the free moveable estate in preference to collaterals or to the whole free moveable estate if the intestate left no collaterals.

Collaterals of the half blood uterine had at common law no rights of succession to moveables at all, although the half blood consanguinean had full rights postponed only to collaterals of the full blood. Section 5 of the 1855 Act gave uterine collaterals a right limited in all circumstances to one-half of the moveable estate. (The balance went to the Crown if there were no other heirs.) This right applied only if the intestate died without issue, without collaterals of the full blood or of the half blood consanguinean, and predeceased by both parents.

C. Collation inter haeredes was a doctrine which arose as a result of the existence of different rules of succession applying to heritable and to moveable property respectively. In mixed estates with both heritage and moveables it qualified the separation of the two lines of succession by permitting, in appropriate circumstances, the massing together of the heritage and the moveables and the distribution of the combined fund by the rules normally applicable to moveable property only. Accepting the inequality which arose from giving all the heritage of an intestate to his heir at law, the object of collation *inter haeredes* was to make some show of equality in the distribution of the intestate's moveable property.

A person succeeding as heir at law to the heritage was normally barred from sharing in the moveable estate.[28] However, provided that he was a member of the class entitled to succeed to the moveables of the intestate (which was not always the case)[29] he could choose to throw his heritage into a common pool with the moveables and to take his proportionate share with the other heirs *in mobilibus* in the composite fund. He had a completely unfettered option and naturally, a decision to collate would normally be made only when the heir's share of the combined fund was more valuable than the heritage to which he succeeded as heir at law.

However, if there was no heritage, no question of collation could arise. Collation was a doctrine applicable only to mixed estates and if the estate was wholly moveable, the heir at law simply took his appropriate share of moveables along with the other heirs *in mobilibus*. He was excluded from sharing in the moveables only so long as he actually took heritage from the intestate's estate. Equally there could be no collation if there were no other heirs *in mobilibus* to share the moveables. In that situation he simply took the whole estate, heritable and moveable, since there was no one with whom to collate.

---

[28] *Law* v. *Law* (1553) Mor. 2365.
[29] *McCaw* v. *McCaws* (1787) Mor. 2383; *Colville's J.F.* v. *Nicoll*, 1914 S.C. 62.

History of the attempts to achieve reform

For the earlier background one can do no better than to quote the Report of the Mackintosh Committee on the Law of Succession in Scotland published in 1950.

> "Amendment of our law of intestate succession is a matter which has been under the consideration of the legal profession in Scotland at least since 1924. Following on the passing of the Law of Property Act 1922 (now embodied in the Administration of Estates Act 1925), which made radical reforms upon the law of succession in England, the whole question of the alteration of the law of intestate succession in Scotland was fully explored by Committees of the Society of Writers to H.M. Signet and of the Faculty of Procurators in Glasgow, and Reports recommending change were made by the Committee of the former body in 1924 and again in 1927 and by the Committee of the latter body in 1925. The most detailed of these Reports was that of 1927 which was approved by the W.S. Society on May 30, 1927. From these Reports and the investigations which preceded them the following common factors of agreement were separately arrived at by the two Committees and represent, we were informed, what is still the considered view of their parent bodies:
>
> "(1) That for the purpose of intestate succession, heritable and moveable property should be blended and form one estate.
> "(2) That the law of primogeniture should be abolished.
> "(3) That the differentiation between the sexes in intestate succession should be abolished.
> "(4) That there should be succession through the mother as well as through the father, and
> "(5) That in any alteration of the law the principle of legal rights should be retained, though these would require readjustment consequent on the abolition of primogeniture and the blending of heritable and moveable estate.
>
> "In 1927 a Bill was promoted by a private member of Parliament entitled 'The Succession (Scotland) Bill' which proposed *inter alia* certain alterations in the law relating to intestate succession including the abolition of primogeniture. This Bill did not proceed, the view taken of it by the legal societies being that a much more sweeping and general amendment of the law of succession was required, and that the legislative action which was necessary in the matter was not such as should be left to the initiative of individual Members of Parliament. In their Report of 1927 the W.S. Society recommended that the Law Officers of the Crown be memorialised with a view to the appointment of a Departmental Committee for consideration of the subject. For one reason or another no such appointment was made until our Committee was set up. . . .
>
> "During the Bill stage of the recent Adoption of Children Act 1949 the question arose as to whether sections 9 and 10 of the Act—which in

effect for all purposes of succession gave adopted children the status and rights of children born in wedlock—should be applied to Scotland. The conclusion then reached was that the sections in question should not be applied to Scotland because of the legal complications which might ensue under our existing law of intestate succession, more particularly because of its rules of primogeniture and preference of males over females. This in turn brought to the fore once more the issue as to whether a comprehensive review of our law of intestate succession ought not now to be undertaken. It will be seen, however, from what has been said above, that while the question which arose under the Adoption of Children Act 1949 may have furnished the immediate occasion which led to the present Inquiry, the causes for this Inquiry lie deeper and are of long-standing duration."

The Committee was appointed on July 30, 1949, and reported on December 9, 1950,[30] but the history of delay noted in the section of the Report quoted above was by no means over.

The Morton Committee on the law of intestacy in England was appointed on October 13, 1950. A Bill giving effect to most of its recommendations received the Royal Assent as the Intestate's Estates Act 1952 on October 30, 1952. Although time was thus speedily found for the English measure, the proposals for Scotland in the Mackintosh Committee Report were allowed to languish despite periodical prodding by Scottish Members of Parliament. In February 1952, in answer to a question in the House it was "hoped to make a statement at an early date," but in November 1953 it was "not proposed to introduce legislation on this subject during the present session." Not until May 1957 was another question asked in the House, when the reply was again evasive. It is perhaps symptomatic of the consistent delay that a letter to the editor of the *Scots Law Times* on the anomalies of the law of succession, printed early in 1957, could reappear in that journal, identically worded, late in 1958.

Pressure for the introduction of legislation was stepped up from then on. Two questions were asked in the House in 1958, and some concrete results were achieved when a private member's Bill to raise the amount of the surviving spouse's prior right from £500 to £5,000 received governmental blessing and was enacted as the Intestate Husband's Estate (Scotland) Act 1959. This appeared to provoke action, and in the Queen's Speech at the opening of the new session of Parliament in October 1959, legislation to effect the long-awaited reform of the law of succession was promised for that session. A draft Bill was in fact circulated for comment but ran into a variety of technical objections, and the Bill lost its place in the legislative queue. A series of questions in 1960 and 1961 could elicit no more than the stock reply that it could not yet be said when it might be possible to introduce a Bill.

---

[30] Cmd. 8144.

In April 1961 the Intestacy (Scotland) Bill was introduced by a group of Scottish private members, including those who had been most active in putting pressure on the Government, but it made no progress. Admittedly however, the drafting would not have been satisfactory as an Act. 1962 appears to have been quiescent, and finally in May 1963, completely out of the blue, came the publication of the Law Reform (Succession, etc.) (Scotland) Bill. While too late to be enacted in that session of Parliament, it was at least an earnest of good intentions, and provided an opportunity for detailed consideration of the proposals. Some of the fruits of that consideration were apparent when the Bill, under its new title of the Succession (Scotland) Bill, was reintroduced in the following session of Parliament on November 14, 1963. The Act came into force on September 10, 1964, since when certain amendments have been effected, particularly by the Law Reform (Miscellaneous Provisions) (Scotland) Acts of 1966 and 1968.

Further major reform is likely when the Scottish Law Commission's Report on Succession[31] is accepted and the proposed Bill is introduced into Parliament. The possible effect of these reforms is discussed in Chapter 10.

---

[31] Scot. Law Com. No. 124.

CHAPTER 2

INTESTATE SUCCESSION AFTER THE 1964 ACT

Commencement

The 1964 Act came into force on September 10, 1964 to regulate the succession to the estates of persons dying after midnight on the night of September 9–10, 1964.[1]

The provision in section 5 of the Law Reform (Miscellaneous Provisions) (Scotland) Act 1966[2] designed to cure a hiatus in the succession rights of some adopted persons (see p. 70) came into force on August 3, 1966. It applies to cases where the adopting parents died before September 10, 1964, and the natural parents died on or after August 3, 1966.

The increased but limited succession rights of illegitimate children created by Part I of the Law Reform (Miscellaneous Provisions) (Scotland) Act 1968[3] came into force in respect of the estates of persons dying on or after November 25, 1968, as did the provisions in Part II of the same Act bringing crofting tenancies within the scope of the Succession Act. Virtual abolition of the status of illegitimacy and the creation of equality in succession for children formerly classed as illegitimate has applied in respect of deaths on or after December 8, 1986.[4]

Substantial increases in the financial limits of the prior rights of a surviving spouse were effected by the Succession (Scotland) Act 1973[5] for deaths on or after May 23, 1973. That Act also gave the Secretary of State power to effect further increases by statutory instrument and such increases have so far been made by the Prior Rights of Surviving Spouse (Scotland) Orders of 1977 (deaths on or after December 31, 1977), 1981 (deaths on or after August 1, 1981) and 1988 (deaths on or after May 1, 1988).

Policy of the changes

The main policy of the alterations made by the 1964 Act was one of taking account of changing social conditions. The previous law was framed in such a way as to be relevant mainly to the large landed estate and, although modifications had been made from time to time, it still bore the marks of the feudal system in which these landowners might be

---

[1] s. 38 (3).
[2] c. 19.
[3] c. 70.
[4] Law Reform (Parent and Child) (Scotland) Act 1986, c. 9.
[5] c. 25.

called on as such to provide military services. Changed conditions, however, demanded a different approach. Not only had the typical estate left by a deceased person changed from one of the few large landed estates to one of a large number of much more modest estates, but there had been steady progress in the equalization of the sexes and a growing feeling that a surviving spouse, especially a widow, was not properly catered for by the law of intestate succession.

All this meant that the law of intestate succession in Scotland was completely out of touch with the expectations of a large section of the population. Many a solicitor was abused, or suspected of improper dealings, by disappointed relatives who found that they were to get no share of the estate. It was not easy to justify the privileged position of the heir at law to his younger brothers. It was not easy to tell a mother that she had no right to her deceased child's heritable estate and that it might go to the Crown rather than to her. Even if, as an act of grace, the Crown did make a gift of the heritage to her, she rightly would consider that the fact that this was necessary, and the deductions to which the estate might be subject on the way, were ridiculous. It was not easy to tell the cousin who had nursed the deceased for years prior to his death that, because the deceased had made no will, the whole of his moveable estate went to his Aunt Jemima in Timbuktu, and that, devoted or not, the cousin got nothing. And in particular, it was not easy to tell a widow that the amount of capital which she had to live on after her husband's death might be substantially less than she had expected. Many a widow imagined that the whole estate of her husband automatically passed to her on his death and was disappointed when the truth emerged.

The reforms therefore attempted to bring the law of intestate succession into line with modern conditions. In the well-known phrase of the Mackintosh Committee Report, "we have throughout kept in view the principle that when a man dies without a will the law should try to provide so far as possible for the distribution of his estate in the manner he would most likely have given effect to himself if he had made a will."

It is probably true that no general provision for intestacy can provide a result which will be that most likely to have been selected by every deceased person, whatever the size of his estate. Fears were expressed in Parliament as to the effect the Act would have on larger estates, but it was pointed out that intestacy was far commoner in small estates than in large ones. Thus, although ideas as to what constituted a "small" estate varied widely, the Act was framed with the medium to small estate in mind.

Figures obtained from a survey of confirmations granted in 1961 were quoted in the House of Lords to illustrate the proposition that the Succession Act had to be mainly concerned with the smaller estates. Of 26,943 confirmations granted in 1961, 17,273 (or approximately two-thirds) were cases where wills had been made. Only 9,670 (approximately one-third) were intestacies. Of the 9,670 intestacies only 32 were estates with a gross value over £25,000, and in only five cases was the heritable portion of an intestate estate valued at over £10,000. Intestacy was thus rare when the estate was large, and extremely rare when there was substantial heritable estate. As this would suggest, experience since 1964 has allayed fears that the Act would cause wholesale subdivision of country estates and farms.

Even these figures do not give the full picture. Although there were 26,943 confirmations in 1961 there were 63,928 deaths in Scotland that year. Since 1946 the annual number of deaths in Scotland has in fact been stable at around 63,000 (which is almost the same as the number of deaths in 1855). Thus although deaths in a given year need not necessarily lead to confirmation in that year, the proportion of confirmations to deaths in any year gives useful evidence, being set against a relatively stable number of deaths. Some of the deaths will have been of persons whose estates were wound up elsewhere, but that should be counter-balanced by deaths elsewhere of domiciled Scots. Allowing for these factors, there were therefore in 1961 approximately 37,000 cases, over and above those in which confirmation was granted, in which it must be assumed that the estate was so small that confirmation was not obtained.

A survey carried out at Aberdeen in the mid-1980s produced similar results. In the five years from 1980 to 1984, the Scottish average of confirmations as a proportion of total deaths was about 43 per cent. This conceals variations between different parts of the country. In Aberdeen and Stonehaven sheriff court districts confirmations averaged around 50 per cent. of relevant deaths, with the obvious conclusion that in other areas the proportion was less than the national average of 43 per cent. It is rather startling to the solicitor accustomed to winding up estates and obtaining confirmation to realise that only about two-fifths of the persons who die in Scotland leave estate of sufficient value to be worth the expense of obtaining confirmation of an executor.

It seems probable that there is a correlation between the proportion of estates in which confirmation is obtained and the proportion in which there is a will. Although not yet fully established, it seems that there is a higher proportion of testate to intestate confirmations in areas where the proportion of confirmations to deaths is also higher than average. If this correlation exists, then there seems to be a strong possibility that the deaths in respect of which no confirmation was obtained will include a high proportion of intestacies. Although the estates may have been small, the rules of intestate succession would still be of importance. The figures clearly indicate the need for the law of intestate succession to be relevant to the small and very small estate rather than to the large estate.

These figures also cast doubt on the frequently quoted ratio of one-third intestacy to two-thirds testacy. Although the figure is not readily verifiable, it may be true that about 66 per cent. of *confirmations* are in respect of testate estates. However if one makes the heroic assumption that not more than one-fifth of the 57 per cent. of people whose deaths do not lead to confirmation will have left any testamentary provisions, the result would be a true figure of about 39 per cent. testacy to 61 per cent. intestacy.

In order to bring the law into harmony with changed conditions, the 1964 Act effected a variety of changes. First, there was a greatly reduced emphasis on the importance of heritage in succession. While the distinction between heritage and moveables in succession was not totally removed, the privileged position of the heir at law was. Apart from the special case of titles and coats of arms, he no longer has any rights which are not shared by the other heirs. Scotland cannot reasonably be accused of undue haste in making this change, for it was one of the very last countries in the world to abolish the special rules of succession to land.

Similarly, there was a substantial reduction of the feudal emphasis on direct blood relationship through the male line. This shows itself in various ways. The position of the surviving spouse of an intestate was substantially improved, partly by changes in prior rights, and partly by being for the first time included in the list of heirs to the free estate after providing for prior and legal rights. Previously, whatever rights a surviving spouse might have had in the other's estate, he or she was never an heir of the other, and this change represented a substantial breach in the doctrine that succession depends on direct blood relationship. So also did the grant of full rights of succession to adopted children in the estates of their adopting parents. Despite pressure in Parliament, however, stepchildren were not given rights of succession. In this situation the principle of blood relationship was apparently too strong to be overcome.

In addition to the widow's increased rights, there were other changes in the position of women. The preference for males disappeared with the abolition of the need to look for the one member of a given class to take the heritable estate as heir at law and the substitution of the principle that all members of a class share equally in the whole, but equating the sexes was carried further. The mother and relations through her were given the same rights as the father and the relations through him, and this had effects such as giving collaterals of the half blood uterine exactly the same rights as collaterals of the half blood consanguinean. Bringing in the maternal relatives substantially widened the potential field of research into the family tree but was clearly necessary in the interests of justice and logic. The argument which was presented against the Mackintosh Committee's Report that "it is contrary to all Scottish feeling for heritage to go out of the family to which it belongs" merely begged the question and was completely out of touch with the practical aspects of the situation. No one is now prepared to justify the preservation of the purity of the male line in succession to heritage.

As a result of all these changes, not only have the common law principles for the selection of the heir at law become virtually obsolete, but so also have the common law principles for identification of the next of kin. Previously relevant for the purpose of ascertaining the heirs *in mobilibus*, who were a class including the next of kin, but not limited to them, these common law rules now drop out of the picture altogether—apart from competitions for the office of executor. In place of the principles previously applicable in intestate moveable succession there is now a statutory list contained in section 2 of the 1964 Act.

Assimilation of heritage and moveables

As already noted, part of the policy of the Act was to assimilate heritage and moveables for the purposes of succession, and in so far as this was achieved, it was done by section 1 of the Act. However the distinction between heritage and moveables has by no means been abolished. Although terce and courtesy are no longer exigible from the deceased's heritable estate, section 10 preserves the rule that *jus relicti, jus relictae* and legitim are exigible out of the deceased's moveable estate only. In addition the items excepted from the operation of the Act by section 37 (principally titles and coats of arms) pass under the pre-existing rules.

The preservation of the distinction between heritage and moveables for the purposes of legal rights has the effect that the distinction must also be preserved for the purposes of the surviving spouse's prior rights under sections 8 and 9 so that precise values may be maintained for the calculation of legal rights. Equally the law relating to the incidence of liabilities between heritage and moveables remains unimpaired.[6]

The result is that the assimilation of heritage and moveables affects only the free estate after satisfaction of the prior rights of a surviving spouse and of the legal rights of a surviving spouse and descendants. When dealing with the free estate, property consisting of heritage to the value of £3,000 and moveables to the value of £5,000 is simply a fund of £8,000 to be divided up according to the provisions of Part I of the Act. These are broadly similar to the old law of intestate moveable succession.

Another consequence of the assimilation of heritage and moveables is the virtual abolition of the status of heir at law. Apart from the items excepted by section 37, where the status is still relevant, the heir at law and his anomalous privileges vanish from the law. Sections 27 to 50 of the Titles to Land Consolidation (Scotland) Act 1868, dealing with service of heirs, were repealed by the 1964 Act, but had to be revived in 1980 by section 6 of the Law Reform (Miscellaneous Provisions) (Scotland) Act for the limited purpose of enabling the heir of a last surviving trustee to establish the propinquity on which his right to office depended. It was expected that there would be very few cases of this sort, and that services of heirs of persons dying before the commencement of the Succession Act would form a minuscule and vanishing jurisdiction of the Sheriff of Chancery to whom the whole jurisdiction over services was transferred.[7] However the flow of cases where title to land depends upon succession to someone dying before 1964 has continued virtually unabated, with an average of over 40 new cases every year. New procedural rules for services of heirs have been required to cope with the cases.

Among other changes consequential on the partial assimilation of heritage and moveables, the 1964 Act empowered minors to dispose of

---

[6] s. 14 (3).
[7] S.I. 1971 No. 743.

their heritage by will as they already could in respect of their moveables. This has now been extended by the Age of Legal Capacity (Scotland) Act 1991[8] (which abolishes the concepts of pupillarity and minority) to the effect that all children (male or female) have testamentary capacity from the age of 12. The doctrine of collation *inter haeredes* was also abolished by the 1964 Act. For some time after the Act collation remained relevant in cases where the heir at law succeeded to the tenancy of a croft and had to collate the value of that tenancy in order to share in the moveable estate.[9] However, crofting tenancies, formerly excluded from the operation of the Succession Act, were brought within its scope by Part II of the Law Reform (Miscellaneous Provisions) (Scotland) Act 1968. Thus the heir at law no longer has, as such, any right of succession to crofts, and collation disappeared in that situation also.

The estate subject to the operation of the Act

Peerages excluded

Under section 37 (1) (*a*), nothing in the Succession Act applies to any title, coat of arms, honour or dignity transmissible on the death of the holder thereof or affects the succession thereto or the devolution thereof. This has the result, for example, that succession to peerages is still governed by the principles of primogeniture and preference for males. It also means that adopted and illegitimate children, whose rights of succession are conferred by the Act, cannot succeed to them.[10] Legitimated children can however succeed to titles. This was always true of those legitimated at common law, while those whose legitimation depends upon the Legitimation (Scotland) Act 1968[11] have rights independent of the Succession Act.

Definition of "estate"

Apart from this exception, "estate" is defined in section 36 (2) as follows:

> "Any reference in this Act to the estate of a deceased person shall, unless the context otherwise requires, be construed as a reference to the whole estate, whether heritable or moveable, or partly heritable and partly moveable, belonging to the deceased at the time of his death or over which the deceased had a power of appointment and, where the deceased immediately before his death held the interest of a tenant under a tenancy or lease which was not expressed to expire on his death, includes that interest."[12]

---

[8] c. 50. s. 2 (2).

[9] 1965 S.L.T. (News) 209.

[10] The extension of the rights of illegitimate children by the Law Reform (Miscellaneous Provisions) (Scotland) Act 1968 took the form of inserting the provisions into the Succession Act, while the further liberalization in the separate Law Reform (Parent and Child) (Scotland) Act 1986 contains in s. 9 (1) (*c*) an express exemption of succession to titles, etc.

[11] c. 22.

[12] See *Cormack* v. *McIldowie's Exrs.*, 1975 S.L.T. 214 on the nature of qualifying tenancies.

In addition to the general definition there are two provisos. One is that heritage subject to a special destination in favour of a third party is not part of the deceased's estate unless he could and did evacuate that destination. The other provides that if heritage over which the deceased held a power of appointment has not been disposed of under that power, and it is in those circumstances subject to a power of appointment by some other person, it is not to be treated as part of the deceased's estate. Considerable care must be taken over the terms of this definition which is central to the whole scheme of the Act.

Special destinations

The definition expressly states that property subject to an unrevoked special destination is not part of the deceased's estate for the purposes of the Act. It is probably therefore incompetent for the deceased's executor to confirm to it, although it will still be part of the estate liable to taxation.[13]

The commonest example of a special destination is probably the survivorship destination in a title to heritage taken to husband and wife and survivor.[14] Although not necessarily true of other types of property, in this case registration of the disposition immediately confers on each a one-half *pro indiviso* share of the heritage. The survivorship destination concerns only the survivor's right to receive in addition the predeceaser's half. Whether this half forms part of the predeceaser's estate for the purposes of the Act depends upon two factors. One is whether there was power to revoke the destination. The other is whether, even assuming the power to exist, revocation has in fact occurred.

There is no limitation on the power of either of the parties to a survivorship destination to alienate his share during his lifetime, thereby evacuating the destination to that half. The possible limitation applies only to testamentary deeds.[15]

In the absence of express contractual provisions, the existence of a power to revoke by testamentary deed is normally dependent on the source of the finance used in the purchase of the property. If the price was provided at least to a significant extent by both parties the destination will be a contractual arrangement which neither has power to revoke.[16] Equally if the property was a gift from a third party, the destination will be a condition attached to the gift which neither spouse has power to revoke.[17] If the purchase price was provided wholly by one of the spouses, and the terms of the conveyance do not contradict that fact[18] that spouse may be entitled by will to revoke the destination so far as it provides that

---

[13] See *post*, p. 33.
[14] If the Scottish Law Commission's proposals in its report on succession (Scot. Law Com. No. 124) are accepted, this will be the only form of special destination to remain in future.
[15] *Steele* v. *Caldwell*, 1979 S.L.T. 228; *Smith* v. *Mackintosh*, 1989 S.L.T. 148.
[16] *Perrett's Trs.* v. *Perrett*, 1909 S.C. 522.
[17] *Brown's Trs.* v. *Brown*, 1943 S.C. 488.
[18] See *Gordon-Rogers* v. *Thomson's Exrs.*, 1988 S.L.T. 618; *Smith* v. *Mackintosh* (*supra*).

his or her one-half of the property is to pass to the other spouse.[19] In the absence of power to revoke, any purported revocation of a destination is totally ineffective.

However, if the power exists, the question of whether revocation has occurred so as to bring the property into the "estate" of the deceased has been simplified by section 30 of the 1964 Act. Briefly, revocation of a destination occurs only if there is an express reference to the destination and a declared intention to evacuate it.[20] The old practice of including a general reference to destinations without specifying them is no longer effective.

Powers of appointment

The provisions concerning powers of appointment are also worth closer attention. For the purposes of the Act, the general proposition in section 36 (2) is that the "estate" of a deceased person includes property over which he had a power of appointment, subject only to the proviso excluding heritable property from his estate if his failure to exercise a power of appointment gives rise to a power of appointment in someone else. This might have been thought to mean that (apart from the situation in the proviso) where the deceased had a power of appointment, whether general or special, whether or not he exercised it and indeed whether or not he had a right of fee in the property concerned, the deceased's family could claim rights of beneficial succession in it. The prospect of the widow acquiring prior rights out of property which her husband did not own would have been a startling one. However, this provision appears in fact to be a purely administrative one giving the executor power to obtain a title to the property for the purpose of conveying to those beneficially interested by virtue of the appointment or of the deed creating the power. By a classic example of tortuous draftsmanship, rights of succession to the donee of the power are excluded unless he had the fee of the property over which his power of appointment extended.

The case where the deceased was owner of the property would arise where the power was completely general or where he was given a full liferent with an unqualified power of disposal.[21] No greater problem arises in applying the Succession Act to this type of property than to any other property which he owned.

However, if the deceased had no right of fee in the property over which he had the power of appointment—*e.g.* if either the liferent or the power was qualified in some way—then it will be found that the various rights of succession are set out in such a way as not to apply.

The surviving spouse's prior rights under sections 8 and 9 come out of the intestate estate of the deceased. Similarly, the provisions of Part I for

---

[19] *Hay's Tr.* v. *Hay's Trs*, 1951 S.C. 329.
[20] See *post*, p. 87.
[21] *MacKenzie's Trs.* v. *Kilmarnock* (1908) 16 S.L.T. 676; 1909 S.C. 472; *Ewing's Trs.* v. *Ewing*, 1909 1 S.L.T. 104; 1909 S.C. 409.

succession to the free estate apply solely to the intestate estate. If the deceased exercised the power of appointment, he was not intestate *quoad* the property subject to the power. However, even if he did *not* exercise the power, the property is still not part of his "intestate estate" as that phrase is defined in section 36 (1), because it has been disposed of by "testamentary disposition" within the meaning of the same section. The definition there given is not limited to deeds by the deceased and includes "*any* deed taking effect on his death whereby any part of his estate is disposed of." If he failed to exercise his power of appointment, the deed by which the power was created takes effect on his death and disposes of part of his "estate." Hence property subject to a power is not part of the intestate estate for the purposes of prior rights or the free estate.

So far as legal rights are concerned, section 10 (2) provides that they are to be calculated by reference to so much of the net moveable estate as remains after satisfaction of prior rights. "Net estate" is defined as so much of an estate as remains after "estate duty[22] and other liabilities of the estate having priority over legal rights, the prior rights of a surviving spouse and rights of succession." It would seem that one of the liabilities of the estate having this priority would arise from the duty to transfer property which the deceased did not own to those who have a vested right to it.

Hence one is left with the proposition that property subject to a power is part of the deceased's estate solely for the purpose of completion of title.

Another point is raised by this. It must be carefully noted that the word "estate" is used in different senses in different parts of the Act. Not only must the interpretation section (section 36) be studied closely, but one must also consider special interpretations in particular sections. Thus in Part I of the Act, which deals with the succession to the free estate, the words "intestate estate" are used as meaning only the free estate after prior and legal rights (section 1 (2)). In section 9, "intestate estate" is defined as meaning so much of the net intestate estate as remains after satisfaction of the surviving spouse's housing right under section 8 (section 9 (6) (*a*)).

Agricultural property

The special administrative provisions for agricultural units which appeared at one stage of the Succession Bill's history were eventually dropped. The purpose was to ensure as far as possible that farms would be kept in the ownership of a single member of the family. The provisions were highly complex and seemed likely to cause many practical difficulties in operating them. It was also pointed out in the House of Lords that from a survey of the estates of persons dying in 1961, intestacy was

---

[22] Includes CTT and IHT. Inheritance Tax Act 1984 (c. 51), Sched. 6, para. 1 and Finance Act 1986 (c. 41), s. 100 (1) (*b*).

extremely rare among those with heritable estates of over £10,000. (Of 9,670 intestacies recorded, only five involved heritage of over £10,000 in value.) As £10,000 even then represented a very modest farm, there seemed to be no real substance in the fears that, without special provisions, farms would be split up, or pass out of the family's hands altogether. From the figures, the vast majority of farmers regulate the succession to their farms by will. In any event it would be extremely unlikely that a farm would be subdivided on intestacy, for the economic facts of life would dictate its continuance as a unit.

Similar reasoning has now led to crofting tenancies being brought within the scope of the Succession Act by the Law Reform (Miscellaneous Provisions) (Scotland) Act 1968. Originally they were excluded from the reforms effected in 1964 and had special rules of succession giving the primary right to the tenancy (and its value) to the heir at law. Now, however, a crofting tenancy is just another item of heritable estate to be dealt with like any other. It has a value, whatever difficulties there may be in ascertaining it, and that *value* may now have to be divided among those beneficially interested in the estate, although only one person can be the new tenant. This may lead to competition for the office of executor, as the executor controls the transmission of the tenancy.[23]

Death and survivorship

The fundamental nature of the law on this point remains as before. The deceased whose estate is in question must be proved to have died and any person claiming to be a beneficiary must be affirmatively proved to have survived him or her. The onus of proof lies on the person relying on the death or survivorship, and the consequence of failure of proof is the failure of that person's claim on the estate.

Death certificates are sufficient, though not conclusive, evidence of the death, and an action is available under the Presumption of Death (Scotland) Act 1977 for fixing the date of death in cases of disappearance.

Common calamities

The 1964 Act, however, effected a very valuable change in establishing survivorship. In a common calamity, section 31 creates what it calls presumptions of survivorship based on age. In truth they are not really presumptions but rules of law as they cannot be rebutted. If there is proof on the balance of probabilities[24] that one person in a common calamity survived the other, effect is given to that order of deaths. It is only if there is no proof of survivorship that the Act's "presumptions" come into play, so that, by definition, there cannot be evidence to rebut the presumptions.

---

[23] MacCuish & Flyn, *Crofting Law*, para. 7.05.
[24] *Lamb* v. *Lord Advocate*, 1976 S.L.T. 151.

The general rule in section 31 is that where two persons have died in circumstances indicating that they died simultaneously or rendering it uncertain which, if either, of them survived the other, the younger is presumed to have survived the elder for all purposes of succession.[25]

However, in two particular cases, different presumptions apply. Where the persons concerned are husband and wife, section 31 (1) (*a*) states a positive presumption that neither survived the other. The different treatment for spouses is intended to avoid a situation in which the estate of the elder spouse would pass to the younger by virtue of the presumption and then to the younger spouse's relatives to the exclusion of the elder spouse's relatives. For example, if a childless couple perished in a car crash, or died in independent incidents, without proof of survivorship, the husband's estate might pass out of his family and into his wife's family. It was felt in Parliament that this would be likely to be contrary to the husband's wishes, and thus the presumption in this case is that neither survived the other.

One wonders, however, whether in the case of the husband and wife common calamity is properly catered for. The positive presumption that neither survived is admittedly better than the old lack of any presumption. On intestacy, the husband's estate can be wound up on the basis that the wife did not survive to become a beneficiary and vice versa. But if one spouse makes a will in favour of the other and makes alternative provision in the event of the other "predeceasing," he will none the less die intestate if both spouses perish in a common calamity. The statutory presumption that the other "did not survive" is not proof of predecease as the deaths might have been simultaneous. Hence the essential precondition of the alternative provision cannot be shown to exist and it cannot take effect. It might have been better to direct the logically impossible presumption that each predeceased the other. The common practice of making testamentary provisions for a spouse conditional upon that spouse surviving for a specified period avoids the problem.[26]

The other special case where a different presumption of survivorship applies is a somewhat complicated one specified in section 31 (2). Where two persons other than husband and wife have perished in circumstances making survivorship uncertain, the presumption would normally be that the younger survived the elder. But, if the elder has left a testamentary disposition containing a provision in favour of the younger, and failing the younger, in favour of a third party, and if the younger has died intestate, then it is presumed *for the purposes of that survivorship destination* that the elder person survived the younger. The effect is that the elder's property will go to the nominated third person. Without such a provision, in spite of the known wishes of the elder person as specified in the survivorship destination, the property so bequeathed would have

---

[25] s. 31 (1) (*b*).

[26] The Scottish Law Commission's proposed reforms would introduce a fixed period for all cases.

passed via the younger to those who would be entitled to succeed on the intestacy of the younger person.

The drafting of section 31 (2) does not appear to be beyond criticism, even if one accepts the need for this exception to the usual presumption of survivorship. The younger person must die "intestate" before the reversed presumption applies. This is defined in section 36 (1) as "leaving undisposed of by testamentary disposition the whole or any part of" one's estate. Thus one dies "intestate" if any part of one's estate is undisposed of.[27] Thus, in the situation envisaged in section 31 (2), even if the younger person has made explicit provision in his will for the property which he expects to pass to him on the elder person's death, he has died "intestate" within the meaning of section 31 (2) if he has failed to dispose of any item of his estate. The younger person being "intestate," the presumption for the purpose of the destination would be that the elder survived him, and the property would pass to the third party nominated in the destination. Only if he had also made a testamentary disposition of every item of his estate would the younger person avoid being "intestate." One might have thought that, if this exception to the usual presumption of survivorship is necessary (which seems doubtful) it would have applied whether or not the younger person made a will or alternatively only in cases where he was intestate as to the property subject to the survivorship destination. To make it apply where he is intestate as to any part of his estate seems to be a defect in drafting. The Scottish Law Commission proposes reform.

It is to be noted that the reversed presumption in section 31 (2) applies only for the purposes of the third party destination, to ensure that the third party in fact receives the property in question. For all *other* purposes of succession, the younger person will still be presumed to have survived the elder.

The comment has been made that the presumptions contained in section 31 do not cover cases where more than two persons perish in a common calamity, but in fact all cases are dealt with. In any situation one is concerned only with two people at a time. One is winding up X's estate and the question is whether Y survived, or is to be presumed to have survived, so as to qualify as a beneficiary. If Z also died in the same calamity, an entirely separate question of survivorship arises between X and Z.

For purposes of Inheritance Tax, persons dying in a common calamity without proof of survivorship are deemed to die at the same instant.[28]

Posthumous children

A different question of survivorship arises in connection with posthumous children. Wills frequently refer to a beneficiary being "survived by issue," and under the Succession Act there are references to

---

[27] *Munro's Trs., Petrs.*, 1971 S.L.T. 313.

[28] Inheritance Tax Act 1984 (c. 51), s. 4 (2).

survivorship in sections 9 (1), 11 (1) and 2 (1) (*a*) in connection with prior rights, legitim and rights in the free estate respectively. The question is whether a posthumous child counts as such a survivor.

In *Elliott* v. *Joicey*[29] it was held that the deceased did not "leave issue him surviving" when his only child was born posthumously. This was apparently on the basis that a child which was *in utero* at the deceased's death had no separate existence at that time and could not be said to "survive" him in the ordinary meaning of that word.

One may think that the ordinary meaning does include a posthumous child and it might still be possible to present that argument in an appropriate case. However, whatever the ordinary meaning may be, it is clear that the courts are ready to deduce that a meaning including posthumous children was intended if the result of that construction would be to the benefit of the child. The main reason for the decision in *Elliott* v. *Joicey* seems to have been that there was no benefit to the child in holding that it survived its parent. In the vast majority of cases, and in particular cases arising under the Succession Act, there is clear benefit to the child in holding that it survives, and thus this interpretation would be adopted. The maxim "*Qui in utero est pro jam nato habetur*" is of very long standing and gives the posthumous child the same benefits as one born before the parent's death, providing it is born alive.[30] The consequence of prenatal death is that the child is treated as never having existed.[31]

The unworthy heir

In order to qualify as a beneficiary in the division of an estate, it may not always be enough for the person apparently entitled under the rules of testate or intestate succession to establish that he survived the deceased. In certain situations, the person otherwise entitled to succeed may be passed over because of some factor making it inappropriate that he should succeed to that particular deceased. The theoretical basis of this disqualification, and therefore the precise area of its application, are not entirely certain, but considerations of public policy are clearly involved in a determination that an heir is so unworthy that he ought not to be permitted to inherit.

The main situation for invoking the disqualification arises when the potential beneficiary has killed the person whose estate is being distributed. There is statutory provision in the Parricide Act 1594[32] disinheriting anyone convicted by an assize of "slaying" a parent or grandparent, but the Act is limited to these relationships and may apply only to the succession to heritage.[33] It seems, however, that there is also a

[29] 1935 S.C. (H.L.) 57.
[30] *Cox's Trs.* v. *Cox*, 1950 S.L.T. 127; 1950 S.C. 117.
[31] Bankton, *Inst.*, I, xlvii; Walker, *Intestate Succession*, p. 10.
[32] 1594 c. 30; 12 mo. c. 224.
[33] Bankton, *Inst.*, II, ccci, 30.

more general rule of common law that a person who has culpably and deliberately killed another is debarred from succeeding to that other's estate. A rule of this nature is well established in England, where a common formulation is that it is contrary to public policy for a person guilty of feloniously killing another to take any benefit in the deceased's estate.[34]

Although it was generally accepted in Scotland that there was also a general disqualification at common law, and estates were indeed wound up on this basis when one spouse killed another,[35] there was little direct authority. Such as there was could be found in the principle of insurance law that an insured cannot deliberately produce the circumstances under which he may recover under his policy, which is not very different from the case of the heir accelerating his succession by deliberately creating the death under which his right emerges. Public policy demanded that the same approach be taken to killing the deceased and the sheriff court case of *Smith, Petr.*[36] for the first time expressly held that a wife convicted of culpably killing her husband was barred from taking any benefit in his estate. The degree of culpability was not high, but was sufficient to bring in the exclusion. Since then several cases have confirmed the existence of the common law rule.[37]

The common law disqualification is based upon so important a fundamental principle that it is the only known case in which British courts are prepared to ignore the express and precise terms of statute in favour of a common law rule based upon morality. The statutes regulating intestate succession have no qualifications permitting the exclusion of the deceased's killer, but the courts have been prepared to ignore the statutes in such cases. Despite the strength of the principle of unworthiness, it is interesting that a power to exempt from the forfeiture was introduced so soon after the existence of the forfeiture was formally recognised in Scotland. The Forfeiture Act 1982[38] was introduced as a private member's Bill and became law in a form which leaves many questions unanswered. Except in cases where the killer has been convicted of murder, a court is given power to "modify" what the Act calls "the forfeiture rule." It has not been clear whether power to modify includes power to exclude the rule totally, and in Scotland the courts have proceeded on the assumption that it does not. However they have been prepared to go so far as to remove all practical difference between modification and exclusion by awarding the killer the whole of the deceased's heritage and 99 per cent. of his moveables.[39]

---

[34] *Re Dellow's Will Trusts* [1964] 1 All E.R. 771.
[35] *e.g.* the estate involved in *Garvie's Trs.* v. *Still & Anor.*, 1972 S.L.T. 29.
[36] 1979 S.L.T. (Sh. Ct.) 35.
[37] *Burns* v. *Secretary of State for Social Services*, 1985 S.L.T. 351 (1st Div.); *Paterson, Petr.*, 1986 S.L.T. 121; *Cross, Petr.*, 1987 S.L.T. 384; *Gilchrist, Petr.*, 1990 S.L.T. 494; *Hunter's Exrs., Petrs.*, 1992 S.L.T. 1141.
[38] c. 34.
[39] *Cross, Petr.* (*supra*); *Paterson, Petr.* (*supra*); *Gilchrist, Petr.* (*supra*).

In its application to Scotland the Forfeiture Act runs into another problem over its definition of the forfeiture rule from which exemption may be granted. It is defined in section 1 as the "rule of public policy" which excludes the person who has unlawfully killed another. It is not clear that this includes the statutory disqualification created in Scotland by the Parricide Act 1594, but the Act was not considered in *Cross*, *Petr.* where a son killed his father and extensive exemption was granted. The result of a disqualification is clearly spelt out in the Parricide Act for the situations to which it applies, although the disqualification of the killer's posterity may have been repealed in the general repeal of sentences involving corruption of blood.[40] At common law the result is not clearly established. Although there is English authority that the share of the unworthy heir falls to be distributed as if that person died before the deceased,[41] and this will often have to be the practical result, the principle will not be carried so far as to bring into play testamentary provisions depending on the "predecease" of the killer. The Inner House has held in *Hunter*[42] that the disqualification should be applied only to the extent necessary to achieve its object.

As between husband and wife another disqualification may arise under the Conjugal Rights (Scotland) Amendment Act 1861.[43] Property acquired by a wife after she has obtained a decree of judicial separation passes on her intestacy as if her husband had been then dead.[44] In effect this creates a statutory unworthiness of husbands (though not of wives). The disqualification ceases if the spouses again cohabit.

The order of applicability of rules of succession

Under the 1964 Act, as under the old law of intestate succession, there is a fragmentation of approach in deciding how a particular estate is to be divided up. After payment of the deceased's debts and any other liabilities and charges to which his estate is subject, there are under the Act three sets of rules to be considered in their proper order, before the final division can be established. The order is as follows:

1. Prior rights

(*A*) *The housing right under section 8.* Under section 8, the surviving spouse of an intestate is entitled to the deceased's interest in any one house owned or tenanted by the deceased at the time of his or her death. The surviving spouse must have been ordinarily resident in the house in question at the intestate's death, and the maximum value of the benefit conferred under this section is £65,000. If the value of the deceased's

---

[40] Criminal Justice (Scotland) Act 1949 (12, 13 & 14 Geo. 6, c. 94), s. 15 (1).
[41] *Re Callaway, deceased* [1956] 2 All E.R. 451. See also for Ireland, Succession Act 1965, s. 120 (5) and for Germany B.G.B. 2344.
[42] 1992 S.L.T. 1141.
[43] 24 & 25 Vict. c. 86.
[44] s. 6.

interest is more than £65,000, the surviving spouse receives that sum. Even if the value is below that limit, in some cases it is only the value of the deceased's interest (and not the interest itself) which passes to the survivor. In addition, the surviving spouse is entitled to the furniture and plenishings of the house, up to a maximum value of £12,000, and subject to special provisions in respect of heirlooms.

The fact that the housing right under section 8 is the first in order of priority emerges when it is found that all the other rights are postponed to it.

(*B*) *The monetary right under section 9.* From what is left after any right under section 8 has been met,[45] the surviving spouse of an intestate is entitled to £21,000 if the intestate is survived by children or to £35,000 if there are no children.

The values of the prior rights are likely to be substantially increased in late 1993.

2. Legal rights

These are the traditional legal rights, still resting partly on the previous common law. Under section 10 (2), legal rights, as amended by the Act, are exigible from any moveable estate remaining after the satisfaction of the prior rights under sections 8 and 9. The main amendments are the abolition of terce and courtesy, the introduction of representation in legitim, and the grant of rights to illegitimate children, so that legal rights are now available to the surviving spouse and to the descendants of the intestate, but in his moveable estate only.

3. Succession to the free estate

These rules, specified in Part I of the Act, deal with the succession to the free intestate estate after both of the above sets of rules have been applied,[46] precise values being maintained at each stage.

As before, the rules of succession to the free estate are a modified version of the parentelic system. Apart from specialties such as bringing the surviving spouse into the list of heirs to the free estate and dividing the estate equally between parents and brothers and sisters when both categories survive, one exhausts one class (as represented if need be) before moving on to the next class. As before, the order of the classes is issue, then collaterals, then parents, then parents' collaterals and so on *ad infinitum*.

---

[45] s. 9 (6) (*a*).
[46] s. 1 (2).

CHAPTER 3

DEBTS AND OTHER CHARGES UPON THE ESTATE

Before any estate is available for distribution to beneficiaries, whether under a will or on intestacy, there must be deducted from the gross estate any debts incurred by the deceased and any liabilities to which his estate is subject. It is in the balance after these items have been deducted that the beneficiaries share. Even although a surviving spouse and children are sometimes classed as creditors in respect of their legal rights in a competition with others having ordinary rights of succession, this does not entitle them to participate in the gross estate along with genuine creditors. They are limited to sharing in the net estate after deduction of debts and liabilities and thus in a competition with true creditors, those entitled to legal rights are ordinary beneficiaries.[1] The special privilege of an illegitimate child of being regarded as a true creditor for aliment was removed by the Law Reform (Miscellaneous Provisions) (Scotland) Act 1968.[2] Thus all the rights of succession, under the three different sets of rules mentioned in the previous chapter, are in the net estate after satisfaction of debts and liabilities.

There is no obvious limit to the way in which a deceased person may have incurred liabilities falling to be paid out of his estate. Contractual obligations, for example debts on the deceased's own account or guarantees of the debts of others, may be liabilities of the estate. So also may delictual claims arising from wrongful acts by the deceased. However, typical examples of debts which commonly have to be paid or allowed for before division of the estate are outstanding loans secured over the deceased's house, local poll tax or council tax, suppliers' accounts, funeral expenses and the expenses of administration of the estate.

Apart from the ordinary run of debts met with in most estates there are some of rarer occurrence. McLaren[3] gives the example of the expenses connected with the birth of a posthumous child, citing the authority of Erskine and two early cases in Morison's *Dictionary*. One can perhaps regard this as a liability incurred by the deceased husband by fathering the child, and it is certainly consonant with reason that the expenses should be treated as a debt due from his estate. In view of the existence of the National Health Service, the point will rarely be of much importance nowadays, but if, in the case of complications, the mother were to be in a private nursing home for a lengthy period, the sum

---

[1] *Naismith* v. *Boyes* (1899) 1 F. (H.L.) 79, *per* Lord Watson at p. 82.

[2] c. 70.

[3] *Wills & Succession*, i, 127.

involved could be substantial, and could make a considerable difference to the shares to be taken by the beneficiaries from the estate. At least if the deceased husband expressly or impliedly authorised private treatment for the birth, such an expense should clearly be treated as a debt due from the estate rather than a private liability of the mother.

The right of the deceased's widow (but not, apparently, widower) and family to a reasonable allowance for mournings on a scale suitable to the family's social position is a debt of the estate. Erskine,[4] Bell[5] and McLaren[6] all refer to the cost of mournings as a debt, while Bell goes so far as to treat it as a privileged debt payable even although the estate should be insufficient to meet the claims of the deceased's creditors. The right to mournings is however likely to be abolished as anachronistic if the proposals of the Scottish Law Commission are enacted.[7]

Another debt which appears nowadays to be rarely invoked is the right of a surviving spouse to aliment till the next term after the deceased's death. As stated by Erskine[8] and in *McIntyre* v. *McIntyre's Trs.*[9] this is a right available to a widow only, the purpose being to provide funds for her maintenance until her provisions, either on intestacy or under a will, become payable. It would seem, however, that section 4 of the Married Women's Property (Scotland) Act 1920[10] gave a surviving husband a reciprocal right—if he was indigent. Any such rights are specifically saved by the 1964 Act. Section 37 (1) (*c*) provides that nothing in the Act is to "affect any right on the part of a surviving spouse to claim from the representatives of his or her deceased spouse payment of aliment out of the estate of that spouse." In view of the extensive provisions now made for a surviving spouse, it may be that it will rarely be necessary to invoke this right, but it could still be of importance in cases where the deceased has left a will making very little provision for his or her spouse. This right is also liable to be abolished if the Scottish Law Commission's proposals are accepted.[11]

Classification of debts as heritable or moveable

Although there has been an assimilation of heritage and moveables for some purposes, it is still necessary to classify debts as either heritable or moveable. Not only must there be a precise value for the moveable estate from which the legal rights of spouses and issue are due, but the prior rights of a surviving spouse may also be affected. The prior right to the deceased's interest in the matrimonial home is "subject . . . to any

---

[4] *Inst.*, III, ix, 22, 43.
[5] *Comm.*, i, 679.
[6] *Wills & Succession*, i, 127; see also *Sheddan & Ors.* v. *Gibson* (1802) Mor. 11855.
[7] *Report on Succession* (Scot. Law Com. No. 124), recommendation 54.
[8] *Inst.*, I, vi, 41.
[9] (1865) 3 M. 1074. See also *Barlass* v. *Barlass's Trs.*, 1916 S.C. 741.
[10] 10 & 11 Geo. 5, c. 64—repealed Family Law (Scotland) Act 1985 (c. 37), Sched. 2.
[11] *Report* (*supra*), recommendation 56.

heritable debt secured over the interest."[12] Thus the benefit taken by the surviving spouse is directly reduced by the whole amount of any debt which can be classed as both heritable and secured over the deceased's interest.

The result is that the liabilities of the estate must still be allocated to heritage and moveables under the old principles regulating the liability *inter se* of heir and executor, even although the heir at law now exists only for succession to titles. Section 14 (3) expressly preserves all the old rules, with the general result that debts secured over heritage are payable out of, or form a deduction from, the value of the heritage while all other debts are payable out of the moveable estate.[13]

One aspect of the general rules which has achieved a new significance in a number of cases is however the method of dealing with debts for which the creditor holds both heritable and moveable securities. It is not uncommon for a bank or insurance company which has provided a loan for the purchase of a house to take both a heritable security over the house and an assignation of policies of assurance on the life of the purchaser. If the purchaser dies, the lender will be very generously secured, as the life policies will frequently be sufficient by themselves to pay off the debt. Nonetheless the situation remains that there is a heritable debt secured over the house at the time of death. Assuming that the house is one in which the deceased's spouse is ordinarily resident, the result would be that the value of the surviving spouse's prior right to the house would be reduced by the whole amount of the heritable security if no account could be taken of the creditor's concurrent moveable security.

Thus, as was also the case between heir and executor it is necessary to apportion the debt between heritage and moveables so that only the appropriate proportion of the debt is classed as a heritable debt. The heritable element is therefore the same proportion of the total debt as the proportion between the value of the heritable security held by the creditor and the whole value of all the securities held by the creditor. If the heritage held in security is worth £20,000 and the moveable security is worth £10,000, only two-thirds of the debt is a heritable debt.[14] Very difficult questions arise if a life policy assigned in security is a joint one on the lives of two spouses. Depending on the precise terms of the policy, there can arise a debt due by the estate to the survivor of half of the proceeds of the policy.[15]

Inheritance Tax

Whatever its name, Inheritance Tax is not in fact a tax upon inheritances received, like the former legacy duty and succession duty, but a tax

---

[12] 1964 Act, s. 8 (6) (*d*).

[13] What little authority exists is very general. See McLaren, *Wills & Succession*, ii, 1305 and Wilson, *Law of Debt*, 2nd ed., para. 29.10.

[14] *Graham* v. *Graham & Ors.* (1898) 5 S.L.T. 319.

[15] Gretton, 1988 J.L.S. 141.

on capital transferred out of a deceased person's estate. There could be much to be said for the fairness of a tax based on the total sums received by individuals from all inheritances. In particular, the rate of tax could be varied according to the total benefits from inheritances and according to the degree of relationship between the deceased and the beneficiary. However the administrative complications and the record-keeping involved mean that a true inheritance tax is not a practical possibility. Capital Transfer Tax ran into the same problems when it purported to record and tax all chargeable transfers, even lifetime transfers. Hence when the Capital Transfer Tax Act 1984[16] was retrospectively renamed the Inheritance Tax Act (I.H.T.A.) by the Finance Act 1986,[17] the opportunity was taken to convert the tax back to a basic principle not dissimilar to the old estate duty levied on the estates of deceased persons. Further review is however now under consideration (late 1992).

It would not be appropriate in a work of this nature to enter into an extended discussion of the implications of Inheritance Tax upon the distribution of the estate of a deceased person, and there are, in any event, a number of specialist works dealing with the subject in detail. The main point is that the amount of the tax due is deducted from the estate available for the beneficiaries of the estate. A specific legacy of heritage no longer bears its own tax.[18] The deceased's personal representatives are primarily liable for payment of the tax in the ordinary case.

Inheritance Tax is charged on the value transferred by a chargeable transfer, and tax is charged on death as if the deceased, immediately before his death, had transferred the value of his estate as it then stood.[19] Certain gifts ("potentially exempt transfers") made within the seven years prior to the deceased's death are also subject to Inheritance Tax.[20] Gifts, even outwith the seven-year period, may still be liable to Inheritance Tax as "gifts with reservations" if the deceased had retained an interest in the subject of the gift.[21] The value of the estate takes account of the liabilities of the deceased[22] and it seems that the liabilities which were accepted as deductions for estate duty and for Capital Transfer Tax are also accepted for Inheritance Tax. Thus the allowance for mournings remains an allowable deduction for tax purposes.[23] The cost of a tombstone was formerly thought not to be allowable, but since the decision in *Prentice* v. *Chalmers*[24] it is established that the reasonable cost of a tombstone is now allowable. However, it should be remembered that a particular debt may well be a liability of the estate to be deducted before distribution to beneficiaries even although it is not an allowable deduction for tax.

---

[16] c. 51.

[17] c. 41, s. 100.

[18] *Cowie's Trs. Petrs.*, 1982 S.L.T 326, *sub nom. Re Dougal* [1981] S.T.C. 514. Inheritance Tax Act 1984 (c. 51) s. 211.

[19] IHTA 1984, s. 4 (1).

[20] IHTA 1984, s. 3A (1), added by Finance Act 1986, Sched. 9.

[21] Finance Act 1986, s. 102.

[22] IHTA 1984, s. 5 (3).

[23] Extra Statutory Concession F1 (1992).

[24] 1985 S.L.T. 168; Practice Statement 7/87.

Exempt transfers arise in several situations. Thus small transfers of up to £3,000 in any one year are exempt from Inheritance Tax[25] and so also are marriage gifts up to specified limits.[26] Gifts to charities and to public bodies are also exempt.[27] The most important exemption is however that all transfers between spouses are exempt from Inheritance Tax.[28] Thus the former problems in the estate duty legislation whereby the value of a surviving spouse's prior rights varied according to whether he or she took the house itself, or a cash sum in lieu, no longer cause trouble.

It is also possible to alter the disposition of an estate (whether by will or on intestacy) by a deed of variation (family arrangement) or similar instrument. This affirmation of the very important rule that beneficiaries may rearrange benefits among themselves is significant for several purposes. So far as Inheritance Tax is concerned, such a variation effected within two years of the deceased's death has the result that the tax charge is on the basis that the agreed variation was the distribution prescribed by the will or the intestacy rules.[29]

[25] IHTA 1984, s. 19.
[26] IHTA 1984, s. 22.
[27] IHTA 1984, ss. 23–27.
[28] IHTA 1984, s. 18.
[29] IHTA 1984, s. 142.

CHAPTER 4

SURVIVING SPOUSE'S PRIOR RIGHTS

The prior rights created by the Succession Act are probably the most important single feature of the Act. They are in two parts, the first of which is set out in section 8. This was entirely new, and consists of a right to the house (with its furniture and plenishings and up to specified values) in which the surviving spouse was ordinarily resident at the date of death of the intestate. The second part, stated in section 9, gives a surviving spouse a right to a fixed sum of money, the amount depending on whether the deceased was or was not survived by issue. This was patterned upon the right formerly conferred by the Intestate Husband's Estate (Scotland) Acts 1911 to 1959, but there are important differences. Provision is now made for the spouse even when the deceased is survived by issue (who may be legitimate or illegitimate) and the prior right is now part of the general law of succession of Scotland, instead of being confined to the estates of persons dying domiciled in Scotland.[1]

The rights to the house, to the furniture and plenishings and to a sum of money are quite independent of each other. The fact that the deceased may have had no interest in a house does not increase the value of the monetary right, and therefore the total value to the surviving spouse of prior rights varies according to the form of the estate as well as its total size.

The great social significance of these rights lies in the fact that in the large majority of intestacies, prior rights will exhaust the estate and ensure that the surviving spouse is the sole beneficiary, even although others may have nominal rights of succession.

Intestacy

It is, however, important to emphasise that prior rights can arise only when the deceased died intestate. They do not function as family protection devices, so that if the deceased has disposed of the whole of his estate by testamentary disposition, his surviving spouse has no claim to prior rights, however unjust the will. In that situation the spouse must claim the legal right of *jus relictae* or *jus relicti* if she or he is not satisfied with the provisions of the will, possibly supplemented by claims for mournings and aliment for so long as these claims are possible.

For prior rights to operate, however, the intestacy need not be complete. Thus if the deceased dies partially intestate the surviving

[1] See Intestate Husband's Estate Act 1911 (1 & 2 Geo. 5, c. 10), s. 1.

spouse has prior rights in so much of the estate as is undisposed of by will. This appears from the definitions in section 36 (1) of the Act, which include the statement that " 'an intestate' means a person who has died leaving undisposed of by testamentary disposition the whole or any part of his estate, and 'intestate' shall be construed accordingly." The rights are required by sections 8 (1) and 9 (1) to be met out of the "intestate estate" which by section 36 (1) is defined as "so much of his estate as is undisposed of by testamentary disposition." The only qualification in cases of partial intestacy is contained in the proviso to section 9 (1). This provides that legacies left to the surviving spouse in the deceased's will may have to be deducted from the claim for prior rights in the estate which was not disposed of by the will.[2] Thus prior rights are available only to a surviving spouse and operate only in that part of the deceased's estate which has not been disposed of by testamentary disposition.[3]

The housing right under section 8

No recommendation that a surviving spouse should receive the deceased's house was made by the Mackintosh Committee, and this provision did not appear in the pilot version of the Bill introduced into Parliament in May 1963. Concern was, however, expressed in the Scottish Grand Committee on that occasion about the position of a surviving spouse, particularly a widow. It was pointed out that under the previous system it was not unknown for a widow of an intestate to find herself without a roof over her head if the heir at law decided to sell the house. Family squabbles, of the type that every solicitor has encountered, sometimes led to her being put out of the house or feeling bound to go. Sometimes a widow who had worked in order to help her husband to buy a house found on his death that the title was in his name and that it passed to, say, his brother or uncle. While solicitors always endeavoured to ensure that the purchaser of a house considered the question and made a will, there was, and still is, often a reluctance to settle down to consider the terms of a will. The result was that there were from time to time very hard cases which tended to discredit the law and the legal profession. The government took account of the concern expressed and what is now section 8 appeared in the Bill when it was reintroduced in November 1963.

Briefly, the effect is that on intestacy of the deceased spouse, the surviving spouse is entitled to receive, subject to any burdens affecting it, the ownership or tenancy of any one house owned, or tenanted otherwise than under the Rent Acts, by the deceased spouse, plus its furniture and plenishings. Maximum limits of £65,000 and £12,000 are stipulated for the values of the house and furniture respectively. The surviving spouse, but not necessarily the deceased spouse, must have been ordinarily resident in the house in question at the date of death of the intestate.

---

[2] See *post*, pp. 45–46.

[3] *Munro's Trs., Petrs.*, 1971 S.L.T. 313.

The right to the house

The substantive right is set out in section 8 (1). This provides that where the intestate estate includes a "relevant interest" in a dwelling-house to which the section applies, the surviving spouse is entitled to receive that interest, if its value does not exceed £65,000. If it does exceed that figure, the surviving spouse is entitled to the sum of £65,000. The concept of a maximum limit on the value of the housing right was intended to meet the difficulties which might arise if very valuable houses or mansions passed to the deceased's widow. At one stage in the Succession Bill's progress through Parliament, it was proposed to give the surviving spouse only the value of the house, and not the ownership (or tenancy) of it, if there were "special circumstances of a historical nature" connected with it. This being so vague as to be probably unworkable, the provision was dropped in favour of a maximum value for the interest which is transferred to the surviving spouse.

The limit of £65,000 has not, however, kept up with inflation, despite increases in 1973, 1981 and 1988.[4] The original figure of £15,000 then represented approximately three times the value of a substantial city house. The current figure of £65,000 is less than half of the value of the same house and the protection afforded by the housing right may now be illusory. The intention was that a surviving spouse would be enabled to continue to live undisturbed in the house in which he or she was ordinarily resident before the deceased's death, but values have so changed that the surviving spouse may not be able to afford to remain in it. If the value of the house is over the limit, or if one of the exceptions stated in section 8 (2) applies, the survivor receives a cash payment rather than the house itself. If the value of the deceased's interest in the house is below the limit, but one of the exceptions applies, the payment is "a sum equal to the value of the relevant interest." However if the value of the interest exceeds the limit, the surviving spouse is entitled to receive "the sum of £65,000." It is not said that this is in lieu of the interest or that it is a surrogatum for the interest. Some doubt may therefore exist whether this right falls to be treated as an interest in heritage or as an interest in moveables.[5] The better view, and the only one which makes sense, is that the right falls to be treated as heritable, as being a surrogatum for the house itself.

Relevant interest

It is very important to an understanding of this prior right to observe that it transfers to the surviving spouse not the house itself, but the deceased's "relevant interest" in the house. This is to cope with the various forms of interest which an occupier of a house may have. The purpose is to ensure that the surviving spouse obtains whatever interest

[4] Succession (Scotland) Act 1973 (c. 25), s. 1; S.I. 1981 No. 806; S.I. 1988 No. 633.

[5] For possible effects of this doubt on the calculation of the legal rights fund and on private international law, see *post*, p. 117.

the deceased had and can continue to live as before. In contrast to the position with the furniture and plenishings, which must have belonged to the deceased before they can pass as a prior right, it is whatever interest the deceased may have had in the house which is transferred. The deceased may have been the owner or a tenant or may have had some lesser right, but it is that interest which is transferred. The exception—and it is a large one—is that tenancies subject to the Rent Acts 1971 to 1974 do not pass to the surviving spouse as a prior right, but this is because Rent Act tenancies already have their own code of transmission on the tenant's death.

The "relevant interest" as defined in section 8 (6) (*d*) is subject to any heritable debt secured over the deceased's interest. In addition to the problem of how much of a debt is heritable when there is also moveable security (*supra*, pp. 31–32) this means that it is the net value after allowing for the heritable debt which determines whether the limit on value has been reached. The surviving spouse takes the deceased's interest when the value of the *interest* (and not of the house) does not exceed £65,000.

If there is a "mortgage protection" policy on the life of the deceased owner of a house, the surviving spouse commonly assumes that this clears the house of debt and that the whole value is transferred as a prior right, subject to the limit. However this is incorrect, for such a policy is just an ordinary policy of life assurance which pays into the estate a moveable sum which happens to be the amount needed to pay off the heritable debt. It does not alter the fact that at the moment of death, a heritable debt is secured over the house, and the prior right is to the value subject to the burden of that debt. There is no compensation in the monetary right for the reduced value of the housing right and attempts to devise a scheme for tying mortgage protection policies directly to the debt so as to cancel the debt at the moment of death have so far failed.

"Ordinarily resident"

Section 8 applies, by virtue of section 8 (4), to any dwelling-house in which the surviving spouse of the intestate was ordinarily resident at the date of death of the intestate. The deceased spouse need not have been resident there, and if the deceased was not resident there, the separation may have been friendly or otherwise. The only qualification for this right is that the surviving spouse was ordinarily resident there (and of course that the interest in the house belonged to the deceased spouse).

It is, of course, possible to be ordinarily resident in more than one dwelling-house at a time. It may be a rare situation, but could arise, for example, if the spouses had town and country houses and used both regularly, keeping two establishments in being. To meet this possibility, the proviso to section 8 (1) ensures that the surviving spouse's right applies to the predeceaser's interest in only one of the houses in which the survivor was ordinarily resident. When this situation arises, the surviving spouse has an unfettered discretion to choose the house which is to fall under the right with a period of up to six months within which to reach a decision. In the cases when this right of election arises, the surviving spouse will probably be influenced by the capital values, at least if it is a right of ownership that is involved. Unless there is some particular reason for preferring to occupy the less valuable house, the surviving spouse can always opt to take the more valuable, selling it if need be to provide capital for the purchase of a more conveniently located house. This would apply even more strongly if one of the houses was owned and the other merely leased by the deceased spouse. It will be noted, however, that the value of the furniture and plenishings in the two houses need not be a factor, since an entirely separate election is involved in that case.[6]

Dwelling-house

The right is not limited to the actual structure—the stone and mortar. "Dwelling-house" is defined in section 8 (6) (*a*) as including any garden or portion of ground attached to, and usually occupied with, the dwelling-house or otherwise required for the amenity or convenience of the house. This would seem to cover not only garden ground physically contiguous to the house but also such things as *pro indiviso* shares in the garden ground in the centre of a square.

It is not clear whether such mobile or temporary residences as caravans and houseboats come within the definition of "dwelling-house." The Matrimonial Homes (Family Protection) (Scotland) Act 1981[7] expressly includes them, along with any "other structure" which has become a family residence, within the definition of a matrimonial home for the purposes of that Act. However, the Matrimonial Homes Act definition sets out to be a comprehensive one, while the Succession Act's definition of a dwelling-house does not. The latter merely specifies that some things are included, without stating that others are excluded, and the view is ventured that the definition can extend to caravans, etc.

Exceptions where the surviving spouse receives only the value of the house

Recognising that, in some circumstances, considerable difficulties might be created by the transfer of the ownership or tenancy of a house to the surviving spouse, two exceptions are stated in section 8 (2). In these cases the surviving spouse is entitled to receive the value of the deceased's interest up to the maximum limit, but is not entitled to insist upon a transfer of the interest itself.

The first of the exceptions arises under section 8 (2) (*a*) when, although the other conditions are satisfied, the dwelling-house forms part only of the subjects comprised in one tenancy or lease under which the intestate was the tenant. A dwelling-house for the purposes of section 8 need not be a complete structure in itself. By virtue of section 8 (6) (*a*) the term includes a part of a building occupied (at the date of the death of the

[6] s. 8 (3) proviso.
[7] 1981 c. 59, s. 22.

intestate) as a separate dwelling. Thus a flat in a large block clearly falls within the definition. No problem arises if the flat was *owned* by the deceased spouse, whether or not his title also included the other flats in the block. The flat in which the surviving spouse was ordinarily resident can readily be hived off and conveyed separately to the survivor. But if the deceased had only a lease of the block of flats, in one of which the survivor was ordinarily resident, the landlord could not reasonably be required to grant a separate lease of that flat to the surviving spouse. Hence the exception applies to a dwelling-house forming part of larger subjects tenanted by the deceased and does not arise in cases of ownership.

This exception may prove to be of relatively rare occurrence in practice, but the second exception is a specialized application of the first which is likely to be of greater importance. It arises in cases of both ownership and tenancy by the deceased spouse, and is stated in section 8 (2) (*b*). Again the surviving spouse is limited to the value of the house in question if it "forms the whole or part of subjects an interest in which is comprised in the intestate estate and which were used by the intestate for carrying on a trade, profession or occupation, and the value of the estate as a whole would be likely to be substantially diminished if the dwelling-house were disposed of otherwise than with the assets of the trade, profession or occupation."

The typical example of this exception is a farmhouse. Farming would seem to fall under the heading of "trade, profession or occupation"; the house is part of the subjects used for that trade, etc., and the value of the estate as a whole would undoubtedly be substantially diminished if the farmhouse were not available along with the farming land. If the purchaser cannot have a house from which to run the farm, the amount by which the value of the farm is reduced is likely to be much greater than the value of the house as such, due to the inconvenience to the purchaser. Similar considerations might apply to cases such as that of the doctor's house with surgery attached. In either case, if the whole unit was merely tenanted by the deceased, the house would also come under the first exception in section 8 (2) (*a*), but even if the deceased was the owner, it would seem that the surviving spouse would be entitled only to the value, and not to the ownership, of the deceased's interest in the house. The fall in the value of the whole unit by reason of the absence of the house would be greater than the value of the house itself, *qua* house, and hence the "value of the estate as a whole would be likely to be substantially diminished" if the house were not disposed of along with the farm or surgery.

The surviving spouse may not regard the cash value of the house or of the tenancy thereof as adequate compensation for loss of the living accommodation, but the general policy that the survivor should not be left without a roof over his or her head gives way in this instance to the general benefit of the estate as a whole.

It is worth remembering that many farms (and surgeries) are owned by partnerships rather than by individuals. If a farm is owned by a partnership of which the deceased was a partner, his interest is a moveable interest in the partnership. He does not have a direct interest in the individual assets of the partnership, and in particular he would not seem to have any "relevant interest" in the farmhouse unless he has a tenancy agreement with the firm. In the normal case he would be neither owner nor tenant and his occupancy would not be a "relevant interest" so that nothing would pass to his spouse as a prior right under this heading.

Valuation of dwelling-houses

Where any question arises as to the value of a house, or interest therein, for the purpose either of the maximum limit or of the substituted value in cases failing within section 8 (2), it is provided by section 8 (5) that the question is to be settled by arbitration by a single arbiter. In default of agreement on an arbiter, he is to be appointed by the sheriff of the county in which the intestate was domiciled at the date of his death, or if that county is uncertain, or the intestate was domiciled furth of Scotland, by the Sheriff of the Lothians and Peebles at Edinburgh.

The value to be ascertained will presumably be the market value of the deceased's interest, taking into account any heritable debt secured over it, which should mean that in most cases the net value agreed for estate duty purposes will be accepted by those concerned.

Furniture and plenishings

The right to the house would be of little practical use if the surviving spouse had to restock it. The general aim of section 8 is to further the presumed intention of the intestate spouse that the survivor should be enabled to continue to live in the house which he or she previously occupied with as little disturbance as possible. Accordingly, section 8 (3) provides that in addition to taking over any interest which the deceased may have had in the dwelling-house in which the survivor was ordinarily resident and indeed whether or not the deceased had any interest in the house, the surviving spouse is entitled to receive that house's furniture and plenishings so far as belonging to the intestate, subject to a maximum value of £12,000.

It will be noted that this excludes furniture being acquired by the deceased on hire-purchase. Section 8 (3) gives rights to the survivor when "the intestate estate includes the furniture and plenishings." The whole point of a hire-purchase agreement being that the articles concerned do not belong to the hirer until fully paid for, furniture on hire-purchase is not included in the deceased's estate and does not pass to the surviving spouse under this provision. Subject to any specialties in the terms of the contract, this would presumably also be true even if insurance had been effected to pay off the outstanding debt in the event of the hirer's death. Credit sale agreements do not give rise to this problem as the property in the goods does then pass to the purchaser leaving the seller with only a claim of debt.

Definition of furniture and plenishings

The "furniture and plenishings" which fall under this right are more restrictively defined than on the first appearance of the Bill. The definition appears in section 8 (6) (*b*), and is not exhaustive of all possibilities, for the term is said to include "garden effects, domestic animals, plate, plated articles, linen, china, glass, books, pictures, prints, articles of household use, and consumable stores." It does not include "any article or animal used at the date of death of the intestate for business purposes, or money or securities for money or any heirloom." No mention is made of motorcars although they, with carriages and horses, were included in the version of the Bill which had its first reading in May 1963. One imagines that it might still be possible in some cases to argue that a car was part of the plenishings of a particular house if it were treated as an appurtenance of the house, *e.g.* an estate car kept at a country mansion and used solely for ferrying people and their luggage to and from the nearest station. In most cases, however, a car will prove either to have been used for business purposes, or not to be part of the plenishings of the house at all. Professional practice in drawing up inventories of estates would tend to indicate that a car is rarely regarded as part of the plenishings of a house, for cars are usually entered as separate items of estate.

The heirlooms which are not to be treated as part of the furniture and plenishings of any particular house are (by section 8 (6) (*c*)), any articles which have associations with the intestate's family of such nature and extent that they ought to pass to some member of that family other than the surviving spouse of the intestate. This is a magnificently vague provision which has so far produced surprisingly little litigation. The type of item envisaged by those who pressed for this provision in Parliament was a regimental trophy, but one wonders whether it will not lead to disputes over Grandmother's silver teapot or Great-grandmother's best tea dishes.

The definition of furniture and plenishings is, of necessity, in fairly general terms, and there is obvious scope for considerable argument over what does and what does not fall within it. It is unfortunate, therefore, that the uncertainty, and the scope for litigation is further increased by employing this form of definition as "including" certain items. This merely throws one back on the common law concept of what is furniture and plenishing, with a number of specific examples and exceptions pointed out by the Act. Since every item which is held to pass to the surviving spouse under this head automatically reduces the share falling to other persons interested in the succession, a considerable amount of litigation may arise. Any family animosities are at their bitterest when an estate is being divided up, and these provisions give full scope for this bitterness to erupt into litigation. An executor would be wise to treat the classification of particular items as furniture and plenishings with considerable caution.

Limit on value

Where the value of the furniture and plenishings included in the intestate estate does not exceed £12,000 the surviving spouse is entitled to the whole thereof. If the value is over £12,000, the survivor may select the items which he or she wishes to have up to that value. This limit will be adequate in most estates, and is certainly nearer to a realistic figure than the upper limit placed on the house itself. Its function is to provide for the possibility that the deceased spouse had extremely valuable paintings hanging on the walls of the house.

Disputes as to valuations are to be settled by a single arbiter under section 8 (5), as in the case of valuations of the house. However, despite the terms of the arbitration provisions, valuation of the furniture and plenishings can be undertaken only when the deceased was domiciled in Scotland, for only in that situation will Scots law govern the succession to his moveable estate.[8]

The house from which the furniture and plenishings may be taken

In the normal case where the surviving spouse was ordinarily resident in only one house in which the deceased had a "relevant interest" there is no problem. It is the furniture and plenishings of that house which the survivor is entitled to receive.[9] The survivor is still entitled to the furniture and plenishings when the deceased spouse's interest in the house falls within one of the exceptions specified in section 8 (2) (or has a value over the limit), so that the survivor receives only the substituted value. Despite the exception, the house in that case is still one to which section 8 applies,[10] and therefore the surviving spouse is entitled to such furniture and plenishings in it as belonged to the intestate by virtue of section 8 (3).

In cases where the surviving spouse was ordinarily resident in more than one house at the date of death of the intestate, the survivor is entitled to the furniture and plenishings belonging to the deceased in such one of them as he or she may elect within six months of the death of the intestate.[11] This election is entirely separate from the election of a house from two or more belonging to the deceased in which the survivor was ordinarily resident under section 8 (1). It will therefore be possible to elect to take one of the houses with the furniture and plenishings of another, although one imagines that any difference in value of furnishings would rarely justify the removal expenses involved.

The right to furniture and plenishings may arise completely independently of the right to a house, as where the deceased spouse did not have a "relevant interest" in any house in which the survivor was ordinarily resident, but did own some or all of the furniture. Section 8 (3) expressly provides that the right to furniture and plenishings exists whether or not the house is comprised in the intestate estate. The commonest case is that of the wife dying intestate when the house is owned or tenanted by the husband. Here no interest in the house is included in the wife's estate,

[8] See Chap. 9 *infra*.
[9] s. 8 (3).
[10] s. 8 (4).
[11] s. 8 (3) proviso.

but the husband is entitled to receive as a prior right such of the furniture and plenishings of the house as belonged to the wife, subject always to the £12,000 limit.

Order of priority of the rights under section 8

The surviving spouse's rights to the house and furniture and plenishings under this section are the first items to come out of the deceased spouse's estate. Section 9 (6) (*a*) postpones the second set of prior rights—the monetary provision—to the housing right under section 8. Section 10 (2) postpones the traditional legal rights, as amended, to both of these prior rights, and section 1 (2) postpones the operation of the rules of succession to the free estate to both prior and legal rights. Hence the housing right is the first to be considered.

Monetary right under section 9

Section 9 (1) entitles the surviving spouse to £21,000 if the deceased left children, or to £35,000 if the deceased left no children. This right comes out of the intestate estate left after the housing rights under section 8 have been met[12] and is therefore in addition to the right to house, furniture and plenishings.

Interest is payable on the £21,000 or £35,000 as the case may be from the date of the intestate's death until payment. Although the Succession Act originally specified a fixed rate of interest (4 per cent.) the rate is variable by the Secretary of State, and currently is 7 per cent.[13]

When the Succession Act 1964 came into force, the surviving spouse's right was restricted to the lower figure only when the deceased was survived by lawful issue. This included adopted children but not illegitimate children. Thus, if a deceased wife was survived only by an illegitimate child, her husband was entitled to a prior right at the higher level even if that entirely defeated the child's claim in the mother's estate. This had also been the case under the corresponding provisions prior to the 1964 Act[14] and still applies in the division of the estates of persons who died on or after September 10, 1964, up to and including November 24, 1968.

However, on November 25, 1968—the commencement of the Law Reform (Miscellaneous Provisions) (Scotland) Act 1968—the first major improvement of the position of illegitimate children came into force. Illegitimate children were put on the same footing as legitimate children in the succession to both parents (although only in succession directly to the parents). The result is that since that date the surviving spouse's prior monetary right has been restricted to the lower figure (currently £21,000)

---

[12] s. 9 (6) (*a*).
[13] S.I. 1981 No. 805. From 1964 to 1981, 4 per cent.
[14] *Osman* v. *Campbell*, 1946 S.C. 204.

whenever the deceased was survived by children, legitimate or illegitimate.[15] From November 25, 1968, until the Law Reform (Parent and Child) (Scotland) Act 1986[16] came into force on December 8, 1986, the existence of *lawful* issue, however remote, of a predeceasing child of the intestate also restricted the surviving spouse's right, but illegitimate offspring of a predeceasing child were not taken into account.

This was because the policy was to grant illegitimate children rights of succession in the estates of their parents, but not to permit them to represent their parents in, *e.g.* the division of the estates of their grandparents. When this policy was applied to prior rights, the result was that the existence of an illegitimate child affected the division of the estate of its father or mother, but not any other estate. Thus, if the intestate's sole child (legitimate or illegitimate) had predeceased him, only the existence of legitimate offspring of that child reduced the surviving spouse's right.[17]

However, the status of illegitimacy has for practical purposes been abolished by the Law Reform (Parent and Child) (Scotland) Act 1986. Section 1 of that Act sets out the fundamental principle that the fact that a person's parents are not or have not been married to one another shall be left out of account in establishing the legal relationship between the person and any other person. The consequence is that the existence of any issue of the deceased spouse reduces the right of the surviving spouse under section 9 to the lower figure of £21,000. The terms legitimate or illegitimate have ceased to have any meaning.

The children or issue concerned must, of course, be the offspring of the deceased spouse but need not be the offspring of the surviving spouse. Children of the deceased by a previous marriage or children who would formerly have been classed as illegitimate automatically reduce the surviving spouse's entitlement.

Effect of legacies in cases of partial intestacy

A surviving spouse has prior rights in cases of partial as well as total intestacy. The rights exist in the intestate estate as defined in the Act, and the definition refers to such part of the deceased's estate as is undisposed of by testamentary disposition.[18] If the intestacy is partial, the surviving spouse still receives the house and its furniture and plenishings except to the extent that they have been disposed of by the deceased in his will.[19] Equally, the surviving spouse is still entitled to either £21,000 or £35,000 from the rest of the undisposed-of estate, but must deduct from that sum the amount or value of any legacy which he or she is entitled to receive out of the estate of the deceased. However, the survivor does not require

---

[15] 1968 Act (c. 70), s. 3 and Sched. 1, amending s. 9 (1) of the Succession Act.

[16] c. 9.

[17] Succession (Scotland) Act 1964, s. 9 (1) (*a*), as amended, read with the definition of "issue" in s. 36 (1).

[18] s. 36 (1). See *supra*, p. 36.

[19] s. 8 (1) and (3).

to deduct the value of a legacy of any house in which he or she was ordinarily resident at the deceased's death, nor need a legacy of any furniture and plenishings of any such house be deducted.[20] If the survivor was ordinarily resident in more than one house, he or she may take a legacy of all the houses, and of all the furniture and plenishings in all of them, with no limits on value, without having to deduct the legacy from the prior right. This is because section 8 (4) applies the section to *any* dwelling-house in which the survivor was ordinarily resident, while the proviso to section 9 (1) discounts a legacy of *any* house to which section 8 applies. If the surviving spouse chooses to renounce any legacy affecting the monetary prior right, as might be done if the legacy were of dubious value, the full sum may be claimed.

Section 9 (6) (*b*) defines a legacy for these purposes as including "any payment or benefit to which a surviving spouse becomes entitled by virtue of any testamentary disposition." This gives a very wide interpretation to the term legacy and many benefits may be conferred in deeds which rank as testamentary dispositions which are not normally thought of as legacies. For example, the definition would seem to cover special destinations in favour of the surviving spouse. In a situation where the deceased spouse had purchased heritage with his own funds and recorded a destination, which he did not thereafter revoke, to himself and his wife and the survivor, that part of the destination having testamentary effect, namely the destination to his wife of the one-half share belonging to him at his death, would be a "legacy," the value of which might have to be deducted by the widow from her claim for the monetary element of her prior rights. Provisions in marriage contracts might also be such as to rank as "legacies." Although the definition of legacy in section 9 (6) (*b*) is not limited to testamentary dispositions made by the deceased spouse, what falls to be deducted is a legacy "out of the estate of the intestate."[21]

The valuation of any such legacy is to be made as at the date of the deceased's death.[22]

Estate affected by the surviving spouse's monetary right

Where the amount of the estate available to meet the monetary payments, after deducting the rights under section 8, is less than the £21,000 or £35,000 due to the surviving spouse, that spouse's right is held to be satisfied by the transfer to him or her of the whole of the available balance, thereby exhausting the estate.[23]

This can have surprising effects, as illustrated by example 1 in Appendix 2. A man dies intestate leaving a widow and two children, *i.e.*

---

[20] s. 9 (1) proviso.
[21] s. 9 (1) proviso.
[22] s. 9 (6) (*b*).
[23] s. 9 (2) and (6) (*a*).

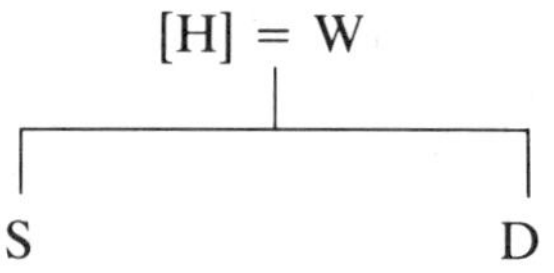

The net value of his estate is £88,000 consisting of a house valued at £60,000, furniture and plenishings thereof valued at £8,000, and net moveable estate of £20,000. The widow's prior right under section 8 gives her the house and furniture and plenishings. Her prior right to a monetary provision under section 9 is to £21,000, there being lawful issue of the deceased spouse. The balance available to meet this right is only £20,000, and hence the widow takes the whole of it in satisfaction of her rights. Thus the whole of the deceased's estate has gone to his widow. The son and daughter have a right to legitim in any moveable estate available after the spouse's prior rights have been met and to any free balance of the estate after *jus relictae* and legitim have been deducted. Here, however, the estate is not large enough to reach the stage of calculating legal rights, let alone dividing up any free balance under the rules in Part I of the Act. Hence the widow takes the whole estate, and the children get nothing.

Take, however, exactly the same family with exactly the same items of estate, but postulating that the husband had not believed what he had been told about intestate succession, and that he had decided to make sure his widow received his whole estate by saying so in his will. Since he has made a will dealing with his whole estate, his widow has no prior rights. There is, therefore, estate from which legitim is exigible, despite the will. The moveable estate amounts to £28,000 (furniture, etc., plus the net moveable estate) and the legitim fund for division between the children is therefore £9,333. The widow receives the remaining £18,667 of the moveable estate and the house by virtue of the will.

It is therefore possible, by dying intestate, to achieve an exclusion of the children's right to legitim although it is not possible to achieve this by express testamentary provision. Indeed the children can be better off when their parent makes a will attempting to cut them out of any share in his estate than when he does nothing at all. At first sight it seemed that there might now be situations in which a solicitor would find himself in the position of advising his client not to make a will. This would have been unsatisfactory, since much depends on the precise value of the estate at the intestate's death and ingenious drafting devices were suggested to achieve the best of both worlds.

The simple answer was, however, pointed out by Professor McDonald.[24] If a client seeks to ensure that his widow will receive his whole estate, he should make a will wholly in her favour without a destination over in the event of her failing to take the testamentary gift. If

[24] (1965) 10 J.L.S. 4.

the issue do not claim legitim the will operates whatever the values. If the issue do claim legitim and the estate is above the limit of value at which intestacy ceases to be more beneficial to the widow than testacy, then the widow takes under the will subject to the legitim. If the issue claim legitim and the estate is below that critical value (which is rather above the amount that would pass wholly to the widow by prior rights) the widow simply renounces her benefit under the will. This necessarily results in intestacy, there being no other beneficiary under the will.

The Kerr, Petitioner problem

The question of whether such a renunciation in fact created an intestacy was closely argued in *Kerr, Petr.*[25] The decision by the sheriff-substitute, affirmed by the sheriff on appeal, was that intestacy did result, so that the widow became entitled to the whole estate by virtue of her prior rights to the total exclusion of her step-daughter. This result was probably inevitable, for the alternative would have been to postulate a species of property which, though not intestate, fell to be divided as if it were, apart from prior rights.

Where the amount of the estate available to meet the monetary payment under section 9 is greater than the amount due to the surviving spouse, section 9 (3) provides that the amount concerned "shall be borne by, and paid out of, the parts of the intestate estate consisting of heritable and moveable property respectively in proportion to the respective amounts of those parts." Despite the assimilation of heritage and moveables for some purposes of succession, this is necessary because the distinction between heritage and moveables has been kept for the purposes of the legal rights of *jus relicti*, *jus relictae* and legitim. After the prior rights under sections 8 and 9 have been satisfied, the surviving spouse is entitled to *jus relicti* or *jus relictae* in the surplus moveables, and issue of the deceased have the right to legitim, also in the surplus moveables. A precise value for moveables must therefore be maintained at the stage of prior rights so that the estate from which legal rights can be taken may be accurately ascertained.

The proportion of the section 9 prior right payable by heritage and by moveables is the proportion which the net capital value of each bears to the net capital value of the *whole* estate available to meet the monetary payment. As an example, if the net estate after satisfaction of the housing right under section 8 is £40,000, consisting of heritage to the value of £10,000 and moveables to the value of £30,000, heritage represents one-quarter of the estate and bears one-quarter of the payment to the surviving spouse—*i.e.* £5,250 or £8,750 as the case may be. Moveables, representing three-quarters of the estate, bear the remaining three-quarters of the payment. The balance of the moveables is subject to *jus relicti* or *jus relictae*, and to legitim if applicable (see also example 2, Appendix 2).

[25] 1968 S.L.T. (Sh. Ct.) 61. See (1968) 13 J.L.S. 192.

It is not necessary actually to pay the amount due from heritage out of the proceeds of sale of the heritage or to create a security right over the heritage. All that is needed is a notional figure for heritage and moveables for the computation of legal rights. After legal rights have been computed, heritage and moveables are assimilated into one estate and pass under the same rules. No rights are affected if the surviving spouse is actually paid out of available moveable assets or by transfer of heritage to those values.

The surviving spouse is entitled to insist upon the furniture and plenishings and the deceased's interest in the house being transferred in view of the express terms of the statute. However for other intestate assets the executor has a discretion whether to realise the asset and distribute the proceeds or to distribute *in specie*.[26] The discretion must be exercised in the interest of the estate as a whole, and if distribution is made *in specie* the executor may distribute equally to the beneficiaries (which will normally be appropriate). However circumstances may be such that it is appropriate for the executor to be selective and to transfer different assets to individual beneficiaries.[27]

No representation in prior rights

The rights under sections 8 and 9 are available only to a spouse who does actually survive, and cannot be claimed by issue of a predeceasing spouse as there is no provision for representation in the sections creating prior rights. The scheme of infinite representation set out in sections 5 and 6 applies only to Part I of the Act, dealing with the free estate available after prior rights and legal rights, and the scheme of representation contained in section 11 is limited to representation in legitim.

Previous figures for prior rights

For deaths from September 10, 1964, to May 22, 1973, inclusive

s. 8	(1)	—	£15,000
s. 8	(3)	—	£ 5,000
s. 9		—	£ 2,500 or £5,000

For deaths from May 23, 1973, to December 30, 1977, inclusive (Succession (Scotland) Act 1973)

s. 8	(1)	—	£30,000
s. 8	(3)	—	£ 8,000
s. 9		—	£ 4,000 or £8,000

---

[26] *Cochrane's Trs.* v. *Inland Revenue*, 1975 S.L.T. 6 where the Lord President stated that the executor was not bound to take directions even from a residuary legatee. See also *Murray's J.F.* v. *Thomas Murray & Sons (Ice Merchants)*, 1992 S.L.T. 824.

[27] See also *post*, p. 113.

For deaths from December 31, 1977, to July 31, 1981, inclusive (S.I. 1977 No. 2110.)

s. 8	(1)	—	£30,000
s. 8	(3)	—	£ 8,000
s. 9		—	£ 8,000 or £16,000

For deaths from August 1, 1981, to April 30, 1988, inclusive (S.I. 1981 No. 806.)

s. 8	(1)	—	£50,000
s. 8	(3)	—	£10,000
s. 9		—	£15,000 or £25,000

CHAPTER 5

LEGAL RIGHTS OF THE SURVIVING SPOUSE AND OF DESCENDANTS

The Succession (Scotland) Act 1964 is not a complete restatement of the traditional legal rights of spouses and children so that in this field much of the older law is still relevant. However, the various particular changes made by the Act were the first substantial alterations in legal rights for some centuries so that care has to be taken in assimilating the old and the new.

The Succession Act also abolished the former rule that legal rights were due on divorce as if the guilty spouse had died.[1] Thus references to legal rights in marriage contracts which were entered into before September 10, 1964, but which take effect on divorce granted in an action commenced on or after that date are now to be construed as references to rights which the spouse might obtain under the new schemes of financial provision on divorce.[2] Any reference to legal rights in a pre-1964 marriage contract tended to take the form of a renunciation of them by the parties. The result now is that the clause will be treated as a renunciation of any claim for financial provision on divorce. It may also exclude the right to seek a variation of the marriage contract on divorce.[3]

While this chapter attempts to state the law as it now affects legal rights, taking into account the subsisting parts of the old law as well as the amendments made by the Act, it would not be appropriate in a work of this nature to enter into a full and elaborate discussion of the surviving parts of the old law with full citation of authority. The cases on various aspects of legal rights are legion and no attempt is made here to vouch every proposition. Such cases as are here noted, relating to the unamended parts of the older law, are cited merely as illustrations of what may be regarded as tolerably well-settled principles. Against this background, the changes effected by the Act are examined.

Order of priority of legal rights

In their application to intestate succession, legal rights are exigible from the moveable estate available after any prior rights under sections 8 and 9 of the Succession Act have been satisfied.[4]

---

[1] Succession (Scotland) Act 1964, s. 25, repealed and replaced by Divorce (Scotland) Act 1976 (c. 39), Sched. 2 and ss. 5 & 6.

[2] 1964 Act, s. 33 (2). See Divorce (Scotland) Act 1976, s. 5; Matrimonial and Family Proceedings Act 1984 (c. 42), s. 29 or Family Law (Scotland) Act 1985 (c. 37), s. 8.

[3] *Thomson* v. *Thomson*, 1982 S.L.T. 521.

[4] s. 10 (2).

If the deceased is survived by a spouse the practical result of the postponement to prior rights will often be that legal rights are of no significance. If the composition and size of the deceased's estate are such that the prior rights of the surviving spouse are greater than the value of the estate, the whole estate passes to the surviving spouse and there will be no legal rights.[5] While Scots tend to be proud of the way in which legal rights operate as a bar to capricious disinheritance by a testator, the fact that a child's right to legitim may be defeated if the parent does not make a will, and indeed sometimes even if he does make a will, leaves an interesting jurisprudential question of whether the child can be said to have a right at all if there is no estate on which the right can operate.

The rights available

The legal rights formerly exigible from the heritage of a deceased person, namely the widow's terce and the widower's courtesy, are abolished in respect of any deaths occurring on or after September 10, 1964.[6] References in any other enactment to courtesy or terce are of no effect.[7] This total abolition of rights which were of very long standing in the law was generally welcomed. Terce, in particular, was of very little value to the recipient in the vast majority of cases and had largely a nuisance value as a trap for unwary conveyancers (if such beings exist!).

However, the opportunity was not taken to extend legal rights to the whole estate. Despite strenuous efforts in Parliament during the consideration of the Succession Bill, the government insisted on retaining the distinction between heritage and moveables for the purposes of legal rights. Consequently the abolition of terce and courtesy means that there are now no legal rights—as opposed to prior rights—in a deceased's heritable property. The legal rights which are now available to the deceased's surviving spouse and to his descendants are exigible from his *moveable* estate only, and the moveable estate in question is that remaining after satisfaction of any prior rights. It is therefore still essential to classify property correctly and to allocate debts to heritage and to moveables.

The surviving wife's right is *jus relictae* while the corresponding right of a husband is *jus relicti*. They are identical in all but name and entitle the surviving spouse to one-third of the deceased's moveable property if the deceased is survived by qualified descendants or to one-half of the moveables if there are no such descendants. The legal right of descendants (not merely immediate children of the deceased as was the case pre-1964) is legitim. If the deceased parent has left a surviving spouse, the descendants share a legitim fund consisting of one-third of the available

---

[5] This is now less often true than it was in 1964, as the values for prior rights have not kept pace with inflation, particularly of house values.

[6] s. 10 (1).

[7] Sched. 2, para. 4.

moveable estate of the deceased parent. If the deceased left no surviving spouse the legitim fund to be shared among the descendants consists of one-half of the moveables.

In other words, when legal rights are involved, there are three possible units of division of the moveable fund from which they are exigible. These units are:

(1) surviving spouse's share—*jus relicti* or *jus relictae*;
(2) descendants' share—legitim (bairn's part);
(3) dead's part—this, along with heritage not required to meet prior rights, passes on intestacy under the rules of succession to the free estate contained in Part I of the Act.

If the intestate was survived by both spouse and issue, the moveables available to meet legal rights are split into three parts, one part to each of the units of division. If the intestate was survived by a spouse, but not by issue, or conversely was survived by issue but not by a spouse, the available moveables are split into two parts, one being dead's part and the other being the surviving spouse's share or the legitim fund for division among the issue.

Interest on legal rights

Interest is payable on the ascertained amount of the legal rights from the date of death until paid.[8] Although there is little theoretical discussion of the basis for payment of interest, it is well established that it is payable.[9] In only two of the reported cases was interest refused altogether, and in both of these other factors seem to have been taken into account.[10] It may be that interest arises from the same considerations as apply to interest on debts where the general rule is that, apart from contract, interest is payable as a result of a principal sum having been wrongfully withheld and not paid on the date when it ought to have been paid.[11] There is scope for considerable discussion of what that date is[12] but in the case of legal rights it is established that the relevant date from which interest runs is the date of death.[13] It may seem odd that this should be so, for the law is in the peculiar position of notionally requiring the executor to pay the legal rights on the very day of death while also erecting the principle of vitious intromission against anyone attempting to comply with the requirement. Despite the terms of the decision in *Young*

[8] No interest was payable on terce or courtesy, they being rights to the income arising from the heritage.

[9] McLaren, *Wills & Succession*, i, 125.

[10] *Wick* v. *Wick* (1898) 1 F. 199; *Young* v. *Young*, 1965 S.L.T. (Notes) 95.

[11] See *Kolbin & Sons* v. *Kinnear & Co.*, 1931 S.C. (H.L.) 128, *per* Lord Atkin at p. 137.

[12] Wilson, *The Scottish Law of Debt*, 2nd ed., para. 11.7.

[13] *Gilchrist* v. *Gilchrist's Trs.* (1889) 16 R. 1118, *per* Lord Fraser at 1120. See also *Russel* v. *Att.-Gen.*, 1917 S.C. 28; *Sanderson* v. *Lockhart-Mure*, 1946 S.C. 298; *Kearon* v. *Thomson's Trs.*, 1949 S.C. 287.

v. *Young*[14] interest on legal rights in succession does not depend upon unreasonable delay in payment. In *Kearon* v. *Thomson's Trs.*[15] interest was awarded from the date of death even although it was expressly held by Lord President Cooper that the legitim claim had been promptly complied with by the executors and no objection to their administration had been raised.

The rate of interest is at the discretion of the court,[16] taking account both of prevailing rates and of the interest actually earned by the estate in this period. Factors such as that substantial parts of the estate may not be in a state of productive investment at the time of the deceased's death mean that the rate of interest to be awarded will be somewhat below the current going rate for commercial investments. In practice, the figure of 7 per cent. currently specified for the monetary element of a spouse's prior rights is often acceptable and is commonly recommended by advisers. The Scottish Law Commission has recommended that future legislation should remove the uncertainty of the present discretionary rate by specifying a fixed rate and that in current circumstances the same figure of 7 per cent. should be adopted.

The persons entitled to legal rights

Jus relictae and *jus relicti* are available only to a surviving spouse, there being no representation of a predeceasing spouse at any stage in the division of an intestate estate. The only provisions permitting representation are those in sections 5 and 6 of the Act dealing with the free estate (which do not in any event apply to spouses) and those in section 11 dealing with legitim.

Legitim was formerly confined to surviving legitimate children related by blood to the deceased, but important changes have now been effected.

Adopted children were given by the Succession Act full rights of succession (including legitim) in the estates of the adopting parent or parents.[17] Adopted children now fall to be treated as legitimate children of the adopter for all purposes, including the calculation of prior and legal rights. This remedied a major anomaly of the older law that adoption had no effect upon rights of succession. Adopted persons retained any rights of succession which they had in the estates of their natural parents but gained none in the estates of the adopting parents. A belated transitional provision for the case where the adopting parent died before the Succession Act came into force on September 10, 1964, and the natural parent died on or after August 3, 1966, is contained in the Law Reform (Miscellaneous Provisions) (Scotland) Act 1966.[18] In these circumstances,

---

[14] 1965 S.L.T. (Notes) 95.

[15] 1949 S.C. 287. (The rubric to the report at 1949 S.L.T. 286 is misleading in this respect.)

[16] *Kearon* v. *Thomson's Trs.*, *supra.* There is a comprehensive citation of earlier authority in Lord Cooper's opinion.

[17] s. 23 (1).

[18] (c. 19), s. 5.

any right to legitim which the child has in the estates of its natural parents is preserved.

Illegitimate children, by an even more far-reaching series of provisions, now have the right to legitim in the estates of both parents. The first step came in the Law Reform (Miscellaneous Provisions) (Scotland) Act 1968[19] which added a new section 10A to the Succession Act. The result then was that in the division of the estates of its parents dying on or after November 25, 1968, an illegitimate child had exactly the same right of legitim as a legitimate child. A decree of affiliation and aliment established paternity for this purpose unless the contrary was proved.[20] There were however anomalies even after the 1968 reforms, as a grandchild which was illegitimate could not represent its predeceasing, legitimate, parent to obtain legitim from the estate of a grandparent.[21] The full assimilation of the position of the illegitimate child to that of the legitimate child finally came in the Law Reform (Parent and Child) (Scotland) Act 1986.[22] In the succession to persons dying after the commencement of that Act on December 8, 1986 no distinction is made between legitimate and illegitimate children (except for succession to titles and arms) and in particular, grandchildren will always be able to represent their predeceasing parents for the purposes of legitim in the estates of their grandparents. For practical purposes, illegitimacy has now been abolished. A declarator of parentage (which requires "sufficient evidence") establishes paternity.[23]

The introduction of representation in legitim was another major change effected by the Succession Act. There is no representation of a spouse so as to give that spouse's issue *jus relictae* or *jus relicti*, but legitim is no longer confined to surviving children. This remedies what was widely regarded as one of the major anomalies of the law prior to the Succession Act. In a situation such as the following:

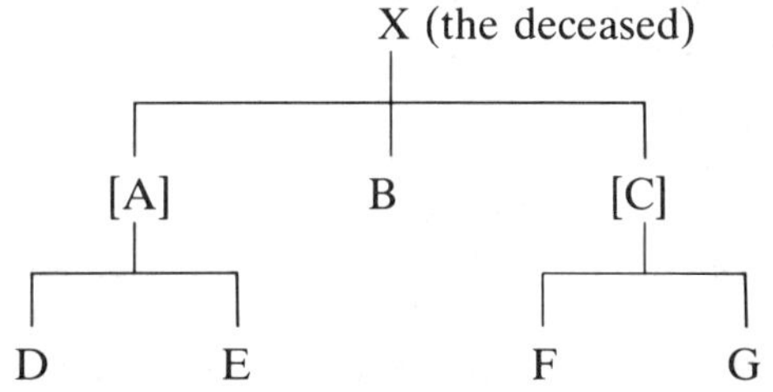

[19] (c. 70), s. 2.

[20] Law Reform (Miscellaneous Provisions) (Scotland) Act 1968 (c. 70), s. 11. Repealed by Law Reform (Parent and Child) (Scotland) Act 1986 (c. 9), Sched. 2.

[21] The "issue" who could represent their parents were defined by s. 36 (1) of the Succession Act as lawful issue, however remote, with the result that an illegitimate child could not claim the legitim to which its parent would have been entitled by survivance.

[22] c. 9.

[23] *Ibid.* s. 5 (3).

B, the surviving child of the intestate, used to take the whole legitim fund to the exclusion of D, E, F and G, the issue of predeceasing children. The lack of representation arose from the wording of the definition of "moveable estate" in section 9 of the Intestate Moveable Succession (Scotland) Act 1855. This provided, *inter alia*, that "moveable estate" included the "whole free moveable estate on which the deceased, if not subject to any incapacity, might have tested." As the deceased could not test on that proportion of his estate subject to legitim (or *jus relicti* and *jus relictae*), this meant that the proportion of the moveables available for legitim was not part of the "moveable estate" in which a right of representation *was* created by section 1 of that Act. (Equally it meant that there was no representation in a spouse's rights.) As there was no representation at common law in the division of moveables, the pre-existing position was preserved for legitim and other legal rights in moveables, so that a single surviving child took the whole legitim fund to the exclusion of grandchildren. There was never any doubt that estate subject to legitim was not estate on which the deceased "might have tested." If in fact he made a will dealing with the whole of his estate, it was effective in respect of the property subject to legitim only if the children entitled to claim refrained from doing so.

The Mackintosh Committee on the Law of Succession recommended the introduction of infinite representation in legitim and so far as this was done, it was done by section 11 of the Succession Act. Section 11 (1) makes the general provision that where a person dies predeceased by a child who has left issue who survive the deceased, and the child would, if he had survived the deceased, have been entitled to legitim out of the deceased's estate, such issue shall have the like right to legitim as the child would have had if he had survived the deceased. "Child" refers to an immediate child of the deceased, and, in respect of deaths occurring on or after November 25, 1968, includes also an illegitimate child.[24] Thus the legitimate children of an illegitimate child could represent it from 1968 onwards, but it was not until 1986 that illegitimate children could actually be the representatives.

In itself, section 11 (1) would have the effect of requiring a division of the legitim fund *per stirpes* into as many parts as there were children of the deceased, irrespective of whether any of the children had survived. The division *per stirpes* would always be at the level of immediate children because the right of representation gives the issue "the like right to legitim as the child would have had if he had survived the deceased." However, section 11 (1) is stated to be "subject to the next following subsection" which requires the use of the anomalous method of division previously in force in relation to moveable estate rather than the true representation which was applied in heritable succession. Briefly, section 11 (2) provides that there is a division *per stirpes* at the level of the class nearest in degree to the deceased of which there are surviving members.

---

[24] See above.

If the deceased's children predecease him, but he is survived by grandchildren, a situation such as the following may arise:

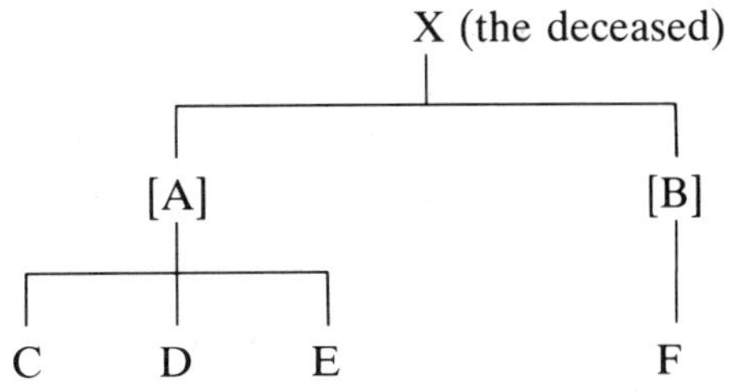

In this situation C, D, E and F are the class nearest in degree to the deceased of which there are surviving members. By virtue of section 11 (1) they are entitled to legitim. As they are all of the same degree of relationship to the deceased, the effect of section 11 (2) (*a*) is that the legitim fund is divided among them equally, *i.e.* a *per capita* division. The division is not one-half to A's family and one-half to B's family, but a division into quarters at the level of grandchildren. A's children have benefited substantially by the fact that both A and B predeceased their grandparent X.

However, take a case where the claimants are not all of the same degree of relationship to the deceased, for example:

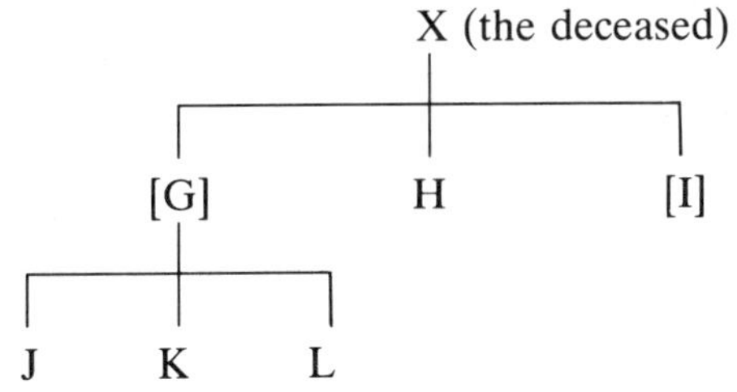

Those entitled to legitim are the child H, and the grandchildren J, K and L. The class nearest in degree to the intestate of which there are surviving members is the class of children, H being the survivor. The division of the legitim fund is therefore *per stirpes* into two parts, there being two children either surviving or represented by surviving issue. Of these parts, H takes one, giving him one-half of the legitim fund, and the other part is divided equally between J, K and L, giving them one-sixth of the fund each.[25]

Property subject to legal rights

With the abolition of terce and courtesy, there are now no legal rights in heritage. Legal rights are exigible from such of the moveable estate

---

[25] s. 11 (2) (*b*).

owned by the deceased at the time of his death as is available after deduction of the appropriate proportion of any surviving spouse's prior rights.

The distinction between heritage and moveables for the purpose of legal rights remains almost completely unaffected.[26] Land; buildings; things annexed to, growing in, or destined for use on, land; and rights having a tract of future time[27] are heritable. Things capable of movement and most incorporeal rights are moveable. Assets which have been held to be moveable for the purpose of legal rights include insurance policies on the deceased's own life,[28] or taken out by him on the life of another,[29] the deceased's vested right in the succession to a third party, even where that third party's estate included heritable bonds[30] and certain bonds and debentures issued under statutory powers.[31] An interest in a partnership is moveable, and this can have dramatic effects when farms are involved. If the deceased owned a farm and was in partnership solely for the purpose of working the farm, his interest in the farm itself is clearly heritable and not subject to legal rights. He will normally have granted a lease of the farm to the partnership which includes himself. However if he had conveyed the farm to the partnership as one of its assets, his interest in the partnership is wholly moveable, even if it mainly represents the value of the land which he had conveyed to the firm. He has no direct interest in the assets of the partnership.[32] This can make a very big difference to the value of legal rights claims in his estate.

One perennial problem is whether particular assets were *in bonis* of the deceased at the time of his death, as only such assets are available for legal rights. In *Beveridge* v. *Beveridge's Exrx.*[33] a question arose over a Treasury gratuity paid to the legal representatives of a deceased civil servant. This was held to be part of the moveable estate subject to legal rights, despite the argument that the deceased had no enforceable right to the sum and thus it could not have been *in bonis* of the deceased at his death.

There are also certain points worth notice in connection with bonds. By section 117 of the Titles to Land Consolidation (Scotland) Act 1868,[34] a "heritable security" is moveable in the general succession of the creditor. It remains heritable, however, *quoad fiscum*; it does not pertain to the wife *jure relictae* (nor to the husband *jure relicti*)[35] and is not to be treated as part of the creditor's moveable estate in computing the legitim fund. In

---

[26] See Walker, *Principles of Scottish Private Law*, 4th ed., Vol. III, pp. 4–17.

[27] This somewhat esoteric concept refers primarily to regular payments to a creditor although not related to any particular capital sum. An annuity is the standard example.

[28] *Muirhead* v. *Muirhead's Factor* (1867) 6 M. 95.

[29] *Chalmers's Trs.* (1882) 9 R. 743. The actuarial value was used.

[30] *Borland's Trs.* v. *Borland*, 1917 S.C. 704.

[31] *Robertson's Trs.* v. *Maxwell*, 1922 S.C. 267.

[32] Gretton, "Who owns partnership property," 1987 J.R. 163.

[33] 1938 S.C. 160.

[34] As amended by Succession (Scotland) Act 1964, s. 34 and Sched. 3.

[35] Married Women's Property (Scotland) Act 1881 (44 & 45 Vict. c. 21), s. 6.

other words, it is heritable for the purposes of legal rights, and as there are now no legal rights in heritage, this means that investment in heritable securities is not subject to legal rights at all. Even when the new standard security was created by the Conveyancing and Feudal Reform (Scotland) Act 1970,[36] the anomaly of its classification was not removed. It is also declared to be a "heritable security" for the purposes of section 117 of the 1868 Act, so that the former difficulties of heritable bonds remain for standard securities.

It is surely nonsensical to preserve this classification of a given type of property as heritable for some purposes and moveable for others, the more especially as the distinction between heritage and moveables is abolished for the purpose of succession to the free estate after prior rights and legal rights. The only thing that is achieved by this chameleon-like nature is confusion and uncertainty as to how the executor should deal with a heritable security in allocating funds to meet a surviving spouse's monetary prior right under section 9.[37]

However, it was startling to discover that not only did the Succession Act preserve the existing situation, but it even brought an additional type of property into the same situation. Schedule 3 repeals a proviso to section 30 of the Conveyancing (Scotland) Act 1874, with the result that ground annuals fall to be treated in the same way as heritable securities under section 117 of the 1868 Act even although they are still expressly excluded from the definition of "heritable security" in that Act. Ground annuals are now also moveable in the creditor's general succession, but heritable *quoad fiscum* and *quoad* legal rights. Surely such property should now be either heritable or moveable for all purposes. It is not now even possible for the creditor to make securities heritable for all purposes as he could formerly do by taking a destination excluding executors. That part of section 117 of the 1868 Act which made the bond heritable for all purposes in such a case has now been repealed, presumably because executors now administer the whole estate, heritage and moveables alike. The result is that section 117 now baldly states that such securities are moveable, except *quoad fiscum* and *quoad* legal rights. It would not matter greatly whether they were to be called moveable or heritable, though, since they can be just another form of investment, it might be preferable to class them as moveable so as to make them subject to legal rights. A complete repeal of section 117 would make them heritable for all purposes by reverting to the common law position. A repeal of the proviso to section 117 would make them moveable for all purposes. Either course would be preferable to the present position.

Personal bonds may also be in an anomalous position. At one stage of the Succession Bill's progress it was proposed to repeal the Act 1661, c. 32.[38] That Act made personal bonds moveable in the succession of the

---

[36] c. 35.

[37] See *supra* p. 48 and Appendix 2, Example 4.

[38] A.P.S. c. 244.

creditor, unless they excluded executors or contained an obligation to infeft. When the difficulties which would have arisen from such a repeal were pointed out, the proposal to repeal was dropped and the Act remains in force. The snag is that the part of the Act which should have been repealed, namely the reference to bonds excluding executors, also remains in force. Executors can no longer be excluded, inasmuch as they now administer both heritable and moveable estate, but nonetheless, it would seem that a personal bond which purports to exclude executors still becomes heritable in the creditor's succession, at least after the first term of payment of interest has arrived, and is thus not subject to any legal rights.

The sensible answer would be to apply legal rights to the whole estate, thereby completely abolishing the distinction between heritage and moveables for all purposes of succession. The Scottish Law Commission proposes just such a reform in its Report on Succession. The new "legal share" which they propose will take the form of percentages of the whole estate and this is greatly to be welcomed.

Date of valuation of assets

Legal rights are entitlements to fixed fractions of the value of the moveable estate of the deceased at the time of his death. That value is normally that shown in the Inheritance Tax inventory and in the confirmation, less the moveable debts of the deceased. However, if the value actually realised after proper administration with due despatch is different from the value in the inventory, it is that realised value which will be used for calculation of legal rights. It is important that the administration has been carried out with all due speed.[39]

Collation *inter liberos*

This doctrine remains applicable in the division of the legitim fund.[40] As collation *inter haeredes* has been abolished with the abolition of the distinction between heritage and moveables in the succession to the free estate, collation *inter liberos* is now the only form of the doctrine of collation still applicable in the law of succession. The purpose of the doctrine is to preserve equality in the division of the legitim fund when more than one of the persons entitled does in fact claim legitim, and one or more of the claimants has received certain types of advances during the parent's lifetime.

The effect is that if a claimant for legitim has received any advances of the appropriate type during the parent's lifetime, other claimants for legitim may require him to add the amount of the advance to the legitim

---

[39] *Russel* v. *Att.-Gen.*, 1917 S.C. 28; *Alexander* v. *Alexander's Trs.*, 1954 S.C. 436; 1954 S.L.T. 342. In *Alexander* the realised value was so much lower than the original valuation that legal rights calculated on the original figure would have been greater than the whole estate.

[40] s. 11 (3).

fund calculated in the ordinary way from the estate owned by the parent at death. The total of the legitim fund plus the advances is then available for distribution among those entitled to legitim. The person who received the advance is required to impute his advance against his rateable share of the combined fund of legitim plus advances.

An example may illustrate the result more clearly. A dies intestate, leaving a widow B and three children, C, D and E.

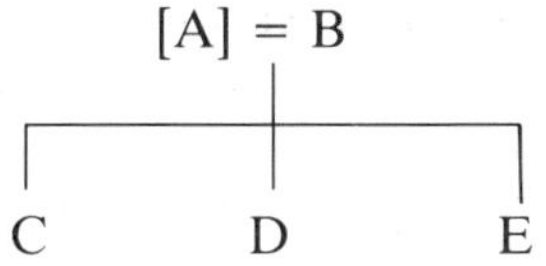

A's net estate amounts to £120,000 in value, consisting of the matrimonial home valued at £60,000, its furniture and plenishings valued at £9,000, and other moveable estate valued at £51,000. By virtue of her prior rights, B, the widow, receives the house and its furniture, etc., plus £21,000. Thus the estate available to meet legal rights is £30,000, all moveable. The legitim fund is therefore £10,000, there being both widow and children.

During his lifetime A had given his child C an advance of £2,000 to enable him to set up in business. This being one of the types of advance covered by the doctrine of collation *inter liberos*, C is required to collate his £2,000 as a condition of claiming legitim. Thus the total value of the fund to be divided among the children as legitim is £12,000, being the £10,000 computed in the ordinary way in the estate owned by the deceased at his death, plus the advance of £2,000. Of this total, C, D and E each are entitled to £4,000 as their share of legitim. In C's case the £2,000 advance already given to him is set against his share of the combined fund, so that he receives only £2,000 from the £10,000 available on A's death, and D and E receive £4,000 each.

The advances which must be collated are limited to those which affect the legitim fund.[41] Thus they do not include payments in discharge of a parent's natural duty of maintenance and education of his child, nor do they include payments by way of remuneration for services which arise out of an onerous contract. Loans made to the legitim claimant are not advances to be collated under this doctrine, for they are due to the deceased's executor and form part of the deceased's gross estate from which the legitim fund is computed. Advances made out of the deceased's heritage are not subject to collation *inter liberos*, because they do not affect the moveable fund from which legitim is taken. Testamentary provisions, as distinct from *inter vivos* advances, need not be collated, as they do not affect the legitim fund. Such testamentary provisions, in so far as they are moveable, are paid out of dead's part of which the

[41] McLaren, *Wills & Succession*, i, 167–169.

deceased was completely free to dispose. In any event, if the beneficiary of such a testamentary provision accepts it, he cannot also claim legitim unless there was a partial intestacy, and, if he is not a claimant for legitim, no one can require the collation of advances made to him. Finally, even if *inter vivos* advances of a type otherwise appropriate for the operation of this doctrine have been made, the donor may expressly or impliedly have indicated that the recipient's right to legitim is to be unaffected thereby.

The typical examples of advances which may have to be collated in securing the equitable division of the legitim fund are advances to set the recipient up in trade, for a marriage portion or for settlement in a station in life. The archaic terminology has to be translated into modern terms.

Under the previous law, only surviving children of the deceased could be called upon to collate under this doctrine, because only surviving children were entitled to legitim. Now, however, with the introduction of infinite representation in legitim, provision is made in the Succession Act[42] for the case where remoter descendants are entitled to legitim. The provision is that where any descendant is entitled to legitim by virtue of representation, "he shall be under the like duty to collate any advances made by the deceased to him, and the proportion appropriate to him of any advances so made to any person through whom he derives such entitlement, as if he had been entitled to claim such legitim otherwise than by virtue of" representation.[43]

No standard of appropriateness is laid down by which to determine the share of an advance to his ancestor which a representative claiming legitim must collate. This can give rise to severe difficulties if the only persons entitled to legitim are grandchildren, the immediate children having predeceased, for *per capita* division means that the share of the legitim fund taken by a grandchild is not the same as the share which his parent—to whom an advance was made—would have taken.[44] The grandchild may be entitled to only, say, one-sixth of the legitim fund where his parent might have been entitled to one-half, but may still be debited with the whole of the advance made to the parent. Worse, the parent may have dissipated the advance and the grandchild may have received no benefit from it at all.

There must be more than one claimant for legitim before the doctrine of collation *inter liberos* comes into play at all. If, as might arise when the deceased has left a will unfavourable to only one of those entitled to legitim, only one of several possible claimants does actually claim, collation cannot arise. The claimant simply takes his or her rateable share of the legitim fund computed in the estate owned by the deceased at his death and advances are not taken into account at all. Collation is an equitable doctrine for the actual distribution of the legitim fund and can be invoked only by actually competing claimants.[45]

---

[42] s. 11 (3).

[43] For an example, see Appendix 2, Example 3.

[44] See 1967 S.L.T. (News) 195, 224 and 247.

[45] *Coats's Trs.* v. *Coats*, 1914 S.C. 744.

Equally, claimants for legitim cannot require other persons who are entitled to legitim, but are not claiming it, to collate advances made to them. *Coats's Trs.* was an unusual case in which the sole claimant for legitim was actively seeking to collate the advances made to her in order to benefit by collation of the much larger advances made to others who were not claiming legitim. The attempt failed.

Characteristics of legal rights

There have been various arguments as to the true theoretical nature and origin of legal rights in Scotland. They could be classified as debts due by the estate or as rights of succession in the estate. They may be the attenuated remnants of a system of community of property in Scotland. Whatever the origin, two aspects of the nature of legal rights are worth further attention. One is that legal rights are indefeasible without the consent of the person entitled to them and the other that they are, nevertheless, subject to evasion.

It is probably the best-known feature of legal rights in Scotland that they cannot be defeated by any testamentary disposition made by the person from whose estate they are exigible. A testator is entitled to test only on that part of his estate remaining after legal rights have been satisfied, and any attempt to go beyond that limitation can be disregarded by those entitled to legal rights. This power to bypass the testator's will is, of course, exercised only when the legal rights are more beneficial than the provisions made in the will. Accordingly, even if a testator directs that his whole estate is to be applied to set up a home for stray dogs in Baluchistan, his surviving spouse and descendants are able to claim their legal rights. Only the dead's part need go to the dogs. In this respect, legal rights operate as a limitation on a testator's freedom and as a bar to capricious disinheritance, thereby ensuring that at least some assets are available for his family. Legal rights have therefore two functions. One is to act as one of the sets of rules in the division of an intestate estate, and the other is to act as a family protection device giving the family automatic rights to fixed shares in the estate.

It used to be the case that the right to legitim could be defeated without the concurrence of the child otherwise entitled thereto if his parents entered into an ante-nuptial marriage contract in which his right was prospectively discharged. This method of defeating a right to legitim was abolished by section 12 of the 1964 Act and it is now true to say of all legal rights, as it was formerly true of the rights other than legitim, that they cannot be defeated without the consent, express or implied, of the person entitled to them.

However, although the entitlement to legal rights cannot be defeated by unilateral action by the person whose estate is in question, the practical effects of the legal rights can be evaded. The ancestor or spouse is perfectly free to deal with his estate as he sees fit during his lifetime, even if the purpose of his dealings is avowedly to evade legal rights. That, combined with the anomaly that legal rights are due only from part of the estate means that he can reduce the proportion of his estate subject to legal rights. To take advantage of the fact that there are no legal rights in heritage, the moveable part of his estate can be sharply reduced by investing in heritage (including heritable securities and also personal bonds purporting to exclude executors). It is true that it is not very convenient to have only heritable assets, as liquidity is then poor. But to the extent that it is suitable in his case, a testator can effectively disinherit his wife and descendants by leaving a will (thereby excluding the surviving spouse's prior rights) and by ensuring that the bulk of his estate consists of heritage. Legal rights would attach only to such portion of his estate as he chose to keep in moveable form. This nonsense will be removed when the Scottish Law Commission's recommendations are eventually enacted.

The result is that legal rights are even more liable to evasion than they were before the 1964 Act came into force, and there remains the even more drastic step by which a person may completely defeat all claims on his estate by transferring the whole of it *inter vivos* to some third party, either as an outright gift or in return for a liferent. Provided the transfer is genuine and irrevocable, this will leave no estate owned by the deceased at his death on which legal rights can operate. All these transactions may be done with the open and expressed intention of evading legal rights, yet no allegations of fraudulent frustration of legal rights will be entertained.[46]

Satisfaction of legal rights

Apart from complete or partial satisfaction of legitim by means of advances which may require to be collated *inter liberos*, legal rights may also be satisfied by testamentary provisions accepted in lieu of the legal rights. The legatee has the choice between the legal right and the testamentary provision, but if the latter is accepted, the legal right is held to be satisfied thereby.

In the case of testamentary dispositions to which section 13 of the 1964 Act applies, *i.e.* wills actually executed after the commencement of the Act,[47] this will be wholly a question of approbate and reprobate. No person can both accept and reject the same instrument, and thus no person can accept the conventional provisions in his favour in a will and also claim legal rights in such a manner as to be inconsistent with the testator's intentions for the disposal of his estate. This, of course, does not *necessarily* bar a spouse or descendant of a testator from claiming legal rights in any estate which has fallen into intestacy as well as the conventional provisions in their favour in the will.[48]

Under the previous law, a claim for legal rights did not automatically involve complete forfeiture of testamentary provisions. Unless there was a

---

[46] *Agnew* v. *Agnew* (1775) Mor. 8210; *Lashley* v. *Hog* (1804) 4 Pat. 581.
[47] s. 36 (3).
[48] *Naismith* v. *Boyes* (1899) 1 F. (H.L.) 79; *Petrie's Tr.* v. *Manders's Tr.*, 1954 S.C. 430.

provision in the testamentary instrument that the provisions thereby made were in full satisfaction of legal rights, or that a claim for legal rights would involve forfeiture of the provisions, the abstruse doctrine of equitable compensation had the effect that the testamentary provision was not irrevocably forfeited by making a claim for legal rights. Instead it was applied in the first instance to restore what was taken from the estate by way of legal rights, and thereafter it remained available to the spouse or child concerned. The cases usually involved a testamentary liferent, in place of which the beneficiary preferred to have an immediate capital sum by way of a claim for legal rights. The action of claiming legal rights does not necessarily accelerate payment of the fee unless the will so provides,[49] and hence the balance of the liferented estate continued to produce income. Once this income had accumulated sufficiently to restore to the estate what it had lost in consequence of the claim for legal rights, the fact that complete compensation had been made to the ultimate fiars usually meant that the liferent again became available to the beneficiary.[50] However a clause in the will declaring that its provisions were in full satisfaction of the legatee's legal rights prevented the beneficiary from relying on equitable compensation. Thus even when full compensation had been made over a period of years, the beneficiary could not then resume his liferent. A full satisfaction clause almost invariably appeared in well-drawn wills.

Section 13 of the 1964 Act reverses this situation. Even if no full satisfaction clause appears in a testamentary disposition executed after the commencement of the Act, it will take effect as if it contained one, unless there is an express provision to the contrary therein. One imagines that there will rarely be such an express provision to the contrary, and the result is therefore virtually to abolish the doctrine of equitable compensation in respect of all wills executed after the commencement of the Act. However *Munro's Trs.*[51] also holds that there may still be equitable compensation for *other* beneficiaries adversely affected by the claim for legal rights.

Testators will sometimes prefer a more stringent type of clause under which the consequence of a claim for legal rights is an express forfeiture of all the beneficiary's rights under the will and sometimes also a forfeiture of the benefits destined to the legatee's issue.[52] Such a forfeiture clause is effective according to its terms, but will be narrowly construed. It is however clearly effective to prevent equitable compensation from being made.

For this purpose, the reference to the date of execution of a will means the date of actual execution, not the date of the testator's death.[53]

---

[49] *Muirhead* v. *Muirhead* (1890) 17 R. (H.L.) 45; *Stair Memorial Encyclopaedia: The Laws of Scotland*, Vol. 25, paras. 953 *et seq.*

[50] *Macfarlane's Trs.* v. *Oliver* (1882) 9 R. 1138; *Munro's Trs.*, 1971 S.L.T. 313.

[51] *Supra.*

[52] See *Tindall's Trs.* v. *Tindall*, 1933 S.C. 419, where the forfeiture was sufficient to cut out the claimant's issue. See also *MacNaughton* v. *MacNaughton's Trs.*, 1954 S.C. 312 and *Walker* v. *Orr's Trs.*, 1958 S.L.T. 63.

[53] s. 36 (3).

Discharge of legal rights

Legal rights may be expressly discharged by the spouse or descendant entitled thereto. Children are capable of granting a discharge from the age of 16 onwards, but as a discharge without full consideration is almost certain to be a prejudicial transaction capable of being set aside by court before the child's twenty-first birthday, executors would be wise to treat a discharge granted by a 16- or 17-year-old with great caution.[54]

It was one of the well-known anomalies of the pre-1964 law that it was possible by ante-nuptial marriage contract for intending spouses to discharge prospectively the legal rights of any children of the marriage. This could not be done after the marriage but the fact that it was possible at all made a severe dent in the protective function of legal rights for children. The children obviously were not parties to the arrangement, and yet their rights might be discharged for them with very little, or even in some cases no, consideration. For example in *Galloway's Trs.* v. *Galloway*[55] the marriage contract made a provision for children, but the fact that the father appointed the whole of the provision to one of them did not alter the fact that the right of the others to claim legitim was discharged.[56]

Section 12 of the 1964 Act now provides that the right to legitim of a child or of remoter issue cannot be excluded by anything contained in an ante-nuptial marriage contract to which section 12 applies entered into between the parents. Whatever such a marriage contract may provide, the descendant has the election between the provisions in his favour in the marriage contract and his legitim. In other words it is purely a question of satisfaction of legal rights and of approbate and reprobate and no longer one of a prospective discharge of the right to legitim at the instance of third parties.

Section 12 applies to any ante-nuptial marriage contract actually executed after the commencement of the 1964 Act (*i.e.* on or after September 10, 1964). Older ante-nuptial marriage contracts may well still be coming into operation, and an exclusion of the children's legitim contained in such a contract would still be effective.

With this anomaly removed, it becomes true to say that legal rights cannot be discharged without the consent in some form of the person entitled. A prospective husband and wife can still contract before marriage for renunciation of *jus relicti* or *jus relictae*, but the contract involves mutual agreement. Any person may voluntarily discharge his or her right to *jus relicti*, *jus relictae* or legitim, but it is up to him or her to decide whether or not to do so. There is, however, a difference between the effect of a discharge granted during the lifetime of the deceased and of one granted after his death.

---

[54] Age of Legal Capacity (Scotland) Act 1991 (c. 50), ss. 1, 3.

[55] 1943 S.C. 339.

[56] In *Callander* v. *Callander's Exr.*, 1972 S.L.T. 209 the exclusion of legitim by the marriage contract still stood even although the children had assigned all their interests to their father and thus received nothing under the contract.

If a discharge is given during the lifetime of the ancestor or spouse from whose estate the rights would have been exigible, the grantor of the discharge is treated as already dead, but not so as to permit the issue of the grantor to claim his share by representation. This therefore increases the share of legitim taken by others.[57]

A discharge of legal rights granted after the death of the ancestor or spouse does not increase the share taken by other claimants for legal rights but benefits the person entitled to the free estate or the residuary legatee as the case may be.

As an illustration, take the case of a man dying, leaving five children and a legitim fund of £5,000. If none of the children has discharged their right to legitim during their father's lifetime, the amount to which any one child is entitled on the father's death is £1,000. This is so even if the others accept testamentary provisions in lieu of legitim, or indeed even if they should now discharge their claims gratuitously. However, if all the others had discharged their claims before their father's death, the one entitled to legitim would take the whole legitim fund of £5,000. In *Panmure* v. *Crokat*[58] the discharges were performed by ante-nuptial marriage contract, and the one child not included in the discharge—possibly in error—was held entitled to the whole legitim fund.

Prescription and legal rights

The right to claim *jus relictae*, *jus relicti* and legitim is extinguished by the negative prescription if no "relevant claim" has been made within a continuous period of 20 years.[59] Time runs from the date the obligation becomes enforceable, which will usually be the date of death. Any period during which the legal rights creditor was under legal disability is ignored.[60] This seems now to mean that prescription will run from age 16. Under the Age of Legal Capacity (Scotland) Act 1991[61] legal capacity to enter into any transaction is attained at age 16 and any statutory reference to disability by reason of nonage is to be construed as a reference to a person under the age of 16.[62] Unless a claim for legal rights has the effect of reducing the amount received by the claimant as compared with the amount due under the will, executors will be in safety to act upon a claim by a 16-year-old. An increased benefit could not be held to be "prejudicial" within the meaning of section 3 of the 1991 Act. Hence it seems highly probable that prescription will now run from age 16.

---

[57] *Hog* v. *Hog* (1791) Mor. 8193.
[58] (1856) 18 D. 703.
[59] Prescription and Limitation (Scotland) Act 1973, s. 7, read with Sched. I, para. 2 (*f*).
[60] *Ibid.*, s. 6 (4) (*b*) read with s. 7 (2).
[61] (c. 50), s. 1.
[62] s. 1 (2).

CHAPTER 6

SUCCESSION TO THE FREE ESTATE

"Free estate"

The rules comprised under this head are mostly stated in Part I (sections 1 to 7) of the Act and deal with the succession to the free estate, heritage and moveables together, after any prior rights and legal rights which are applicable have been deducted.[1] In other words, if the intestate died survived by neither spouse nor issue, these rules apply to the whole estate (apart from the excepted items specified in section 37 of the Act and the effect of section 36 (2) on special destinations and powers of appointment). If the intestate is survived by a spouse and/or issue, the appropriate prior rights and legal rights, in that order, are deducted before the rules of Part I come into play in respect of the balance of the estate. In such cases the provisions in Part I relating to the free estate may apply to only a small proportion of an intestate's estate.

Method of statement in the Act

The pattern of the pre-1964 law was to have a number of common law principles overlaid by specific statutory provisions. This was changed by the Act and there is now a single statutory list of those entitled to succeed. The details of this list are mainly to be found in section 2. While the new list bears a strong resemblance to the previous rules relating to the disposal of moveable estate, the common law concept of the "next of kin" is no longer relevant in finding those entitled to a particular intestate estate.

Section 2 is in the form of a list of specified relations of the intestate, and must be read in conjunction with the scheme of representation applicable to the division of the free estate contained in section 5, and with the rules for division where two or more persons are entitled contained in section 6. For example, section 2 gives a right of succession to "children," but section 5 gives a full right of representation, and in effect converts "children" to "issue," while section 6 deals with the problems of division *per stirpes* or *per capita*.

The list in section 2 (1) is in the order in which relatives of the deceased are called to the succession. Those higher up the list are preferred to those lower down. This is achieved by giving a right of succession in each paragraph, and providing in each paragraph other than the first that the

[1] s. 1 (2).

right applies only if the deceased was not survived by any "prior relative." That phrase is defined in section 2 (2) as a person of any other class who, if he had survived the intestate, would have had right to the free intestate estate or any of it by virtue of an earlier paragraph of section 2 (1) or by virtue of representation of a person entitled by an earlier paragraph.

Thus, children (and their issue by representation) whose rights are stated in section 2 (1) (*a*) are "prior relatives" and therefore preferred in succession, in a question with brothers and sisters and parents whose rights when representatives of both categories have survived are stated in section 2 (1) (*b*). Similarly, uncles and aunts on either side of the house (and their issue by representation) whose rights are stated in section 2 (1) (*f*) are "prior relatives" in a question with grandparents, whose rights appear in section 2 (1) (*g*).

It may still be relevant to refer to the old law to fill *lacunae* in the Act, and accordingly, section 1 (1) (*b*) requires the free intestate estate (heritable and moveable) to be subject to the previous law of intestate moveable succession so far as "not inconsistent with" the particular provisions of Part I of the Act.

The Order of Succession

(1) Descendants

As before, the category of descendants must first be considered in determining the order of succession to the free estate, as their right is preferable to that of collaterals, spouse or ascendants. The main provision, contained in section 2 (1) (*a*), is "where an intestate is survived by children, they shall have right to the whole of the intestate estate."

It is to be noticed that the "intestate estate" referred to is defined for the purposes of this Part of the Act by section 1 (2). Briefly, it means the free estate after satisfaction of prior rights and legal rights.

As already noted, although section 2 (1) (*a*) refers to "children," it does in fact regulate the whole succession of descendants of the intestate when read in conjunction with the scheme of representation contained in section 5 (1) and that of distribution contained in section 6.

Adopted children are now treated as lawful children of the adopter or adopters. The position of adopted children was the final cause of the appointment of the Mackintosh Committee on the Law of Succession, and the provisions of Part IV (sections 23 and 24) of the Act remedy a situation which was a major defect in the previous law of succession. For the present purpose of succession to the free estate by descendants on intestacy, the main provisions are contained in section 23 (1). So far as here relevant, this provides that:

> "For all purposes relating to—
> (*a*) the succession to a deceased person (whether testate or intestate), . . . an adopted person shall be treated as the child of the adopter and not as the child of any other person."

A problem might have arisen over the question of what rights are truly rights of "succession." There has, for example, been considerable discussion of the true nature of the traditional legal rights of spouses and children. Views classing them as debts or rights of succession or something in between have been current for some time. Accordingly, for the purposes of section 23 (1) it is provided that "succession to a deceased person" is to be construed as including the distribution of any property in consequence of his death and any claim to prior rights or legal rights out of his estate. In other words, an adopted child clearly has a right to legitim out of the estates of his adopting parent or parents as well as his right to share in the free intestate estate and any other property being distributed on the adopter's death, as a lawful child of the adopter.

A natural parent of the adopted child being "any other person" within the meaning of section 23 (1), the child's rights of succession in the estates of its natural parents are cut off and replaced by rights in the estates of the adopting parents.

In one situation, however, cutting off the adopted person's rights in the estates of its natural parents had the unfortunate result that the child had no rights in any estate. If the adopting parents died before the Succession Act came into force on September 10, 1964, the child had no rights in their estates. But if the natural parents then died after the commencement of the Succession Act, the child had no rights in their estates either. To remedy this as far as possible, the Law Reform (Miscellaneous Provisions) (Scotland) Act 1966[2] provided that if the adopting parent died before the commencement of the Succession Act and the natural parent died on or after August 3, 1966, the child is to be treated for the purposes of succession to the estate of that natural parent as the child of the natural parent. However, this is only for the purposes of succession to the natural parent. For all other purposes of succession, the adopted child still falls to be regarded as the child of the adopter. If the child was adopted by two spouses jointly, both the adopting parents must have died prior to September 10, 1964, to bring this transitional provision into effect.

The Legitimation (Scotland) Act 1968[3] is still in force although now much less important in view of the virtual abolition of the status of illegitimacy. The effect of the Legitimation Act is that an illegitimate child is always legitimated by the subsequent marriage of its parents instead of only if the parents were free to marry at the time of its conception as was true under the older common law. Since parents whose marriage did not legitimate their child sometimes adopted it, the Act made provision for revocation of such adoption orders on the view that legitimation removed the need for them. However, section 6 (2) of the 1968 Act (as amended) preserves succession rights in intestacies which occurred before the revocation.

---

[2] c. 19, s. 5.
[3] c. 22.

Illegitimate children were the subject of very limited provisions in the Succession Act itself, but there were radical alterations by the Law Reform (Miscellaneous Provisions) (Scotland) Act 1968[4] and by the Law Reform (Parent and Child) (Scotland) Act 1986.[5]

September 10, 1964, to November 24, 1968. The effect of the original section 4 of the Succession Act—applicable in respect of deaths occurring on or after September 10, 1964, up to and including November 24, 1968—was to give the illegitimate child a right of succession to its mother's free estate when the mother died intestate and without lawful issue. The child had no right to legitim and was postponed to the prior rights and legal rights (calculated on the basis that the mother was not survived by issue) of the mother's husband. It had no rights of succession at all if the mother was survived by lawful issue, and could never have rights in its father's intestate estate.

November 25, 1968, to December 7, 1986. The reforms contained in the 1968 Act applied to the estate of any person dying on or after November 25, 1968, up to and including December 7, 1986. The method used was to substitute a new section 4 in the Succession Act.[6] This conferred on the illegitimate child the right to share in the intestate free estate of both parents on a basis of equality with legitimate children. The right to legitim was separately conferred by a new section 10A of the Succession Act inserted by section 2 of the 1968 Act. The result was that legitimate and illegitimate children were now in a position of formal equality so far as succession to the estates of the parents was concerned. A decree of affiliation and aliment established the paternity of the father for succession purposes unless the contrary was proved.[7]

The one substantial difference which remained between the succession rights of legitimate and illegitimate children was that the illegitimate child could not represent its predeceasing parent in a succession opening after the parent's death. The scheme of representation established by section 5 (1) then permitted "issue" to represent their parents but "issue" was defined as lawful issue, so that only legitimate children could represent their parents. This was so even although both legitimate and illegitimate children could succeed *to* their parents. This was reinforced by the statement in section 4 (4) that, except for the specific provisions of section 4 conferring on the child rights in the estates of its parents and the representation provisions of section 5, nothing in Part I of the Act was to be construed as importing any rule of succession through illegitimate relationship. Thus the rights of the illegitimate child in this period were confined to the estates of the persons responsible for its birth.

---

[4] c. 70.
[5] c. 9.
[6] 1968 (c. 70), s. 1.
[7] *Ibid.*, s. 11.

The result was that an illegitimate grandchild could not represent its predeceasing parent (whether that parent was itself legitimate or illegitimate) in the division of a grandparent's estate, but that a legitimate grandchild could represent its illegitimate parent in the grandparent's estate. In the latter case, the legitimate grandchild, being "issue" of the illegitimate child, could take the share which its parent would have taken by survivance.

However, if the deceased whose estate was being distributed was more remote than a lineal grandparent, the illegitimate person himself would not have been entitled to a share if he had survived, so that there could be no representation in such an estate even by his legitimate child.

The effect of the valuable improvements in the lot of the illegitimate child was to implement the Report of the Russell Committee on the Law of Succession in Relation to Illegitimate Persons[8] in the light of the views expressed by the Scottish Law Commission in its Memorandum "Reform of the Law Relating to legitimation *per subsequens matrimonium*."[9]

December 8, 1986, onwards. The present law virtually abolishes the status of illegitimacy.[10] The Law Reform (Parent and Child) (Scotland) Act 1986[11] enacts a general principle of the legal equality of children by the general statement that:

> "The fact that a person's parents are not or have not been married to one another shall be left out of account in establishing the legal relationship between the person and any other person; and accordingly any such relationship shall have effect as if the parents were or had been married to one another."

In its application to succession, this means that whether or not its parents were married to each other a child will have exactly the same rights of succession to its biological parents and also through them by representation. In the older terminology, illegitimate children have full rights of succession.

The general principle is not confined to statutory provisions. Any reference to any relative in any enactment or deed dated after the commencement of the Act is to be construed in accordance with the general principle, unless the contrary intention appears in the enactment or deed.[12] It will however be an expression of contrary intention, even in a deed executed after the Act's commencement, to refer to "lawful" or "illegitimate," etc., children.[13] This will mean that a will could still readily exclude any right of a child formerly described as illegitimate to inherit

[8] Cmnd. 3051.
[9] Cmnd. 3223.
[10] See *supra*, pp. 45 and 55.
[11] c. 9.
[12] s. 1 (2).
[13] s. 1 (4).

under it. However on intestacy, such a child has exactly the same rights of intestate succession as any other child of the parents. The one exception to future deeds being construed according to the principle of equality is that future grants of titles of honour and coats of arms are not affected by the Act and will not therefore have expressly to exclude succession by illegitimate relatives.[14]

(2) Collaterals

If the category of descendants has been exhausted without finding a survivor entitled to succeed, the category of collaterals of the deceased is next in the line of succession. Subject to the qualification in section 2 (1) (*b*) of the 1964 Act giving the surviving parent or parents of the intestate a right to one-half of the free estate when the deceased is survived both by collaterals and by a parent or parents, the category of collaterals of the deceased must be exhausted before ancestors or a surviving spouse have any rights of succession to the free estate.

Assume for the moment that the intestate was survived by collaterals, but left no surviving issue and was predeceased by both parents, so that the right of the collaterals is to the whole of the free intestate estate. The statutory basis for their right to succeed is now section 2 (1) (*c*) of the 1964 Act, replacing the previous common law principle that collaterals succeeded next after descendants. Although this paragraph mentions only "brothers and sisters" of the deceased, it must be read along with section 5 (representation) and section 6 (distribution). It is not limited to the case where immediate brothers and sisters of the deceased have survived him.

Half blood. Giving effect to the recommendations of the Mackintosh Committee, section 2 (2) and section 3 of the Act deal with the rights of collaterals of the half blood. Where collaterals have rights of succession, collaterals of the whole blood, having the same mother and the same father as the intestate, are preferred to collaterals of the half blood, sharing only one parent with the intestate. This restates the pre-existing law on the subject, and has the effect that if the intestate is survived by any collaterals of the whole blood, or their descendants by representation, collaterals of the half blood and those claiming through them have no rights of succession at all. Those related by the whole blood take the whole amount of the estate falling to collaterals. Take the following example:

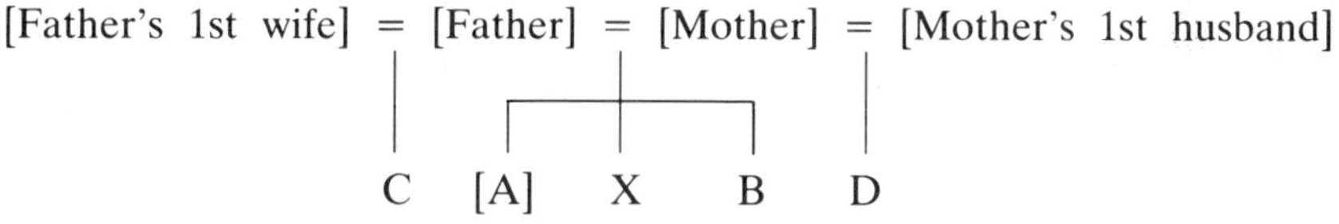

[14] s. 9 (1) (*c*).

X has died intestate, survived by a full brother B and by two half brothers C and D. In this situation B, the sole surviving collateral of the full blood takes the whole free intestate estate, which, if X left no surviving spouse, is the whole net estate after payment of debts and expenses. C and D, collaterals of the half blood consanguinean and uterine respectively, take no share.

If, however, there are no collaterals of the full blood, so that the right of any collaterals of the half blood emerges, section 3 of the 1964 Act made a radical change from the pre-existing law. Collaterals of the half blood now rank "without distinction as between those related to the intestate . . . through their father and those so related through their mother." The words "related through their father" and "related through their mother" were substituted for "consanguinean" and "uterine" in the course of the progress of the Bill through Parliament in the interests of comprehensibility by the layman, but one may wonder whether the same tenderness for the comprehension of the layman might not also have been applied to the rest of the Act. Before the commencement of the Succession Act 1964 the half blood consanguinean had full rights of succession, postponed only to the full blood, but the half blood uterine had rights limited in all circumstances to one-half of the moveable estate, and even then postponed to the half blood consanguinean and to the parents of the intestate. The general policy of the 1964 Act to remove discrimination between the sexes in the law of succession led to the equation of the positions of the half blood consanguinean and uterine by section 3. Both now have full rights of succession postponed only to the full blood.

Taking the same family as that illustrated above, but this time postulating that both collaterals of the full blood have predeceased, *i.e.* a situation such as the following:

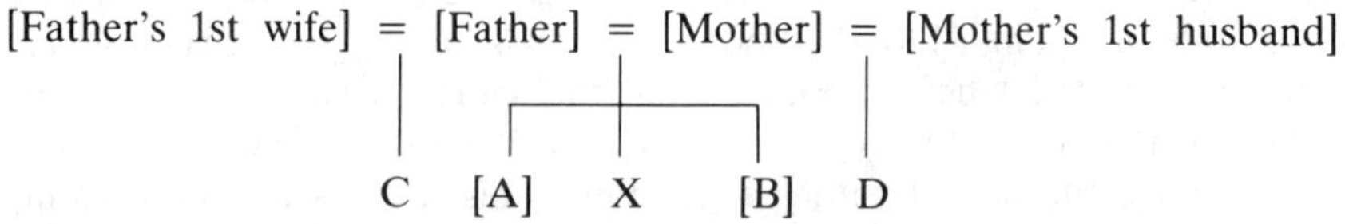

the effect is that C and D share the free intestate estate equally between them as collaterals of the half blood.

Adopted children and collateral succession. Section 24 (1) deals with relationship for the purposes of collateral succession between an adopted child and other children or adopted children of the adopter or adopters. It provides that:

> "an adopted person shall be deemed to be related to any other person, being the child or the adopted child of the adopter or (in the case of a joint adoption) of either of the adopters—
>
> (*a*) where he or she was adopted by two spouses jointly and that other person is the child or adopted child of both of them, as a brother or sister of the whole blood;
>
> (*b*) in any other case, as a brother or sister of the half blood."

Thus if a childless couple adopt a child and subsequently have a child of their own, these two children are, for the purposes of succession, related to each other as brothers or sisters of the full blood. Equally a couple's second adopted child is for this purpose a brother or sister of the full blood to the first. But if either party to a marriage had had a child by a previous marriage, or had previously adopted a child, such child or adopted child would be a collateral of the half blood to any child or adopted child of the present marriage.

Certain odd consequences emerge from the provisions of section 24 (1). An adopted child can be related as a brother or sister of the full blood to any other person only if he or she has been adopted by two spouses jointly and that other person is the child or adopted child of both of them.[15] In any other case the adopted child is related to any other child or adopted child of the adopter or adopters as a brother or sister of the half blood.[16] This means, for example, that if an unmarried woman gives birth to twins and subsequently adopts them in order to get a clear birth certificate for them, these children are related to each other as collaterals of the half blood for the purposes of succession. They cannot be collaterals of the full blood as they do not fall within the provisions of section 24 (1) (*a*) requiring adoption by two spouses jointly. If the mother of the twins subsequently marries someone other than the natural father of the children, and there is a child or adopted child of that marriage, the twins and the subsequent child are all collaterals of the half blood. One twin has no better rights of succession in the other's estate than has the child or adopted child of the subsequent marriage. Until the Law Reform (Parent and Child) (Scotland) Act 1986 came into force it is true that one illegitimate twin was not regarded in law as being in any way related to the other, so that neither had any rights of succession at all in the other's estate without the adoption. However, since 1986, the effect of an adoption by their mother would be to reduce their rights in each other's estate from that of a collateral of the full blood to only half blood status, which might have to be shared with others.

Any question of seniority between collaterals who include an adopted child is resolved by section 24 (1A), added by the Children Act 1975. Briefly, an adopted child ranks in seniority as if born on the date of adoption, while two children adopted on the same day take seniority *inter se* according to their actual date of birth.

Illegitimacy and collateral succession

Deaths occurring before December 8, 1986. The position in intestate collateral succession remained as before—namely that illegitimate relationship was no relationship at all. Various provisions deeming illegitimate relationship to be the same as legitimate appeared in the 1968 Act,

---

[15] s. 24 (1) (*a*).
[16] s. 24 (1) (*b*).

but only for the construction of deeds. Certain similar provisions now appearing in the Succession Act applied only for the purposes of section 6 and that part of section 11 dealing with the division among those beneficially entitled under sections not having the relationship clause. There was no general rule that illegitimate relationship was the same as legitimate relationship[17] and rights of intestate succession existed only between the illegitimate child and its parents, subject to representation of the child by its issue.

In practice the great improvement of the position of illegitimate children introduced in 1968 was very widely accepted, and it was commonly assumed that reciprocal rights of succession had also been created between the illegitimate child and its "brothers and sisters." In fact the situation was that an illegitimate child did not have, and could not have, brothers and sisters for purposes of succession. There was no right of succession before the Succession Act, and neither it nor the 1968 Act created any rights between collaterals. An illegitimate child could acquire collaterals only by leaving the status of illegitimacy through legitimation or adoption.

Deaths from December 8, 1986. The effect of the Law Reform (Parent and Child) (Scotland) Act 1986 was to complete the partial reform begun in 1968. The assimilation of the positions of legitimate and illegitimate children has the result that in the succession to persons who die after the commencement of the 1986 Act a person formerly described as illegitimate has exactly the same rights as he or she would have had if born legitimate. There are now, *de jure*, brothers and sisters who merely existed *de facto* before, and the normal rights of succession apply fully. This automatically increases the burden on an executor of establishing that he has identified all the relations. In at least some cases of collateral succession, the problem will be mitigated by the fact that the formerly illegitimate person may rank only as a collateral of the half blood and be postponed to the succession rights of collaterals of the full blood.

(3) Collaterals and parents

As already noted, parents of the intestate are entitled under section 2 (1) (*b*) to one-half of the free intestate estate when the deceased is not survived by any descendants, but is survived by collaterals and by a parent or parents. The remaining one-half is divided among the collaterals. This is in addition to the right of the parent or parents to succeed to the whole free estate when the category of collaterals has been exhausted. Accordingly, if the intestate is survived by brothers or sisters, or their issue by representation under section 5, and by a parent or parents, one-

[17] Section 4 (4) of the Act provided that, apart from specific sections, nothing in Pt. I of the Succession Act was to be construed as importing any rule of succession through illegitimate relationship.

half of the free estate is divided among the collaterals, and one-half falls to the parent or parents, in both cases according to the rules of division specified in section 6.

Although this provision seems very similar to that in the pre-1964 law of moveable succession, it is to be noted that a substantial difference has been made in the position of the mother of the intestate. As part of the general policy of removing discrimination on the ground of sex, the mother is now put upon an equal footing with the father, and shares the one-half falling to parents in this situation equally with the father. Previously the mother's right in moveables was postponed to that of the father, so that effectively she represented the predeceasing father of the intestate, in moveables at least. She had then no rights in heritage. Now she shares equally with the father, and because heritage and moveables are assimilated in the free estate, she shares in both moveables and heritage.

(4) Parents

If the categories of descendants and of collaterals of the intestate have been exhausted without finding a survivor, the surviving parent or parents of the intestate are next in the line of succession, and are entitled to the whole of the free intestate estate (section 2 (1) (*d*)). This right is additional to, and separate from, their right to share along with collaterals when the intestate is survived both by parents and by collaterals.

As in the case of succession under section 2 (1) (*b*) by parents along with collaterals, the mother's right in the case where parents succeed to the whole free estate under section 2 (1) (*d*) has been substantially improved. She now shares equally along with the father of the intestate, instead of being postponed to the father's right. The division between father and mother is equal by virtue of section 6, they being persons "in the same degree of relationship to the intestate" within the meaning of section 6 (*a*).

Parents of illegitimate children

Deaths prior to December 8, 1986. The Succession Act 1964 largely re-enacted earlier legislation by providing rights of succession between the illegitimate child and its mother only. Where an illegitimate person died intestate, and was not survived by lawful issue, or, if the illegitimate person was a woman, by her illegitimate children (or their issue by representation) the surviving mother of the illegitimate person was entitled to the whole of the free intestate estate.

In the division of the estates of persons dying on or after November 25, 1968, the new right of the illegitimate child to share in the estates of both parents equally with legitimate children was counterbalanced by a right of both parents to succeed to the free estate of the child.[18] Where an

---

[18] Law Reform (Miscellaneous Provisions) (Scotland) Act 1968, s. 1.

illegitimate child died intestate, and was not survived by lawful issue or by an illegitimate child or by lawful issue of such a child, the surviving parent or parents had right to the whole free intestate estate.

The paternity of an illegitimate child may well still be uncertain at the time of his death, but there would be no merit in incurring expenditure to prove the paternity of someone who, by definition, had taken no interest in the child till then, in order to present him with a share of the child's estate. It was therefore presumed that an illegitimate person was not survived by his father unless the contrary was shown.[19]

Parents of an illegitimate child ranked immediately after its descendants, there being no collateral succession.

Deaths from December 8, 1986. As the fact that a person's parents were not married to each other is left out of account[20] both of the biological parents of any person continue to have the full rights of parents in succession, irrespective of any question of legitimacy. The presumption that the father of an illegitimate child had predeceased the child was repealed by the Parent and Child Act of 1986, but there is a protection for trustees. This is achieved by adding to section 7 of the Law Reform (Miscellaneous Provisions) (Scotland) Act 1968 a paragraph (*c*) entitling a trustee or executor to distribute property without having ascertained that no paternal relative of an illegitimate person exists who is or may be entitled to an interest in the property.

Parents and adopted children

An adopted person being now treated as the child of the adopter and not as the child of any other person,[21] the right of the natural parents to succeed to the child's estate is cut off. In its place arises a right of the adopting parent or parents to succeed. This is unaffected by the transitional provisions in section 5 of the Law Reform (Miscellaneous Provisions) (Scotland) Act 1966.

(5) Surviving spouse

The inclusion of the spouse of the intestate in the list of those entitled to succeed to the free intestate estate was one of the major changes from the pre-1964 law of succession dependent upon blood relationship. Previously a surviving spouse might have certain rights in the predeceaser's estate by way of the extraordinary statutory preference and legal rights, but such a spouse was never in any circumstances the predeceaser's heir,[22] and had no right to share in the free intestate estate after the preference and legal rights had been met. That balance of the intestate estate would have fallen to the Crown as *ultimus haeres* rather

---

[19] s. 4 (3) as substituted by Law Reform (Miscellaneous Provisions) (Scotland) Act 1968, s. 1.

[20] Law Reform (Parent and Child) (Scotland) Act 1986, s. 1 (1).

[21] s. 23 (1).

[22] *Brown's Trs.* v. *Brown* (1890) 17 R. 1174.

than to the spouse. Now, as part of the weakening of the emphasis on direct blood relationship and of the improvement of the position of the surviving spouse, the Succession Act has made a spouse one of the ordinary heirs in intestacy as well as having the various extraordinary rights.

The spouse's right is stated in section 2 (1) (*e*) of the 1964 Act, which allows the surviving spouse to take the free estate in the absence of descendants, brothers and sisters or parents of the intestate. In other words, the surviving spouse is preferred to uncles and aunts and all remoter ancestors of the intestate, and in the situation where this right arises, the surviving spouse will therefore take the whole net estate after payment of debts, partly by virtue of prior rights, partly by virtue of legal rights and the balance under section 2 (1) (*e*).

There is no representation of a spouse under these provisions. Section 5 (1) provides representation where a person would have had a right in the intestate's estate "otherwise than as a parent or spouse of the intestate." Thus issue of a predeceasing spouse of the intestate (*i.e.* the intestate's step-children) cannot represent their parent so as to claim the free estate in preference to the intestate's uncles and aunts. Even although the principle of blood relationship has been considerably weakened, it is still felt that the intestate's own uncles and aunts and remoter ancestors have a better claim than his predeceasing wife's children by a previous marriage. Admittedly this may give rise to harsh cases where the step-children have been brought up in his family by the intestate, and find themselves cut off from any share of his estate, but it would be very difficult to frame legislation to cover such cases without including situations where the intestate had no substantial contacts with his step-children. The remedy is to make a will in their favour.

The lack of representation of a spouse means that all the rights which a spouse may have in the deceased's estate, *i.e.* prior rights, legal rights and rights in the free estate, can be stated as being available to a surviving spouse only.

(6) Ascendants other than parents

When an intestate dies without leaving any survivors in the categories of his or her descendants, collaterals, parents or spouse entitled to succeed under the conditions mentioned previously, the succession to the free estate then opens to the ascendants of the intestate other than his parents. The relevant provisions in the 1964 Act are section 2 (1) (*f*), (*g*), (*h*) and (*i*), dealing respectively with uncles and aunts, grandparents, grandparents' collaterals and remoter ancestors.

The different categories of ascendants and the order in which they are called to the succession remain the same as under the old law of intestate moveable succession, but there is the radical change that relationship through the mother as well as through the father has to be taken into account, thus more than doubling the area of search for those entitled to succeed. There is also the important provision that representation does now apply at this level of succession. From the commencement of the Law Reform (Parent and Child) (Scotland) Act 1986[23] illegitimate relationship has been no bar to rights of inheritance. Relationship is traced through illegitimate relatives in exactly the same way as through the legitimate relationship. This further widens the possible area of investigation of relatives, and could lead a solicitor to ask questions embarrassing to his client.[24]

No question of prior rights or of legal rights arises when the succession opens to ascendants more remote than parents, since, by definition, there is no spouse and there are no descendants to make such claims. Thus the free estate for distribution in this case is the whole net estate after payment of debts and expenses.

The principle remains that direct lineal ascendants of a given degree form a class nearer in degree to the intestate than the brothers and sisters of these lineal ascendants, and that brothers and sisters of lineal ascendants of one degree (or the issue of such brothers and sisters by representation) form a class nearer in degree than lineal ascendants of the next degree.

Thus uncles and aunts of the intestate, whether on the paternal side or on the maternal side, succeed in preference to grandparents (section 2 (1) (*f*)). A typical example of the type of situation which arises under these provisions would be as follows:

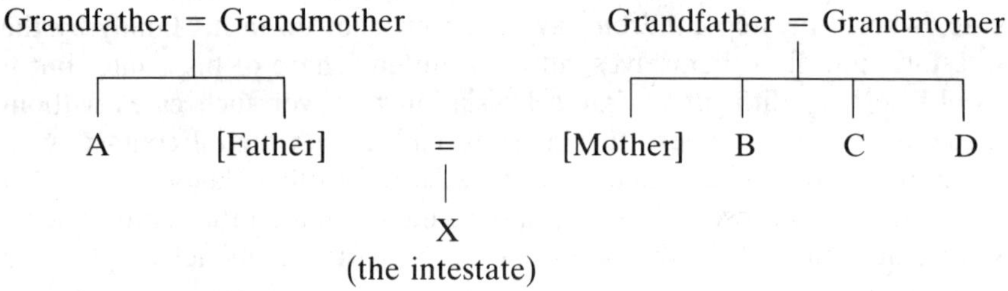

In this case as the father and mother have both predeceased, A, B, C and D, the uncles and aunts of the intestate, divide the free estate equally between them, and the grandparents have no share. It is to be noted that under section 6 the division is equal between all members of the class entitled to succeed. There is no suggestion of a preference for the paternal side over the maternal or vice versa, nor of an equal division between the paternal and maternal sides. It is a *per capita* division between all the persons who fall into a given degree of relationship on either side of the house[25] with representation of any predeceasing members of the class.

Only if the uncles and aunts have also predeceased, without leaving issue to represent them, do the grandparents become entitled to

---

[23] December 8, 1986.
[24] Meston, "Illegitimacy in Succession" (1986) 31 J.L.S. 358.
[25] s. 6 (*a*).

succeed.[26] Again no distinction is made between the paternal and maternal lines. The four grandparents form a class, the surviving members of which share the free estate equally between them when the succession opens at this level.

Failing survivors among the class of grandparents, the brothers and sisters of the grandparents, or their issue by representation, are entitled to the succession.[27] In the absence of any of these, the succession opens to the more remote ancestors of the intestate "generation by generation successively, without distinction between the paternal and maternal lines . . . so however that, failing ancestors of any generation, the brothers and sisters of any of those ancestors shall have right thereto before ancestors of the next more remote generation."[28]

Section 2 (2) provides that references to brothers and sisters include references to brothers and sisters of the half blood, while section 3 provides, as has already been noted in the case of brothers and sisters of the intestate himself, that collaterals of a parent or other ancestor of an intestate related by the whole blood exclude collaterals of the half blood, but that in the absence of collaterals of the whole blood, collaterals of the half blood are entitled to the succession without distinction as between the half blood consanguinean and the half blood uterine.

Taken together, the principle of infinite search among ancestors specified in section 2 (1) (*i*), the rights of collaterals of the half blood, the removal of the significance of illegitimacy and the availability of representation at all levels, mean that an enormous area of search is opened up when the right of succession appears to open to the remoter ancestors. There may be considerable difficulty in practice in drawing up complete and accurate family trees on both the paternal and maternal sides for possibly several generations back and in tracing all the descendants of every member of the trees. The Mackintosh Committee on the Law of Succession did consider this point, and in paragraph 26 of their report stated that they were much attracted by the principle of limiting succession on intestacy to uncles and aunts and their issue. This was partly because the opening of the succession to maternal relatives should in most cases make further search unnecessary and partly because of the difficulty and expense of further search. However, the Committee made no recommendation as all witnesses to whom they suggested a principle of limitation were strongly against any such idea. The draft Bill which was circulated for comment in 1959 also contained a limitation, the proposal being to exclude relatives more remote than the lineal grandparents, but again objection was taken, mainly on the basis that even if much of the estate might be expended in tracing remoter relatives, this was no justification for increasing the rights of the Crown as *ultimus haeres*. When the Succession Bill was introduced in November 1963, it included a

---

[26] s. 2 (1) (*g*).
[27] s. 2 (1) (*h*).
[28] s. 2 (1) (*i*).

proposal that relatives more remote than lineal grandparents should be excluded from the succession, but the principle of infinite search was restored in Committee in the House of Commons.

The English law of intestate succession does contain an exclusion of relatives more remote than grandparents,[29] but it appears now to be accepted in Scotland that an artificial limit on the circle of relations entitled to succeed on intestacy is repugnant to our system of law. We adhere therefore to the long-standing principle that an infinite search must be made following the principles of the version of the parentelic system which we use.

(7) The Crown

In the absence of any person entitled to succeed to the free estate of an intestate by virtue of the specific provisions of Part I of the Act, the right of the Crown to succeed as *ultimus haeres* is saved by section 7 of the Act. The executor, or anyone holding property for which no valid right of succession can be established, has the duty of transferring it to the Queen's and Lord Treasurer's Remembrancer to be administered on behalf of the Crown. The Queen's and Lord Treasurer's Remembrancer takes possession without the need for confirmation.

There was a suggestion in Parliament in debate on the Bill that the Common Good fund of the local authority for the area of the deceased's last residence should be substituted for the Crown as *ultimus haeres*, but the principle was not accepted.

The Crown, through the Queen's and Lord Treasurer's Remembrancer, will normally place advertisements in local newspapers to publicise the fact that an estate has fallen to the Crown. If heirs later establish their relationship, the property will be transferred to them. If no heirs come forward, the Crown continues its practice of making grants to persons who have a moral claim on the deceased (as by rendering significant services without payment) or for whom there is evidence to show that the deceased might reasonably have been expected to make provision. Such persons present a Petition for Gift to the Queen's and Lord Treasurer's Remembrancer. At one time the commonest case was that of "relatives" of an illegitimate person who died without issue, but such persons now are treated as full relatives[30] with the result that fewer estates fall to the Crown.

Representation in, and Division of, the Free Estate

In place of the confusingly limited representation in moveables available under the Intestate Moveable Succession (Scotland) Act 1855 there is

---

[29] Administration of Estates Act 1925, s. 46 (1) (*v*), (*vi*).

[30] Law Reform (Miscellaneous Provisions) (Scotland) Act 1968, Pt. I and Law Reform (Parent and Child) (Scotland) Act 1986, s. 1.

now a full right of representation of anyone other than a parent or spouse of the intestate who would have been entitled to share in the free estate of the intestate had he survived.[31] The exclusion of representation of the intestate's parents is fairly obvious, for in any event the intestate's own issue and collaterals, who would be the representatives of the parents, would normally take before the parents became entitled to any share. It does, however, also ensure that the intestate's collaterals of the half blood cannot represent the predeceasing common parent to the partial exclusion of collaterals of the whole blood. Take, for example, a situation such as the following:

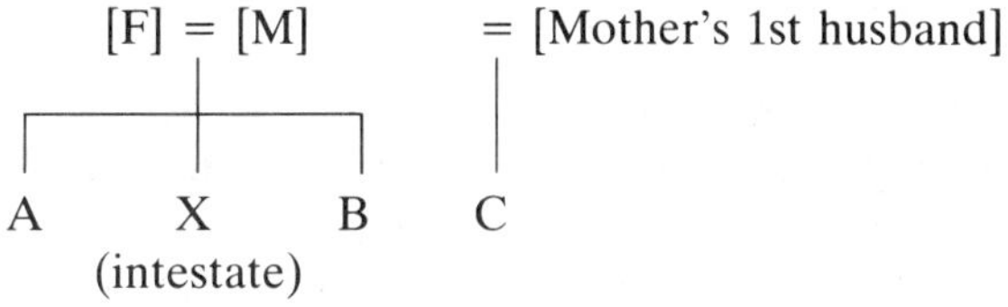

If his mother had survived the intestate, she would have been entitled to one-half of his free estate in preference to A and B under section 2 (1) (*b*). The exclusion of representation of parents means that C, a collateral of the half blood uterine, cannot by representation claim the mother's one-half share of the free estate in a situation where he has otherwise no rights of succession at all.

The exclusion of representation of a spouse in respect of his or her rights in the free estate is designed to ensure that step-children of the intestate do not acquire rights of succession in his estate. Step-children have no place at all in intestate succession, but if representation of a spouse had been permitted, they could have come in by the back door to the prejudice of uncles and aunts and remoter ancestors of the intestate. Strong arguments were presented in Parliament in debate on the Succession Bill that step-children should have some place in the law of succession, but the attachment to blood relationship as the governing principle, though already weakened, proved too strong to permit this radical change.

Apart from these points, the scheme of representation and division specified in sections 5 and 6 in respect of the free estate is very similar to the separate scheme in section 11 for representation in legitim. As in the case of section 11 (1) and (2), section 5 (1) might appear to require that division among representatives must always be *per stirpes*, but is stated to be subject to section 6 which specifies the method of division.

This provides that if all the persons entitled to share in the estate are of the same degree of relationship to the intestate the division is made equally among them *per capita*.[32] Thus, as in the case of the division of legitim,[33] if the intestate is predeceased by his two children but is survived

[31] s. 5 (1)—applying only to the free estate.
[32] s. 6 (*a*).
[33] *Supra*, p. 57.

by four grandchildren, three being issue of one child and one of the other, the division is equal, *per capita*, into quarters.

If, however, those entitled are not all of the same degree of relationship to the intestate, the division is *per stirpes* at the level of the class nearest to the intestate of which there are surviving members—the "nearest surviving relatives."[34]

Since December 8, 1986, the representatives who may take their parent's share are the children of that person without distinction between legitimate and illegitimate children.[35] The former rule that only legitimate issue, however remote, of the predeceaser could represent him now applies only to deaths occurring before December 8, 1986.

Adopted children and representation

The scheme of representation in section 5 (1) is in respect of persons entitled to succeed by virtue of the preceding provisions of the Act. The rights of adopted children are specified later in the Act, but in the form that they are to be regarded as children of the adopter for all purposes of succession. This equates them with the "children" mentioned in section 2 (1) (*a*), and therefore they are entitled to represent their adopting parents in successions in which the adopting parents would have been entitled to share by survivance.

---

[34] s. 6 (*b*).

[35] Law Reform (Parent and Child) (Scotland) Act 1986, s. 1 (1).

CHAPTER 7

TESTATE SUCCESSION

The Succession (Scotland) Act made only limited alterations to the law affecting succession under a will made by the deceased. It was primarily concerned with major reforms in the law of intestate succession. Thus much of the law relating to testate succession was left unaltered by the Act, and such changes as were effected were not so significant reforms as in the case of intestacy.

Types of will

Here the law was largely unaffected. It remains possible to make a purely oral will, provided the words spoken can be vouched by witnesses, but there is a severe practical limitation in that such an oral will can convey property only up to the value of £100 Scots,[1] which is the equivalent of £8.33 sterling. It is therefore of little significance, although an oral legacy of a greater amount is valid up to that sum.

Holograph wills are recognised, and indeed common, in Scotland, although they are not a recognised form in England. To be effective, a holograph will must be wholly in the testator's handwriting and subscribed by him. If the body of the text is not in the testator's handwriting, it is sufficient if he writes, in his own handwriting, the words "adopted as holograph" above his signature at the end of the deed.[2] It seems to be sufficient for a holograph will to be signed on the last page only, although attested wills must be signed on each page, and there is no restriction on the type of surface on which it may be written. A recent will was accepted as valid when it was written on the back of a painting.

Formal, professionally prepared, wills are invariably attested documents. They are signed on each page by the testator[3] and the testator's signature is witnessed on the last page on which there are operative provisions (*i.e.* not merely the testing clause) by two witnesses. The witnesses must know the testator, but this requirement is not a great restriction, as a mere introduction can suffice. It is highly desirable, but not actually essential, that the witnesses should sign immediately after the testator has signed or acknowledged his signature to them.[4] As this

[1] Erskine, *Inst.*, III,ix,7.

[2] In very special circumstances the court may recognise a typed adoption as holograph. *McBeath's Trs.* v. *McBeath*, 1935 S.L.T. 315. *Cf. Chisholm* v. *Chisholm*, 1949 S.L.T. 394.

[3] The Conveyancing and Feudal Reform (Scotland) Act 1970 (c. 35), s. 44 which removed this requirement from other deeds, did not apply to wills.

[4] *Walker* v. *Whitwell*, 1916 S.C. (H.L.) 75.

implies, it is not necessary that the witnesses should both be present to see the testator sign, as it is acceptable if the testator acknowledges his signature to them. The acknowledgment may be to both witnesses together, or it may be done separately to each witness. Persons of 16 years of age or older may act as witnesses.[5] In the case of attestations occurring before September 25, 1991, the minimum age was 12 for females and 14 for boys.

While it is inadvisable for a beneficiary to act as a witness to the will, this is not in Scotland a ground of invalidity of the will and acting as a witness does not deprive a beneficiary of his rights.

A system of notarial execution is available for a testator who is blind or unable to write.[6] The procedure involves reading over the will to the testator in the presence of witnesses, obtaining the testator's agreement and then a signature on his behalf by one of the list of persons qualified to act.

It is a distinctive feature of Scots law that it is possible to incorporate by reference into a validly executed will not only existing documents which are not in themselves validly executed, but even informal documents which may be created in the future. It is common practice to include in formal wills a clause specifying the nature of future informal writings which are to be accepted. The normal use of the clause is to permit disposal of personal effects in writings signed somewhere by the testator, but there is nothing in law to prevent the clause from having a much wider effect in validating past or future writings.[7]

Various devices are sometimes employed to avoid the necessity of executing a formal will. These include the nominations which are statutorily authorised for some types of small savings asset, now mainly benefits from a friendly society, but formerly including National Savings investments.[8] The *Donatio Mortis Causa* is also accepted in Scots law, and has fewer restrictions than in some other countries.[9]

However the main device still used as a will substitute, despite its many dangers, is the special destination inserted into the documents of title to certain types of asset, especially land. This will normally take the form of a direction that when there are two owners the predeceaser's share will pass automatically to the survivor. (In Scotland two owners of a single asset are presumed to be owners in common, not joint owners.) Despite what is commonly thought, a survivorship reference in the heading of bank and building society accounts does not amount to a special destination and has of itself no effect upon the succession to the money in the account, because a bank passbook or its equivalent is not a document of title to the money in the account.

---

[5] Age of Legal Capacity (Scotland) Act 1991 (c. 50), s. 1 (1) (*a*) and s. 9.

[6] Conveyancing (Scotland) Act 1924 (c. 27), s. 18 and Sched. I.

[7] *Macrorie's Exrs.* v. *McLaren*, 1982 S.L.T. 295 (reversed on a different point 1984 S.L.T. 271).

[8] See for example National Savings Bank Regulations 1972 (S.I. 1972 No. 764).

[9] *Morris* v. *Riddick* (1867) 5 M. 1036; *Aiken's Exrs.* v. *Aiken*, 1937 S.L.T. 414.

Although capable of being useful if they are understood and are used properly, special destinations are a relic of a time when it was not technically possible to make a will disposing of heritage and are liable to produce unintended results.[10] They should certainly be abolished and it is unfortunate that the Scottish Law Commission has not been able to recommend their complete abolition, although they will be severely limited when the proposed reforms are brought into effect.

The Succession Act 1964 did make some limited but valuable reforms to the law relating to special destinations. Under section 36 (2), proviso (*a*), heritage owned by the deceased, but subject to a special destination, is not treated for the purposes of the Act as part of his estate unless he could and did evacuate the destination. Section 18 (2) creates a restricted vesting in the executor in a case in which the deceased either could not or did not evacuate such a destination, thus providing a method which can, if necessary, be used to transfer the property to the person called as beneficiary in the destination.

However, the law relating to the acts by a testator which will amount to revocation or evacuation of a special destination (assuming he had the power to revoke it) was not entirely clear before the 1964 Act. This was particularly so when the alleged revocation was merely by implication from a subsequent general settlement which made no specific mention of the special destination. Many difficulties arose from the common practice of taking a title to heritage in the names of husband and wife and the survivor and then subsequently, possibly even on the same day, executing a will which took no account of the survivorship destination. A question of implied revocation frequently arose.

Section 30 of the Act therefore provided that a testamentary disposition executed on or after September 10, 1964 (*i.e.* whose actual date of execution is after the commencement of the Act irrespective of the testator's date of death)[11] shall not have effect so as to evacuate a special destination unless it contains a specific reference to the destination and a declared intention on the part of the testator to revoke it.[12] All this, of course, assumes that the testator has the power to revoke the destination. If he has no power to revoke, no reference, however specific, and no intention, however well declared, can effect revocation. If he has the power, the revocation must be express and cannot arise merely by implication. Power to revoke will be lost if the special destination is contractual in nature, commonly if both spouses have contributed to the purchase of a house, with the result that inserting a special destination amounts to the creation of an irrevocable will of the house. The effect therefore is that special destinations will normally prevail over contrary

---

[10] Meston, "Special Destinations" in *A Scots Conveyancing Miscellany*, ed. Cusine (1987), pp. 62–65. *Weir* v. *J. M. Hodge & Son*, 1990 S.L.T. 266 illustrates a situation in which the existence of the destination was ignored, leading to an action of damages against the solicitor giving negligent advice.

[11] s. 36 (3).

[12] *Stirling's Trs.*, 1977 S.L.T. 229.

provisions in a will. It is not permissible to go behind a statement in the title deeds about the source of the funds used in the purchase.[13]

Confirmation and the probative character of wills

If confirmation is granted in Scotland to an executor who is acting under a will which disposes of property, the will is treated as probative.[14] Whereas the previous procedure merely confirmed the appointment of the executor and made no pronouncement on the validity of the will, the effect now is a judicial statement that the will is validly executed. This is expressly declared to be so even although the will is not in fact probative[15] and indeed the section does not apply if the will is probative without the benefit of the section. Hence confirmation now has much greater validating effects, but it will be noted that confirmation will not be granted to property disposed of in a holograph will unless there is proof of the genuineness of the writing, usually by two affidavits.[16]

Grants of representation issued in England and Wales or Northern Ireland will have the same effect as confirmation without further formality provided that the deceased was domiciled in the jurisdiction issuing the grant and that fact is specified in it. Grants of representation issued outwith the United Kingdom and to which the Colonial Probates Acts 1892 and 1927 apply also make the will probative once they have been sealed in Scotland under that Act.[17]

Revocation of wills

The Succession Act made little alteration in revocation apart from the clarification of how special destinations may be revoked. A testamentary writing may be expressly revoked either by acts of physical destruction carried out by, or on behalf of, the testator with the intention of revoking the will[18] or by a clause of revocation in a subsequent deed executed with testamentary formalities.[19] There may also be implied revocation in whole or in part if a subsequent testamentary deed contains inconsistent provisions although not including a revocation clause.[20] In the circumstances to which it applies, the *conditio si testator sine liberis decesserit* can be invoked by an afterborn child for whom no provision is made in the will and the result will be a total revocation of the whole will.[21] Any form of revocation other than physical destruction may permit the original will

---

[13] *Gordon-Rogers* v. *Thomson's Exrs.*, 1988 S.L.T. 618.
[14] s. 32.
[15] s. 32 (2).
[16] s. 21.
[17] s. 32 (2) (*b*).
[18] *Nasmyth* v. *Hare* (1821) 1 Sh.App. 65; *Thomson's Trs.* v. *Bowhill Baptist Church*, 1956 S.L.T. 302.
[19] *Kirkpatrick's Trs.* v. *Kirkpatrick* (1874) 1 R. (H.L.) 37.
[20] *Park's Trs.* v. *Park* (1890) 27 S.L.R. 528.
[21] *Stevenson's Trs.* v. *Stevenson*, 1932 S.L.T. 510.

to be later revived if the revoking deed is itself revoked by a method which does not affect the original will.[22]

Capacity to execute a will

For wills actually executed on or after September 25, 1991, the minimum age of testamentary capacity is 12.[23] Prior to that date, full testamentary capacity was attained on attaining majority at 12 for females and 14 for males.[24]

A purported will executed by someone incapable of understanding the nature and consequences of a will is void on the ground of insanity.[25] Wills obtained from a testator by undue influence used by a person in a position of authority,[26] and wills executed by someone in the state of mental weakness known as "facility" and obtained by improper acts amounting to circumvention,[27] may be set aside by the court.

Restrictions upon testamentary freedom

The principal restriction upon the freedom of a testator to do as he wishes with his estate is probably the existence of the legal rights of spouses and descendants. These have been discussed above[28] in their role as one of the three sets of rules involved in a division of an intestate estate. Their other function is to protect the spouse and issue of a testator from disinheritance. Whatever the testator may provide in his will, the surviving spouse and issue have an automatic right to their shares of the moveable estate. In theory, the testator has no *power* to dispose of these shares in his will. There will be substantial changes, including the application to the whole estate of the deceased, when the proposed new "legal share" is substituted for legal rights in accordance with the proposals of the Scottish Law Commission.

Other restrictions upon a testator's freedom include the detailed legislation restricting accumulations of income with the capital for excessive periods[29] and the somewhat undefined power of the court to strike down testamentary provisions on the ground of public policy.[30]

A testator is prevented from achieving effects similar to those of an entail[31] by creating a series of successive liferents. A liferent may be

---

[22] *Bruce's J.F.* v. *Lord Advocate*, 1969 S.L.T. 337; Meston, "Revival by Revocation of the Revoking Will," 1974 S.L.T. (News) 153.

[23] Age of Legal Capacity (Scotland) Act 1991 (c. 50), s. 2 (2).

[24] *Stevenson* v. *Allans* (1680) Mor. 8949; Succession (Scotland) Act 1964, ss. 28, 38 (3).

[25] *Sivewright* v. *Sivewright's Trs.*, 1919 2 S.L.T. 261.

[26] *McGilvary* v. *Gilmartin*, 1986 S.L.T. 89.

[27] *West's Tr.* v. *West*, 1980 S.L.T. 6.

[28] Chap. 5.

[29] Trusts (Scotland) Act 1961 (c. 57), s. 5.

[30] *McCaig* v. *Univ. of Glasgow*, 1907 S.C. 231; *Sutherland's Tr.* v. *Verschoyle & Ors.*, 1968 S.L.T. 43.

[31] New entails were prohibited from 1914: Entail (Scotland) Act 1914, s. 2.

created only in favour of someone alive at the date when the deed creating it came into operation. The draconian sanction is that if anyone born after that date is of full age and becomes entitled to a liferent under the deed, the apparent liferenter becomes the outright fiar and the rights of any fiar nominated in the deed are cancelled.[32]

Construction of wills

Adopted persons

Adopted persons are defined for the purposes of the Succession (Scotland) Act 1964 as persons adopted in pursuance of a formal adoption order made under the Adoption Acts either before or after the commencement of the Succession Act or whose adoption is recognised by the law of Scotland.[33]

The general policy of the Act was to remove the anomalies of the previous law in relation to adopted persons. The effect of Part IV of the Act is therefore that they are treated for all purposes, whether of succession or of entitlement under an *inter vivos* deed, as children of the adopter or adopters.[34] This is reinforced by section 39 (1) of the Adoption (Scotland) Act 1978[35] which declares *inter alia* that a child who is the subject of an adoption order is to be treated in law as if he had been born as a legitimate child of the adopter or adopters. Section 24 (1) of the Succession Act specifies the relationship adopted children are to be deemed to have to other children or adopted children of the adopter. The provisions of the Adoption Act 1958 which formerly prevented an adopted child from acquiring any rights of intestate succession or legal rights in the adopter's estate are repealed.[36]

The details of the reciprocal rights of succession between an adopted child and its adopting parents have already been considered in Chapters 5 and 6, along with the place of adopted persons in collateral succession. Briefly, the adopted person's rights either in the estates of its natural parents or through them by representation are cut off, subject to the transitional provisions of the Law Reform (Miscellaneous Provisions) (Scotland) Act 1966.[37] In substitution the adopted person has full rights as a child in the estates of its adopting parents and through them by representation.[38] A person adopted by two spouses jointly has rights of succession as a brother or sister of the whole blood to any other child or adopted child of both spouses. In any other case, however, the adopted person has rights of succession to any other person being the adopted

[32] Law Reform (Miscellaneous Provisions) (Scotland) Act 1968 (c. 70), ss. 18, 22 (5) in respect of deeds executed on or after November 25, 1968.

[33] s. 23 (5).

[34] s. 23 (1).

[35] c. 28. In force September 1, 1984 (S.I. 1984 No. 1050).

[36] s. 24 (4).

[37] c. 19, s. 5.

[38] s. 23 (1).

child of the adopter or of either of the adopters as a brother or sister of the half blood.[39] Equally, since adopted persons are deemed to be related to collaterals in these capacities, they have rights of succession through the collaterals by representation.

There are also provisions in the Act relating to the construction of deeds when adopted children exist. Some confusion has existed over the commencement of these provisions in view of the complex relationship between sections 23 (2), 23 (4) and 36 (3).

Section 23 (4) states that nothing in section 23 "shall affect any deed executed . . . before the commencement of this Act." The effect is that wills actually executed[40] before September 10, 1964, have the same meaning as they had then. In other words, references in such wills to "children" or "issue" are presumed not to include adopted children. It is presumed that the testator was aware of the state of the law at the time and that by not mentioning adopted children he intended not to include them. Such children will, of course, now be entitled to legitim irrespective of the terms of the adopter's will if the adopting parent died after the commencement of the Succession Act. The intention in this, as in other parts of the Act, was to avoid the necessity of disturbing existing arrangements.[41]

Section 23 (2) therefore means that in wills executed on or after September 10, 1964, a general reference to "children" or "issue" will, unless the contrary intention appears, include adopted children. The point of the proviso that for the purposes of section 23 (2) a deed taking effect on the death of any person is to be deemed to have been executed on the date of death of that person is that if a will is executed *after the commencement of the Act* referring to "children," or "issue," and subsequently the testator adopts a child, that child is included. The beginning of section 23 (2) refers to deeds executed after the making of an adoption order, but the proviso ensures that the will is regarded as being executed at the date of the testator's death and hence after the adoption order, so that the adopted child is included in the term "children."

Similarly a deed executed after the commencement of the Succession Act and taking effect on the death of some person other than the grantor of the deed will be deemed for the purposes of section 23 (2) to have been executed on the date of death of that person, and therefore after the adoption of any child who by then had been adopted.

The general policy that an adopted person is to be treated as the child of the adopter is specifically applied to the construction of the terms used in wills and of *inter vivos* deeds disposing of property by section 23 (1) (*a*) and (*b*). This is subject only to the special transitional provision that if the adopting parent died before September 10, 1964, and the natural parent died on or after August 3, 1966, the child is treated as the child of the natural parent for purposes of succession to that parent.[42]

---

[39] s. 24 (1).
[40] s. 36 (3).
[41] "Class Terms in the Construction of Deeds" (1969) 14 J.L.S. 204.
[42] Law Reform (Miscellaneous Provisions) (Scotland) Act 1966 (c. 19), s. 5.

The general policy is made more specific by section 23 (2). In deeds executed after the making of an adoption order (deeds taking effect on the death of any person being deemed to have been executed on the date of his death), any express or implied reference to the child or children of the adopter is to be construed as including a reference to the adopted person. References in any deed to the children of the adopted person's natural parents are to be construed as not including a reference to the adopted person, and references to a person related to the adopted person in any particular degree are to be construed as references to a person who would be related to him in that degree if he were the child of the adopter.

As examples of these situations, a legacy to the "children" of X includes X's adopted children, but a legacy to the "children" of the natural parents of a person who has been adopted by a third party does not include the adopted person. A legacy by an adopted person to, say, his "nephews" is payable to the issue of other children adopted by, or born to, the adopters of the adopted person himself and not to his nephews by natural relationship. The latter aspect of construction in collateral succession is also stated in section 24 (1) and similar situations can be envisaged for *inter vivos* conveyances. For so long as it continues to exist it would seem that the *conditio si testator sine liberis decesserit* would be available to a child adopted after the date of a will for whom no provision is made in it. The proviso to section 23 (2) of the Succession Act is only for the purposes of that subsection, which deals with references to children in deeds.

A question was thought to arise whether a bequest to "the issue of any of my children who fail to survive me" would include the predeceasing child's adopted child. In the view of the present writer, there is no possibility of any doubt upon the matter. Such an adopted child would be included as a beneficiary. It is, of course, open to a testator to make such provision as he wishes, but if he used a phrase such as that quoted above, the whole purpose of the Act is to ensure that its meaning includes the adopted child. In the vigorous correspondence on this topic[43] the most convincing argument was that presented by Professor Clive at page 182 (January 1981) and this is the view which should be acted upon. It will be reinforced by the new section 39A of the Adoption (Scotland) Act 1978 which will be enacted when the Scottish Law Commission's draft Bill in its Report on Succession[44] is eventually enacted.

One of the major difficulties preventing the introduction of full rights of succession for adopted children at an earlier date was the existence of the rules of primogeniture and preference of males in the succession to heritage. While these rules have now largely disappeared, they are still relevant in the case of titles and some other items to which the Act does not apply.[45] Adopted children have no rights of succession to these items,

---

[43] 1981 J.L.S. (Workshop) pp. 159, 165, 172, 182, 191 and 206.
[44] Scot. Law Com. No. 124.
[45] s. 37 (1).

in so far as included in the estate of the adopter. Accordingly, where the terms of any deed provide that any property or interest in property is to devolve along with a title, honour or dignity, nothing in section 23 of the Succession Act 1964 or in the Children Act 1975 or in the Adoption (Scotland) Act 1978 is to prevent that devolution.[46]

If a person has been adopted more than once, in effect only the last adoption is reckoned for the purposes of succession, of establishing relationships and of construction of deeds executed after the last adoption order.[47]

An adoption order may be revoked in various circumstances, *e.g.* when a child who had previously been adopted by his parents is legitimated by virtue of the Legitimation (Scotland) Act 1968. However section 6 of that Act provides that revocation of an adoption order is not to affect an intestacy which occurred, or a deed which came into operation, before the revocation.

Illegitimate persons

The radical improvements in the direct rights of succession of illegitimate children have already been noted in Chapters 5 and 6. However these reforms of the law of intestate succession, even taking into account the right to legitim, by no means exhausted the problem.

At common law there was very serious discrimination against the illegitimate child in the construction of deeds. The rule of construction amounted to a very strong presumption that terms such as "children" or "issue" referred to the legitimate relationship only. This stemmed from the general rule that an illegitimate child is *filius nullius* and the ultimate logic of this rule was well expressed by Lord Watson in *Clarke* v. *Carfin Coal Co.*[48] when he said "at common law the mother is as much as the father, an utter stranger in blood to her child." With this somewhat nonsensical proposition built into the law it is not surprising to find that it could be authoritatively stated[49] that "the mere fact that there were no legitimate children answering the description could scarcely be regarded as a sufficient reason for giving to a designative bequest a construction which would admit persons who in law are regarded as strangers."

In other words, it seemed to be assumed that no testator in his senses would intend to include illegitimate children in the benefits of a bequest to the "children" of a particular person. Thus that construction was avoided unless it was completely impossible to do so—and sometimes even then. For example, in *Mitchell's Trs.* v. *Cables*[50] a testator made a gift to his son "and his lawful children" whom failing to his daughter "and to the whole children procreated or that may yet be procreated of her body." At the date of the will, the daughter had an illegitimate child who

[46] s. 23 (3).
[47] s. 24 (3).
[48] (1891) 18 R. (H.L.) 63 at p. 70.
[49] McLaren, *Wills & Succession*, I, 694.
[50] (1893) 1 S.L.T. 156.

was known to and indeed lived with the testator, and one might have thought that the difference in the wording of the two provisions indicated as clearly as humanly possible that the illegitimate child was intended to be a beneficiary. Nonetheless that construction was rejected.

In the interpretation of deeds executed on or after November 25, 1968, this position was reversed by section 5 of the Law Reform (Miscellaneous Provisions) (Scotland) Act 1968.[51] This provides that in deducing any relationship for the purpose of ascertaining beneficiaries under a deed, the persons concerned are to be taken to be related to each other notwithstanding that the relationship was an illegitimate one only. It is interesting that this part of the 1968 reforms affecting illegitimate children was much wider in scope than the reform of their direct rights of intestate succession. The changed rules of interpretation apply to all deeds creating benefits, not just to deeds by the parents of an illegitimate child, with the result that the further reform in the Law Reform (Parent and Child) (Scotland) Act 1986 was of less significance for the construction of wills than in the creation of rights of succession. The rule of construction contained in the 1968 Act was already a general one, and the main further change effected in 1986 was to apply the principle of equality to most statutes as well as to private deeds.

The main qualification is that the grantor of the deed may express a contrary intention, probably by using such terms as "lawful children" and such a contrary intention will receive effect.[52] Others are that the new rule did not apply to the construction of enactments until 1986 and that it still does not affect the succession to titles, honours or dignities.[53] However the provision in the 1968 Act that the new rule of construction did not prevent property from devolving along with a title does not appear in the 1986 Act. Since 1986 it may therefore be that while a title may pass to the heir at law, property destined along with it may pass to an illegitimate child instead.

Subject to all the same qualifications, section 6 of the 1968 Act also provides that illegitimacy is no longer to prevent the operation of the *conditio si testator sine liberis decesserit*, the *conditio si institutus sine liberis decesserit*, or the principle of accretion. Previously a number of cases had established that the children of a predeceasing illegitimate child for whom a testamentary provision had been made could not invoke the *conditio si institutus*.[54] There was no question of an after-born illegitimate child invoking the *conditio si testator* to set aside a will since it had no ordinary rights of succession to protect, and there was no accretion in a gift to illegitimate children as a class.[55]

---

[51] Deeds exercising a power of appointment are treated as having the date of the deed which created the power: 1968 Act, s. 5 (3).

[52] Law Reform (Parent and Child) (Scotland) Act 1986, s. 1 (4) (*c*).

[53] 1968 Act, s. 5 (5) (*b*) and 1986 Act, s. 9 (1) (*c*).

[54] *Farquharson* v. *Kelly* (1900) 7 S.L.T. 442.

[55] McLaren, *Wills & Succession*, i, 695.

Power to bequeath a lease

When a lease is assignable, the tenant has always been able to bequeath his interest under it to any person whom he chooses. He used to have no power of bequest if there was a condition, express or implied, prohibiting assignation. This is still so if there is an express prohibition on assignation, although the deceased's executor may transfer the interest despite an express prohibition.[56] However, if the prohibition on assignation is only an implied one, section 29 gives the tenant a right to bequeath his interest to any one of the persons who, if he had died intestate, would be, or would in any circumstances have been, entitled to succeed to his estate under the Act.

As in the case of an executor's power of transfer of leases, the power of bequest in the face of an implied prohibition on assignation is intended merely to preserve as far as possible in the new circumstances the effect of the prohibition. The purpose of such a prohibition was to ensure that the tenant's heir at law would succeed to the tenancy. That status being now virtually abolished, provision had to be made to ensure that a single tenant could be found to continue the tenancy. This purpose is largely achieved by giving an executor power to transfer the interest to any one person actually entitled to succeed to the deceased's estate on intestacy, irrespective of express or implied prohibitions on assignation.[57] A wider power is, however, given to the tenant himself to select the single tenant to succeed to him from the whole circle of persons who might in any circumstances succeed to the tenancy on intestacy, provided that the prohibition on assignation is no more than an implied one. In effect transfer by the executor or bequest by the tenant within the circle of relations specifed is another method of finding an "heir at law" to continue the tenancy.

The special provisions relating to bequest of agricultural leases contained in section 16 of the Crofters' Holdings (Scotland) Act 1886, section 11 of the Agricultural Holdings (Scotland) Act 1991 and section 10 of the Crofters (Scotland) Act 1955 are not prejudiced by the power of bequest in the 1964 Act.[58]

---

[56] *Infra*, p. 110.

[57] The nominee must have a direct entitlement to succeed: *MacLean* v. *MacLean*, 1988 S.L.T. 626.

[58] s. 29 (2).

CHAPTER 8

EXECUTORS AND THE ADMINISTRATION OF ESTATES

The Succession Act had a profound effect upon the law affecting executors in the administration of estates. The relevant provisions are mainly contained in Part III of the Act and apply to the administration of the estates of persons dying on or after September 10, 1964.[1]

The general effect was to make the executor, as such, a much more significant figure than he had previously been. Prior to the Act the functions of an executor were confined to the moveable estate of the deceased. In his capacity as executor, he had no concern with the deceased's heritage. Thus while his function was to ingather and distribute moveables after paying moveable debts, the heritage passed on intestacy directly to the heir at law without the intervention of a middleman. The administrative provisions of the Act are designed to extend the executor's competence to the whole estate of the deceased—other than titles of honour, coats of arms, and property falling within the provisos to section 36 (2) of the Succession Act. The general policy is put into effect by section 14 (1) and the modification of existing statutes.[2] The executor thus became the key figure in the transfer of property on death and a number of difficulties, especially in connection with methods of completion of title to heritage, had to be faced.

Right to the office of executor

The effect of the Succession Act on the order of preference of claims to the office is still not entirely clear. In practice there may not be much likelihood of competition for the office, but the principles of the order of preference remain somewhat difficult to determine.

What is clear is that the person entitled to the office of executor in preference to all others is the executor nominated by the deceased. Nothing is said in the 1964 Act about those entitled to office as executors-nominate. Accordingly, the position remains that an executor-nominate may be a person expressly or impliedly appointed by the deceased or one placed in that position by construction under section 3 of the Executors (Scotland) Act 1900.[3]

The normal, and simplest, case is that of the express appointment of an executor, *e.g.* "I appoint X to be my executor." Equally, it is the practice

[1] s. 37 (1) (*d*).
[2] Sched. 2, especially para. 3.
[3] 63 & 64 Vict. c. 55.

to treat as executors-nominate any persons on whom the deceased has conferred the powers of an executor, even although he may not have used the term "executor." For example, in *Martin* v. *Ferguson's Trs.*,[4] where the expression used was "I wish my estate to be managed" by specified persons, those persons were to be regarded as executors-nominate.

Constructive appointment as executor-nominate arises under section 3 of the Executors (Scotland) Act 1900 as amended.[5] This provides:

> "Where a testator has not appointed any person to act as his executor, or failing any person so appointed, the testamentary trustees of such testator, original or assumed, or appointed by the Supreme Court or the sheriff court (if any), failing whom any general disponee or universal legatory or residuary legatee appointed by such testator, shall be held to be his executor nominate and entitled to confirmation in that character."

This is a fairly comprehensive coverage of persons whom the deceased might possibly have wished to act as his executor, and it is to be noted that assumed trustees, even if the original trustees have resigned immediately after the assumption, are still entitled to confirmation as executors-nominate.

Provided that it is clear from the whole tenor of the deceased's will, or from the terms of an appointment of trustees by the court, that there is not intended to be any bar to the persons in question taking up office as executors, they will be entitled to that office in preference to all others whose claim is merely through relationship.

It is when the deceased has not appointed executors, either through dying intestate or by not making a nomination in his will, that the rules of preference are less clear. The only provisions in the 1964 Act regulating the right to appointment by the court as executor-dative appear in sections 9 (4) and 5 (2), and they do not appear to cover the whole situation.

Section 9 (4), restating the corresponding provisions in the Intestate Husband's Estate (Scotland) Acts, provides that where a surviving spouse's monetary prior right exhausts the deceased spouse's estate, so that the survivor is entitled to the whole estate, that survivor has the right to be appointed executor. This right is exclusive of all other claimants to the office, the surviving spouse being the only person beneficially interested in the estate.

The other provision in the 1964 Act is that in section 5 (2). This also bears a relationship to one of the few previous statutory enactments on the subject—namely, the last part of section 1 of the Intestate Moveable Succession (Scotland) Act 1855.[6] That provided that in a competition for

---

4 (1892) 19 R. 474.

5 63 & 64 Vict. c. 55, s. 3, amended Law Reform (Miscellaneous Provisions) (Scotland) Act 1980 (c. 55), Sched. 2.

6 18 & 19 Vict. c. 23.

the office of executor, surviving next of kin were to be preferred to the representatives of predeceasing next of kin, who were given a right of succession for the first time by section 1 of the 1855 Act. Section 5 (2) of the 1964 Act provides that the right of representatives to the office of executor is postponed to the right of surviving members of the class, predeceasing members of which they are representing.

In settling the order of preference of rights to the office of executor, the pre-1964 position was that the next of kin (ascertained according to the common law) were primarily entitled to the office. Failing them, at common law the widow as creditrix in respect of her *jus relictae* was entitled to office, followed by other creditors and special legatees. The various statutory amendments to the common law of intestate moveable succession, particularly the Intestate Moveable Succession (Scotland) Act 1855, had the effect of giving the various statutory beneficiaries rights to the office of executor either along with, or postponed to, the next of kin. For example, the right of succession conferred on a mother by section 4 of the 1855 Act gave her also a right to the office of executor-dative *qua* mother, probably even along with the next of kin if they competed. However, the whole order of preference in the office of executor, as also the order of succession, hinged on the next of kin under the common law rules, with possible additions in respect of statutory beneficiaries.

Under the 1964 Act, however, the common law concept of next of kin is no longer relevant in determining the order of the beneficial succession to the estate of a deceased person. Instead there is a statutory list of those entitled to succeed, mainly specified in section 2. A question therefore arose whether the concept of the next of kin is still relevant in competitions for the office of executor-dative or whether there is now a new basic concept that the right to be executor depends on the existence of a right of beneficial succession under the 1964 Act.

There is no inherent improbability in the existence of a different method of establishing the right to the executorship from that employed in settling the beneficial succession, and it would seem that it is still correct to appoint an executor *qua* next of kin if he falls within the common law category, even although his right of succession may be by a different title under the 1964 Act. There is nothing in the Act to alter the previous rule under which the next of kin had the pre-eminent right.[7] This is fortified by the provisions of Schedules 1 and 2 of the Act of Sederunt (Confirmation of Executors) 1964 which continue to provide for decerniture of an executor-dative *qua* next of kin.

At common law the class nearest in degree to the deceased in which there were surviving members was the class of next of kin, the spouse, mother and maternal relatives not being counted for this purpose. In other words, the order was children and remoter descendants, then brothers and sisters german and their descendants, then brothers and sisters of the half blood consanguinean and their descendants, then the father, then his collaterals and ascendants on the same principles.

---

[7] *Bennett* v. *Rennie*, 1988 S.C.L.R. 307.

On the analogy of the treatment of the purely statutory beneficiaries under the previous law, those who have a right of succession under the 1964 Act, though not being in the category of next of kin, would seem to be entitled in a competition to be executors along with the next of kin. It seems doubtful whether the next of kin could be completely ousted by a statutory beneficiary, although there can be cases where the next of kin have no rights of beneficial succession. For example, a deceased might be survived by a spouse and by a paternal uncle. Even if the estate were large enough to leave a surplus after the surviving spouse's prior rights, the free estate after deduction of legal rights would not fall to the uncle, who is the next of kin, but to the surviving spouse under section 2 (1) (*e*). Admittedly, the uncle would be unlikely to take active steps to seek the office of executor in these circumstances, but it seems very doubtful whether, if he made one, his claim could be rejected in favour of that of the spouse. The more probable course would seem to be to make two appointments, one *qua* next of kin and one *qua* surviving spouse. The surviving spouse's exclusive right under section 9 (4) would not apply here, being limited to cases where the survivor takes the *whole* estate by virtue of the monetary prior right.

The situation which seems to have arisen most frequently in practice since the Succession Act is that of an elderly surviving spouse who is either *incapax* or unwilling to act as executor and a son who is willing to act. In these circumstances, it would seem to be perfectly competent to appoint the son executor in his capacity as next of kin, possibly coupled with a declinature by the spouse if the spouse is the sole beneficiary.

Apart from this type of situation, it is probably true that only those who have beneficial rights of succession under the 1964 Act will seek to be appointed executors. The office is usually regarded as a burden rather than as a benefit to be actively sought. But the result would seem to be that those of the statutory beneficiaries who do not apply and who are also next of kin should be appointed and confirmed in the character of next of kin. Any statutory beneficiary who is not one of the next of kin should be appointed and confirmed in his statutory character. Thus a mother would be confirmed *qua* mother, never being one of the next of kin, while the father would be confirmed *qua* father when there were also brothers and sisters, so that his right of succession was purely statutory, but *qua* next of kin when there were no brothers and sisters. Similarly, when the succession has opened to collaterals of the half blood, there is now no distinction between the half blood consanguinean and the half blood uterine. But only the half blood consanguinean could be next of kin at common law. Hence, if two persons sought appointment as executor, one in each category of collateral of the half blood, the half blood consanguinean would be confirmed *qua* next of kin but the half blood uterine would be confirmed *qua* brother or sister of the half blood "related through their mother" in the words of section 3.

To talk of "competition" for the office of executor can sometimes be misleading, for it is not the case that the number who may be executors is limited or that only those at the head of the order of preference may be appointed. In the words of Currie on *Confirmation*[8]:

> "anyone who is directly entitled to share in the succession may be appointed without special intimation to other persons having an equal or even a preferable claim to the office. All applicants having the same or an equal right in the order of preference are entitled to be conjoined."

Duties of an executor

The executor's first responsibility is to ingather the whole estate of the deceased with due dispatch. The mere nomination, or even judicial appointment, of an executor does not of itself give him the authority to do this. Once his right to the office has been established in this way, he then requires confirmation by the appropriate Commissary Court before he has a title to intromit with the estate, and it is this confirmation which saves him from the penalties applicable to a vitious intromitter. However, confirmation purges the vitiosity of prior intromissions, so he is not debarred from taking interim measures of administration in connection with the estate.

The second major function of the executor is to use the estate so ingathered to meet the liabilities of the estate. No change was made in this position by the Succession Act so that, as before, the executor acts independently of both creditors and beneficiaries, and subject to the limitation of his liability to the value of the deceased's estate, he is *eadem persona cum defuncto*. If he discovers, or should have discovered, that the estate is absolutely insolvent, an executor has the duty to petition for sequestration of the estate or the appointment of a judicial factor. The sanction is that any intromissions after that date render him liable to the penalties of vitious intromission even although he has obtained confirmation from the court.[9]

An executor cannot be compelled to pay any debts (other than privileged debts) before the expiry of a period of six months within which creditors may claim equal ranking. Although the Succession Act does bring both heritage and moveables under his control, it has not entirely assimilated heritage and moveables for the purposes of succession rights. Thus, in order to permit an accurate value to be struck for the moveables subject to legal rights, the executor must still allocate debts between heritage and moveables, and section 14 (3) specifically preserves the rules relating to the incidence of liability for debts. The incidence of Inheritance Tax on heritage and moveables differs from the former rules for estate duty, so that a specific legacy of a house does not now bear the burden of the tax applicable to the house.[10] There is no longer an heir to

[8] 7th ed., p. 98.
[9] Bankruptcy (Scotland) Act 1985 (c. 66), s. 8 (4).
[10] *Cowie's Trs., Petrs.*, 1982 S.L.T. 326 and Inheritance Tax Act 1984, s. 211.

contrast with the executor, so that the division "as between heir and executor" has now become a division "as between heritage and moveables." Indeed references in any enactment to "heirs" now include a reference to executors.[11]

Finally, having satisfied the debts, the executor is under a duty to account for the balance of the estate to those entitled to it. This means that the primary responsibility for determining who is entitled to it falls upon him, although the courts may be invoked by requiring a claimant to establish his claim or by raising a special case or multiplepoinding. In the ordinary case, however, the matter will be settled by the executor and there is some onus on him, possibly only in the interests of self-protection, to search out beneficiaries. It would be at least advisable for him in an intestacy to investigate the family tree sufficiently to establish that there are no relatives closer to the deceased than those of whose claims he has notice.

However, in view of the practical difficulties which would arise when an illegitimate person is, or might be, involved, the Law Reform (Miscellaneous Provisions) (Scotland) Act 1968[12] gives the executor some protection. Section 7 absolves him of the necessity to establish that there is no illegitimate person who has a right of succession or whose existence would affect rights of succession. In addition the executor is not required to establish that there is no paternal relative of an illegitimate person.[13] He is exempted from personal liability to any person whose claim depends on illegitimacy if he had no notice of the claim at the time of distribution. The claimant's right is not barred and he may take any steps open to him to recover property from those holding it, but the executor's personal liability to him is avoided.

If express claims by illegitimate persons (or which depend on the existence of illegitimate persons) are presented to the executor, he will decide on their validity in the usual way, and in cases of doubt will require the claimant to prove his relationship. This proof may now take the form of a declarator of parentage, which gives rise to a general presumption (*i.e.* one not limited in effect to the parties to the declarator) to the same effect as the declarator.[14]

Similarly, section 24 (2) of the Succession Act provides that an executor or trustee may distribute the deceased's estate without ascertaining that no adoption order has been made by virtue of which any person is or may be entitled to an interest therein. An intolerable burden would be placed on an executor if he had to ensure not only that the deceased himself had never adopted a child, but also that his parents, or either of them, or indeed any other relative had never adopted a child. He is therefore freed from liability to any such person of whose claim he had no notice.

---

[11] Sched. 2, para. 2 (*b*).

[12] c. 70.

[13] s. 7 (*c*) added by the Law Reform (Parent and Child) (Scotland) Act 1986 to replace s. 4 (3) of the Succession (Scotland) Act 1964.

[14] Law Reform (Parent and Child) (Scotland) Act 1986 (c. 9), ss. 7 and 5 (3).

For carrying out his extended functions, an executor-dative is given by section 20 all the powers, privileges and immunities of a gratuitous trustee and is subject to all the restrictions on such a trustee. This includes, for example, the duty to avoid acting as *auctor in rem suam*.[15] The term "trustee" in the Trusts (Scotland) Acts 1921 and 1961 now includes executors-dative. This does not however exempt an executor-dative from finding caution for his intromissions nor does it give him any power to resign or to assume new trustees.

A problem which has been the subject of some discussion is whether an executor has a duty to tell a spouse or descendant of the possibility of claiming legal rights instead of accepting the provisions of the deceased's will. It can be argued that an executor has the usual duty of a trustee to uphold the trust and thus to carry out the terms of the will, so that any advice to beneficiaries on how to defeat the trust purposes would be contrary to his duty. In practice, however, an executor will often take the view that some information should be given, possibly in a guarded form suggesting separate advice, and this compromise would seem to be a sound course of action.

Obtaining confirmation

Before obtaining confirmation an executor-dative (but not normally an executor-nominate) must find caution for his administration of the estate.[16] The amount of caution, unless judicially restricted, is the full gross amount of the deceased's estate and is usually provided by means of a bond of caution from an insurance company. There is however considerable doubt whether the rules relating to caution serve a useful purpose. When the executor is also the sole beneficiary there is no need to protect the beneficiary against the possibility that as executor he might defraud himself. The cost of a bond in such circumstances is useless expenditure, and there is now a provision that if an intestate's spouse is executor-dative and is also entitled to the whole estate by virtue of prior rights, there is no requirement to find caution. A serious gap in the protection afforded by bonds of caution arises when items such as Civil Service gratuities are involved. Such gratuities will not normally be included in the estate confirmed to, and if the executor should fail to account to the beneficiaries for the amount of the gratuity, caution may not protect the true beneficiary.[17]

As a consequence of the assimilation of heritage and moveables, and of the extension to heritage of the executor's authority, confirmation is now

---

[15] *Inglis* v. *Inglis*, 1983 S.L.T. 437.

[16] Succession (Scotland) Act 1964, s. 20, proviso.

[17] See (1967) 12 J.L.S. 258, and the remarkable case of *Harrison* v. *Butters & Anor.*, 1969 S.L.T. 183 in which a divorced wife represented herself as the widow and obtained confirmation with the backing of a bond of caution. When the true widow appeared, it seems that the caution provided no protection as it would have been void from essential error as to identity.

granted to the heritage as well as the moveables. Before the Succession Act came into force, an executor, *qua* executor, had authority over moveable estate only and was confirmed only to the moveable estate. He did prepare an inventory which included details of heritage, but that was for taxation purposes. For purposes of confirmation, the inventory was solely of moveable property. Now, however, the inventory reproduced in the confirmation includes the whole estate, heritable and moveable, and the bond of caution is for the same amount.

The inclusion of heritage in the confirmation is provided for by section 14 (2) of the Succession Act, and a general power of regulation of procedure is conferred on the Court of Session by section 22. Section 22 (1) provides that the court shall have power "to regulate the procedure to be followed, and to prescribe the form and content of any petition, writ or other document to be used, in connection with the confirmation of executors in cases where, by virtue of this Act, heritable property devolves upon the executor."

In virtue of these and other powers, the Act of Sederunt (Confirmation of Executors) 1964 as amended by the Act of Sederunt (Confirmation of Executors Amendment) 1966 provides that the inventory embodied in a confirmation must include such a description of heritage "as will be sufficient to identify the property or interest therein as a separate item in the deceased person's estate." The intention is that something less than a full conveyancing description will be adequate, so that, for instance, a mere statement of the street name and number would be acceptable.

An important point of practice in obtaining confirmation arises in connection with holograph wills. For all purposes proof of authenticity is now required whether or not the will is to be used as a link in the title to heritage. Section 21 of the Succession Act provides that "notwithstanding any rule of law or practice to the contrary, confirmation of an executor to property disposed of in a holograph testamentary disposition shall not be granted unless the court is satisfied by evidence consisting at least of an affidavit by each of two persons that the writing and signature of the disposition are in the handwriting of the testator." Thus proof of the genuineness of the writing will now be a prerequisite of confirmation of executors-nominate under a holograph will.

This supersedes the provisions of section 5 of the Wills Act 1963 which came into force on January 1, 1964. The effect of that section was that a holograph will containing *in gremio* a statement that it was in the testator's handwriting and therefore acceptable without further proof for commissary purposes, became probative on confirmation being granted without further proof of genuineness of the writing.[18] Thus it was probative for the purpose of a conveyance of heritable property. There were obvious dangers in not requiring proof that an apparently holograph will was in fact written by the testator. Thus, while section 32 of the 1964 Act substantially re-enacts section 5 of the Wills Act in providing that a

[18] 1963 S.L.T. (News) 161.

will is probative if confirmation has been granted to property disposed of in it, section 21 introduces the general qualification in cases of holograph wills that there must be proof of genuineness before confirmation can be granted. This helps to preserve the pre-existing practice in relation to titles to heritage.

The Wills Act came into force on January 1, 1964, and thus section 5 of the Act was in force from January 1 to September 9, 1964, until repealed by the Succession Act. Any holograph wills which were accepted for confirmation during this period merely on the strength of a declaration *in gremio* that they were in the testator's handwriting are thereby probative for conveyancing purposes, without further proof.

Vesting of estate in an executor

Here one is concerned solely with vesting of property in the executor and not with the separate issue of completion of title through the executor. As a consequence of the general extension of the executor's functions to include heritage, section 14 (1) provides that

> "on the death of any person (whether testate or intestate) every part of his estate (whether consisting of moveable property or heritable property) falling to be administered under the law of Scotland shall, by virtue of confirmation thereto, vest for the purposes of administration in the executor thereby confirmed and shall be administered and disposed of according to law by such executor."

The whole estate to which he has confirmed thus vests in the executor. The heritage which previously vested directly in the heir at law in cases of intestacy or in a trustee (who might of course be the executor) if one was appointed, now vests directly in the executor *qua* executor by virtue of confirmation. As such, the executor may exercise all the powers arising from a vested right, including completion of title.[19] The executor, unless he is an executor-creditor, must confirm to the whole estate, including agricultural leases and interests therein.[20] If any part of the deceased's estate should prove to have been omitted from the confirmation, it is necessary for the executor to expede an eik to his confirmation in order to vest the omitted property in him. It is only estate to which he has confirmed which vests in the executor.

Supplementary provisions about the effect of confirmation in estates including entailed property and special destinations appear in section 18 (1) and (2). Despite the prohibition on the creation of new entails which has existed since 1914[21] there are apparently about 1,000 entails still in

---

[19] *Robertson, Petr.*, 1978 S.L.T. (Sh.Ct.) 30; *Garvie's Trs.* v. *Garvie's Tutors*, 1975 S.L.T. 94. This may possibly mean that the spouse of a single executor could have occupancy rights under the Matrimonial Homes (Family Protection) (Scotland) Act 1981.

[20] *Cormack* v. *McIldowie's Exrs.*, 1975 S.L.T. 214; *Lord Rotherwick's Trs.* v. *Hope & Ors.*, 1975 S.L.T. 187.

[21] Entail (Scotland) Act 1914 (4 & 5 Geo. 5, c. 43), s. 2.

existence in Scotland, justifying special provisions. Section 18 (1) provides that on the death of an heir of entail in possession, the entailed property, though not regarded as part of the deceased's estate, nevertheless vests by confirmation in the executor in order that it may be conveyed to the person next entitled to it under the entail. The vesting in the executor is for that purpose only and, apparently, if no such conveyance to the next person entitled is necessary, there is no vesting in the executor at all.

Section 18 (2) makes very similar provisions in respect of heritage subject to a special destination.[22] On the death of a person entitled to property which is subject to a special destination in favour of a third party, then, provided the deceased had either no power to revoke the destination or has in fact not revoked it, the property in question vests by confirmation in the executor solely for the purpose of conveyance to the person next entitled to it, if such conveyance is necessary.

The basis for this seemingly odd provision is that property subject to an unrevoked special destination is not part of the deceased's estate for the purposes of the Succession Act.[23] Thus the executor could not normally confirm to it at all. However, in most cases the person called in the destination requires to have a title formally conferred on him, and the function of section 18 (2) is to permit a limited vesting in the executor to enable him to grant that title. Thus it is only when the substitute requires a title that confirmation vests the property in the executor, and there is no vesting (indeed it is probably incompetent to confirm) if the substitute does not require a title.

The ordinary survivorship destination is the main example of the situation in which no title is required. Thus in these cases, it appears that his executor should not confirm to the predeceaser's *pro indiviso* share and that a purported confirmation would be ineffective.[24] Of course, if the deceased had validly revoked the destination, the property is part of the deceased's estate and vests fully in the executor by virtue of section 14 (1).

If there has been restricted vesting in an executor of property subject to a destination, the docket procedure for transfer is available and the protection given by section 17 applies.[25]

Completion of title to heritage

Various points in connection with the completion of title to heritage arise out of the provisions of the Succession Act. The basic proposition, contained in section 15 (1), is that confirmation is of itself a valid title in the executor to heritage included in the confirmation and which has

---

[22] One definition of a "special destination" appears in *Cormack* v. *McIldowie's Exrs.*, 1975 S.L.T. 214, *per* L.J.-C. Wheatley at 218. The definition may not cover all types.

[23] s. 36 (2) (*a*).

[24] McDonald (1965) 10 J.L.S., at p. 73.

[25] s. 18 (4).

vested in him by virtue of section 14. This result is achieved by the clumsy device of providing that references to heritable securities in section 5 (2) of the Conveyancing (Scotland) Act 1924 are to be construed as including a reference to any interest in heritage which has vested in an executor. That section of the 1924 Act made confirmation a valid title to heritable securities included in the confirmation and therefore now gives a title to any heritage included in the confirmation.

However, a proviso to section 15 (1) requires that for this purpose an appropriate description of the heritage must be included in the confirmation. This meant that although property might vest in the executor without a description being included at all (*e.g.* in the case of an English probate certified in Scotland) or where the description which did exist was defective (*e.g.* when under the original Act of Sederunt of 1964 a full conveyancing description may have been called for) he had no title in these cases. Any need for the description to be a full and formal one was removed by the Act of Sederunt (Confirmation of Executors Amendment) 1966, but the problem over English probates or letters of administration—which contain no details of the particular items of property in the estate—remained until 1968. Even although the process of certification in Scotland gave them the status of implied confirmation it seemed that the proviso to section 15 (1) prevented them from being used as links in title. The difficulty was eventually resolved retrospectively by section 19 of the Law Reform (Miscellaneous Provisions) (Scotland) Act 1968. Section 15 (1) is deemed always to have had effect as if the proviso requiring a description applied only to confirmations other than implied confirmations. The result is that English probates and letters of administration are now just as valid as links in title as Scottish confirmations. As between England and Wales, Scotland and Northern Ireland, certification and resealing are no longer necessary[26] but this change does not alter the validity of probates as links in title.

Another problem which arose shortly after the Succession Act came into force concerned the continued competency of using the procedure of section 10 of the Conveyancing (Scotland) Act 1874. That section, together with the whole provisions relating to services and petitions by persons having only personal rights, was repealed by the Succession Act. However, the Succession Act is not retrospective and section 37 (1) (*d*) specifies that nothing in the Act is to "affect the administration, winding up or distribution of or the making up of title to any part of the estate of any person who died before the commencement" of the Act. Hence it was readily accepted that a living person might still have himself served heir to someone who died before September 10, 1964, and indeed the Act itself contemplates this in section 35 by giving authority for rearranging the jurisdiction over services. In section 10 cases the issue was clouded by the fact that there was usually a second, post-Succession Act, death of the person who had only a personal right. However, despite this death, the

[26] Administration of Estates Act 1971 (c. 25). See also *post*, pp. 121–122.

question still is one of completion of title to the estate of the last infeft proprietor, who died before the Act, and petitions may still be presented under section 10 of the 1874 Act.[27] However it will be noted that if the proprietor with only a personal right died on or after September 10, 1964, his heirs entitled to petition will be those with rights of succession under the Succession Act.[28]

The effect of the abolition of the process of service of heirs in the case of deaths after the commencement of the Succession Act was that there was no longer any machinery by which an heir of a last surviving trustee, called as heir of provision could establish that he was the heir. His entitlement to office was preserved, but he had no means of proving it. For some time after 1964 the problem had been masked by the fact that title was usually being made up to the estate of a person who died before the commencement of the Succession Act so that service of heirs remained competent under section 37 (1) (*d*). However there was no answer if the last surviving trustee died after the commencement of the Act.[29]

The Law Reform (Miscellaneous Provisions) (Scotland) Act 1980, section 6 provided a remedy by the remarkable process of reviving the sections of the Titles to Land Consolidation (Scotland) Act 1868 dealing with service of heirs. The revival is for the limited purpose of providing machinery for heirs at law to establish that they were the heirs of provision and for that purpose only.

The provisions of the Succession Act making confirmation a link in the title to heritage opened up a new stream of title through the executor. It was not immediately obvious what effect this had upon the alternative method of completion of title through the deceased's will in cases where he left one, and even yet the position is somewhat clouded on certain points. It seems likely that the intention was to make the confirmation the only valid link in title, but this was not in fact done.

The position seems to be that in all cases where a will contains a general conveyance to testamentary trustees or executors-nominate, title may be completed or deduced by using the will as a link. There is, however, grave doubt whether it is competent for a special legatee to whom a direct bequest of heritage is made to complete or deduce his title by use of the will.[30] Difficulties can be avoided by following the strong recommendation of the Professors that the confirmation should be used in preference to the will. It will be noted that use of the confirmation permits the use of the simplified docket procedure for transfer and gives the protection of section 17, which would not seem to apply if title is taken through the will.

---

[27] *Duthie's Trs., Petrs.*, 1966 S.L.T. (Sh.Ct.) 24; *Robertson, Petr.*, 1978 S.L.T. (Sh.Ct.) 30; Allan, *Completion of Title* (1978) 23 J.L.S. 438.

[28] *Findlay, Petr.*, 1975 S.L.T. (Sh.Ct.) 46.

[29] *Skinner, Petr.*, 1976 S.L.T. 60 and *Browning, Petr.*, 1976 S.L.T. (Sh.Ct.) 87.

[30] Opinion of the Professors of Conveyancing (1965) 10 J.L.S. 153 and notes issued by the Law Society (1966) 11 J.L.S. 84.

Section 15 (2) made a very valuable innovation by permitting an executor to transfer heritage to beneficiaries by means of the simplified docket procedure. Where heritage has vested in him *qua* executor and ". . . it is necessary for him in distributing the estate to transfer that property—

(*a*) to any person in satisfaction of a claim to legal rights or the prior rights of a surviving spouse out of the estate, or
(*b*) to any person entitled to share in the estate by virtue of this Act, or
(*c*) to any person entitled to take the said property under any testamentary disposition of the deceased,"

the executor may effect the transfer merely by endorsing a docket in the form specified in Schedule 1 either on the confirmation itself or on a separate certificate of confirmation relating to the particular item of heritage in question. The docket specifies the title of the executor and beneficiary, identifies the property transferred, and is signed by the executor and attested by two witnesses. In view of its simplicity the procedure is widely used, usually by docketing a certificate of confirmation to avoid including the details of the whole of the deceased's estate among the titles.

The docketed confirmation cannot be recorded *de plano* in the Register of Sasines and therefore acts only as a midcouple or link in title. Section 15 (2) specifically envisages its use in this way. It will therefore be necessary to register it for preservation to avoid the possibility of it being lost or mislaid. However, it is a transfer to the beneficiary, not merely a statement of who at the deceased's death was entitled to the heritage, so that it would be incompetent to execute a docket in his favour after the beneficiary's death.[31]

Other methods of transfer are not excluded by the existence of the docket procedure, so that a beneficiary who anticipates no change in his title over a substantial period may choose either to take and record a full conveyance from the executor or to expede and record a notice of title specifying the docket as a midcouple.

Taking advantage of the confirmation as vesting estate in an executor also permits the completion of title in cases where heritage has been sold but not conveyed. It would be possible to proceed through the will if there has been a general trust conveyance, but in any event confirmation to the heritage would give the appropriate executor a title.

Similarly, a method of completing title to heritage in a lapsed trust now exists via the executor of the last surviving trustee. The Executors (Scotland) Act 1900, section 6 as amended by Schedule 2 to the Succession Act, provides that

---

[31] (1966) 11 J.L.S. 36.

"When any sole or last surviving trustee . . . has died with any property (whether heritable or moveable) in Scotland vested in him as trustee . . . confirmation by his executors (if any) to the proper estate of such trustee . . . shall . . . be valid, and available to such executors for recovering such property and for assigning and transferring the same . . . directly to the beneficiaries entitled thereto . . . provided always that a note or statement of such property shall have been appended to any inventory or additional inventory of the estate of such deceased trustee . . . given up by his executors in Scotland, and duly confirmed."[32]

A very valuable measure of protection is given to those acquiring property from an executor. Supplementing the previous provisions protecting those who acquire moveable property from an executor, section 17 protects those who in good faith and for value have acquired title to any interest in, or security over, heritable property vested in the executor. If the title was acquired directly or indirectly from the executor or from a person deriving title directly from the executor, no challenge to the acquirer's title may be made on the ground that the executor's confirmation was reducible or even that it has been reduced. Equally where the title was acquired from a person who himself derived title directly from the executor, it is not a competent ground of challenge that the executor should not have transferred the property to him. This means that there is no need for third parties to investigate the validity of a confirmation.

Leases

The right of a tenant of land is heritable, and thus it is an asset of the estate to which the tenant's executor is required to confirm. Section 16 of the Succession Act expressly confers on an executor certain powers over leases or tenancies included in the estate and to which he has confirmed. Leases cannot however be included in the deceased's estate if they were "liferent leases" expiring on his death. Section 36 (2) includes in the definition of estate only cases "where the deceased immediately before his death held the interest of a tenant under a tenancy or lease which was not expressed to expire on his death." The reference to expiring on the deceased's death qualifies the nouns "tenancy" and "lease" (and not the "interest") so that if a lease carries on or is capable of being carried on past the death of the tenant, the fact that the tenant's interest ceased at his death does not prevent the lease from being part of his estate.[33]

It is essential that executors should confirm to the tenant's interest in a lease. It is true that they have not always in the past done so, presumably

[32] Currie *Confirmation*, 7th ed., pp. 248–253. See *supra*, p. 107 for service as heir of provision in a trust.

[33] *Cormack* v. *McIldowie's Exrs.*, 1975 S.L.T. 214, 217.

because the right of a tenant has not always had a measurable value which could be transferred. However, the importance of confirmation was emphasised in *Lord Rotherwick's Trs.* v. *Hope & Ors.*[34] The executors had not confirmed to the deceased's lease of a farm. The lease had therefore not vested in the executors of the tenant, who therefore did not have the powers conferred by section 16. As they had not disposed of the lease within one year,[35] the lease had terminated and decree of removing was granted. Agricultural and crofting tenancies do have a value which is part of the estate (even if the principles of valuation are not always very clear) and must be confirmed to.[36]

The first of the particular powers granted to executors by section 16 concerns the transfer of the lease or tenancy. Section 16 (2) provides that where the deceased has not made a valid bequest of his lease (as to which see section 29 and p. 95 *supra*), or, such a bequest having been made, it is either not accepted by the legatee[37] or is null and void under the statutory provisions relating to agricultural leases, the executor is entitled to transfer the lease to any person entitled to succeed on intestacy. This is so even if there is in the lease a condition either express or implied prohibiting assignation. (If there is no prohibition on assignation, the executor has no need to rely on this statutory power.) If the executor does have to rely on the statutory power—*i.e.* when there is a prohibition on assignation—he cannot transfer the lease to any person other than one of those with rights of intestate succession without the landlord's consent. However section 16 does not apply where there is a valid destination in the lease itself.[38]

It was pointed out in debate in the House of Commons that these provisions give the executor greater powers over the lease than the deceased himself had. The power of bequest of leases specified in section 29 applies only in the face of an implied prohibition on assignation and is not exercisable in face of an express prohibition. The executor's power of transfer transcends both express and implied prohibitions on assignation in the lease. The apparent anomaly can, however, be explained by considering the purpose of prohibitions on assignation. This used to be to ensure that the tenant's heir at law would succeed to the tenancy. In consequence of the virtual abolition of the status of heir at law, provision had to be made to ensure that a single tenant would be found to continue the tenancy. A landlord could not reasonably be required to accept fragmentation of the tenancy. All heritage now vests in the executor, and therefore there has to be some form of assignation by him if the tenancy

---

[34] 1975 S.L.T. 187.

[35] s. 16 (3) (*b*).

[36] In *Inglis* v. *Inglis*, 1983 S.L.T. 437 the assignee of a farm lease was able to obtain a settlement of £35,000 plus a lease of a smaller area from the landlord. This was held to be part of the deceased's estate in a settlement with the other heirs.

[37] If the bequest *is* accepted (even without timeous notification) an intestate transfer is no longer possible: *Coats* v. *Logan*, 1985 S.L.T. 221.

[38] *Reid's Trs.* v. *Macpherson*, 1975 S.L.T. 101.

is to continue at all. Thus he is given power to transfer the lease, irrespective of the prohibition, to a single member of the class entitled to share in the deceased's estate. In effect this is another method of finding an "heir at law," but it does have the merit that the executor may be able to find a person who is genuinely interested in continuing the tenancy, which was not always the case under the old rules for selection of the heir at law. The different conditions which apply when the question is one of bequest by the tenant himself would seem to justify a different approach there.

Among the consequential modifications to existing statutes specified in Schedule 2 are provisions taking account of the powers of an executor to transfer leases. For example section 21 of the Agricultural Holdings (Scotland) Act 1949, which dealt with the landlord's right to object to the heir at law of the tenant succeeding to the holding, was replaced by a new section 21, which now appears as section 12 of the Agricultural Holdings (Scotland) Act 1991.[39] This deals with the landlord's right to object to the acquirer of a lease. The provisions, although similar to those of the original section 21, are amended to meet the new situation. Thus the first step is now for the acquirer to notify the landlord of his acquisition of the holding within 21 days of the acquisition.[40] Previously the landlord could always find out who was the tenant's heir at law, but he must now be told who is to acquire the lease. Thereafter it is up to the landlord to set the procedure of objection in motion by serving a counter-notice within one month. It will be noted that the landlord may have to possess his soul in patience for a very long time, for at least a year may elapse from the death of the tenant before the landlord can find out who the acquirer of the lease is to be.

Section 16 (3) and (4) of the 1964 Act provide for termination of the lease, irrespective of its provisions or of any statutory or other provisions, either by the executor or by the landlord, if the executor is satisfied that he cannot dispose of the lease to an acquirer or if he has in fact not disposed of it within the time limit specified. Note that if the executor simply delays in disposal of the lease, it is liable to be lost to the beneficiaries. Only he can dispose of it, but if he fails to do so within the time limit, the lease may be terminated.[41] Beneficiaries will have to be vigilant to protect their rights.

The time limit is normally one year from the date of death of the deceased, but in the case of an agricultural lease which is the subject of a petition to the Land Court under the Crofters' Holdings (Scotland) Act 1886, section 16, or an application thereto under the Agricultural Holdings (Scotland) Act 1991, the period of one year runs from the date of the determination or withdrawal of the petition or application. These

---

[39] c. 55.

[40] *Garvie's Trs.* v. *Garvie's Tutors*, 1975 S.L.T. 94: *Coats* v. *Logan*, 1985 S.L.T. 221: Gill, *The Law of Agricultural Holdings in Scotland* (2nd ed.), Chap. 34.

[41] *Lord Rotherwick's Trs.* v. *Hope & Ors.*, 1975 S.L.T. 187; *Gifford* v. *Buchanan*, 1983 S.L.T. 613.

statutory provisions relate to the situation when the landlord seeks to object to the legatee of a lease as his tenant. Similar provisions are now made for crofts also. The one-year time limit within which the lease must be transferred may be extended by agreement between landlord and executor or, failing agreement, by the sheriff on summary application by the executor.[42] However, it is the executor who must seek the extension. It would seem that the beneficiaries could not prevent an executor from procrastinating until the year was up, thereby permitting the landlord to terminate the lease.

Due notice must be given of any such termination by the landlord or executor. For agricultural leases it is such period as may be agreed, or failing agreement, the familiar period of not less than one year nor more than two years ending with such term of Whitsunday or Martinmas as may be specified in the notice.[43] In the case of any other lease, the maximum period of notice for this purpose is six months, without prejudice to any statutory provision prescribing a shorter period of notice for the lease in question.[44] The period of notice required to terminate a lease of an ordinary dwelling-house would normally be substantially less than six months.

The fact that executor and landlord may have a power to terminate a lease does not prejudice any claim by either party to the lease for compensation or damages in respect of the termination. However, to preserve the limitation of the liability of the executor, any award of compensation or damages in respect of a termination by the executor is enforceable only against the estate of the deceased and not against the executor personally.[45]

The special provisions of section 16 (6) and (7) take account of the fact that a lease is vested in an executor only *qua* executor in considering questions based on breaches of the conditions of a lease. In the case of agricultural leases the Land Court is not to make an order for removal under section 3 of the Small Landholders and Agricultural Holdings (Scotland) Act 1931 or section 13 of the Crofters (Scotland) Act 1955, and the arbiter is not to make an order in favour of the landlord in a question under section 22 (2) (*e*) of the Agricultural Holdings (Scotland) Act 1991 unless the court or arbiter is satisfied that it is reasonable, having regard to the fact that the interest is vested in the executor in his capacity as executor, that it should be made.

In the case of non-agricultural leases, the court is not to grant decree in an action of removing based on a breach of a condition of the lease unless it is satisfied that the condition alleged to have been breached is one which it is reasonable to expect the executor to have observed, having regard to the fact that the interest is vested in him in his capacity as an executor.

---

[42] The application must be made within the year and is not competent after the landlord has given notice of termination: *Gifford* v. *Buchanan*, *supra*.

[43] s. 16 (4) (*a*).

[44] s. 16 (4) (*b*) and proviso.

[45] s. 16 (5).

Finally it is provided that the detailed provisions relating to bequest of agricultural leases specified in the Crofters' Holdings (Scotland) Act 1886, the Agricultural Holdings (Scotland) Act 1991 and the Crofters (Scotland) Act 1955, as amended, are to have effect notwithstanding that the lease, or the deceased's interest therein, has vested in the executor for purposes of administration.[46]

One particular difficulty facing executors in connection with agricultural leases shows up in acute form a general problem of Scots law. It is not at all clear in Scotland who owns a deceased's property between the date of his death and the appointment and confirmation of his executor. As there is no longer an heir at law to succeed automatically to heritage, this means that a landlord may encounter severe difficulties in attempting to serve a notice to quit if the tenant's executor has not yet been appointed. If the tenant dies shortly before a term of Whitsunday or Martinmas, the landlord may be at least delayed in exercising his right to obtain possession by being unable to find someone on whom to serve notice before the term. Various suggestions for methods of coping with this problem have been put forward and the Scottish Law Commission has recommended that any notice to be given under a lease should continue to be addressed to the deceased party to the lease as if he were still alive. That notice would be effective.[47]

Satisfaction of legacies in kind

One of the perennial problems facing an executor arises when it is desired to satisfy legacies in kind rather than in cash. In that situation there seem to be unending disputes about the allocation of particular assets and the values to be attached to them.[48] The only real answer is to make proper provision in the will for the transfer of assets *in specie*.

If there is a true special legacy, it operates as an assignation of the particular subject of the gift, and the executor has no discretion about how to satisfy the legacy. He simply transfers the property specially identified. However, apart from special legacies, and the special element of demonstrative legacies, an executor is free to convey any asset to any beneficiary in full or part satisfaction of his share. The choice is that of the executor and not of the beneficiary.

A particularly significant decision is *Cochrane's Trs.* v. *Inland Revenue*.[49] In this case the executors were held liable for Capital Gains Tax even although the residuary legatee, with a vested right to the whole residue, was not so liable. The legatee argued that he was entitled to the

---

46 s. 16 (8).

47 Scot. Law Com. No. 118—*Report on Recovery of Possession of Heritable Property* (1989), recommendation 69. This does not appear to have been adopted in the Agricultural Holdings (Scotland) Act 1991. For the similar problem in crofting law, see MacCuish and Flyn, *Crofting Law*, para. 7.05.

48 See for example *Coats's Trs.* v. *Coats*, 1914 S.C. 723.

49 1975 S.L.T. 6.

whole assets from the moment of the deceased's death and was entitled to call for delivery of the assets. The successful position of the Revenue was that a residuary legatee is entitled to what is left after the executor has exercised his discretionary powers and cannot give directions to the executor about particular assets. It was even emphasised that executors are not bound to consider the views of a residuary beneficiary before realising any part of the estate.[50]

This illustrates that no general beneficiary has any right to any particular asset, with the result that the executor is free to allocate the whole of a shareholding to one beneficiary and is not bound to divide it equally between them all. The important proviso is that a proper valuation of the shares must be used, and the valuation for purposes of division must be that at the date of the distribution, not the date of death values in the inventory. Pecuniary legatees are entitled only to assets which, at the date of transfer to them, amount to the value of their legacy.

---

[50] *Supra*, p. 10.

Chapter 9

PRIVATE INTERNATIONAL LAW

Problems of private international law arise in practice far more frequently than is usually thought, especially in the field of succession. Every Scottish estate of any size tends to include shares in English companies and therefore involves some aspect of private international law, even if it is no more than the question of the validity of a Scottish confirmation in England. The oil industry is international in its personnel, and problems frequently arise about wills and rights of inheritance under different legal systems. The authoritative and essential work is Anton, *Private International Law*.[1] There is very useful material concerning administration of estates with a foreign element in Currie on *Confirmation*.[2] What follows is no more than an attempt to set out the broad principles as they apply to the law of succession in Scotland and reference should be made to these authorities for detailed consideration of problems.

The Succession Act does not purport to affect or alter the rules of private international law. Section 37 (2) expressly preserves the pre-existing law by providing that:

> "Nothing in this Act shall be construed as affecting the operation of any rule of law applicable immediately before the commencement of this Act to the choice of the system of law governing the administration, winding up or distribution of the estate, or part of the estate, of any deceased person."

Intestate succession

Put very briefly, the result is that the Scots law of intestate succession governs the succession to the moveable estate of a person whose last domicile was in Scotland, irrespective of where the property may be situated (subject always to a different view being taken by the legal system having control over the property).[3] It also means that Scots law governs the devolution of immoveable property situated in Scotland, irrespective of the owner's domicile. These follow as aspects of the twin propositions that succession to moveables is governed by the *lex domicilii*

---

[1] 2nd ed., 1990, esp. Chaps. 26 & 27. See also Maher, *Private International Law, Cases and Materials* and *Stair Memorial Encyclopaedia: The Laws of Scotland*, Vol. 25, under "Wills and Succession" and Vol. 17, under "Private International Law."

[2] Major works primarily from the English standpoint include Cheshire & North, *Private International Law* and Dicey & Morris, *Conflict of Laws*.

[3] *Bruce* v. *Bruce* (1790) 3 Pat. 163.

of the deceased whereas succession to immoveables is governed by the *lex situs* of the property.

The classification of particular items as moveable or immoveable falls to be performed by the *lex situs* of the property and is not necessarily identical with any classification used by that system for its own internal purposes. In particular, it is not identical with the classification as heritable or moveable in Scotland or as real or personal in England.[4] Some items may be heritable (*e.g.* by destination) for the purposes of Scots private law, but still moveable as opposed to immoveable for the purposes of private international law. In every case, the classification must be performed so that the appropriate system of law may be determined.

However while it is clear that this is the present state of the law, it is by no means so clear that it ought to be the law. Virtually every country in the world has abolished any special rules for the succession to land so that for its own internal purposes no distinction is made between moveable and immoveable property. The distinction is no longer felt to serve a meaningful social purpose, and yet despite the virtually unanimous international opinion to this effect, Scots law persists with the distinction as if it separated significantly different categories for purposes of choice of law. This can produce bizarre variations in the result in a particular case depending upon where particular items of the estate happen to be situated. Even within the United Kingdom, where Northern Ireland, England and Scotland seek to achieve similar results on intestacy but by very different methods, the present rules for the choice of the appropriate system of law can produce remarkable and quite unjustifiable variations in the amount that a widow will receive depending on the situation of the property.[5] It is submitted that all property ought to devolve according to the law of the deceased's last domicile and that the role of the *lex situs* should disappear.[6] If this were carried out, there would, of course, be difficulties in administering systems of title to land, for rights of a type unknown to the law of the country where the land is situated might have to be catered for and documents of unusual types accepted. However these problems would not be insuperable, and indeed are no more serious than those which already exist, and are already overcome, in our present rules of private international law. It is to be hoped that future legislation will effect this reform.

In the application of the existing rules to the scheme of succession set out in the Succession (Scotland) Act, some points are worth special notice.

---

[4] *Macdonald* v. *Macdonald*, 1932 S.C. (H.L.) 79.

[5] See Morris (1969) 85 L.Q.R. 339.

[6] The Scottish Law Commission had proposed that both moveables and immoveables should devolve on intestacy according to the law of the last domicile, but made no formal recommendation to this effect in its Report on Succession (Scot. Law Com. No. 124) in view of the existence of a draft Convention prepared by the Hague Conference on Private International Law.

Prior rights

The surviving spouse's prior right under section 8 to the deceased's interest in the dwelling-house is clearly a right in immoveable property and is governed by the *lex situs*. Thus the Scottish rule applies to houses situated in Scotland, irrespective of the owner's domicile, provided the conditions of section 8 are met. For example a wife living apart from her English husband in a house belonging to him in Scotland, would have a prior right to the house on his death.

In the situation to which section 8 (2) applies (*i.e.* farmhouses and other business premises including a house)[7] a surviving spouse receives a "sum equal to the value of the relevant interest" held by the deceased. It is fairly easy to regard this cash sum as a kind of surrogatum for the immoveable itself, since it is equated with the interest which the survivor would otherwise have received. Hence there can be little doubt that this right to a cash sum is also to be treated as an interest in an immoveable falling to be governed by the *lex situs*, so that it also could be due out of houses situated in Scotland, irrespective of the domicile of the owner.

However, there is greater difficulty in knowing how to classify the surviving spouse's right to a fixed sum when the value of the house is greater than the maximum limit. Under section 8 (1) (*b*), where the value of the deceased's "relevant interest" exceeds £65,000, the survivor is entitled to "the sum of £65,000" without any words classifying this sum as a surrogatum for the house itself. An argument can therefore be presented that the right is an interest in moveables, and therefore applicable only to domiciled Scots, and is not due when a house in Scotland is owned by someone domiciled elsewhere. However, while this provision of the Act has clearly not been fully thought out, the better view would seem to be that the right to the cash sum is in lieu of the house itself. The purpose of the provision is merely to put an upper limit on the benefit to a surviving spouse of the housing right, and it is an integral part of the right to the house, however it may be expressed. Thus it is suggested that if an appropriate house worth more than £65,000 is situated in Scotland, the surviving spouse will be entitled to the cash sum of £65,000 even if the deceased was domiciled outwith Scotland, on the basis that the right is part of the succession to immoveables. Conversely, the survivor will not be entitled to £65,000 if the house is situated outside Scotland, even if the deceased's domicile was Scottish, but would be entitled to any comparable right granted by the law of the country where the house is situated.[8]

The prior right to furniture and plenishings conferred by section 8 (3) is clearly moveable. Hence this right applies only when the deceased was domiciled in Scotland. It would seem, therefore, that the reference in section 8 (5) to a deceased who was domiciled furth of Scotland is inept so far as concerns the furniture and plenishings. If the deceased was not a

---

[7] See pp. 39–41 above.

[8] Leslie, "Prior Rights in Succession," 1988 S.L.T. (News) 105.

domiciled Scot, the surviving spouse is not entitled to the furniture and plenishings under the Succession Act, and there is little point in having an arbiter of their value appointed by the sheriff. (The main purpose of this subsection is, of course, to provide means for obtaining a valuation of the house itself, and for this purpose it is perfectly effective.)

The prior right under section 9 of the Succession Act might at first sight seem to be purely moveable and thus applicable only when the deceased was domiciled in Scotland. This would, however, be a mistaken view, for the section 9 right is required to be "borne by, and paid out of, the parts of the intestate estate consisting of heritable and moveable property respectively." It is thus part of the Scots law affecting succession to immoveable property (being in effect a charge upon heritage in Scotland) as well as part of the Scots law of moveable succession.

The result is that if the deceased was domiciled in Scotland, the financial right is due from his moveables, wherever situated, and from his immoveable property in Scotland. No account is taken of any immoveable property situated outside Scotland. However, even if the deceased was domiciled outside Scotland, the fact that the section 9 right is part of the Scots law of succession to immoveable property means that the surviving spouse is entitled to £21,000 or to £35,000 as the case may be out of any immoveable property situated in Scotland. The full amount is payable under Scots law to the surviving spouse irrespective of the amount or value of any other estate owned by the deceased, and irrespective of any rights which the surviving spouse may have under any other system.[9]

Legal rights

Legal rights in Scots law now exist only in the moveable estate belonging to the deceased at the time of his death and are classified as rights of succession despite their origin in a form of community of property between husband and wife. As rules governing moveable succession they apply only when the deceased was domiciled in Scotland and affect his moveable property wherever situated. The fact that a foreign system of law may treat land for the purposes of succession as if it were moveable or personal property does not, however, give the widow and children of a Scottish domiciliary legal rights in that land.[10] Any comparable forced share provisions affecting moveables in a foreign system of law would be applied in Scotland in the succession to a deceased who was domiciled in that country.

There are no longer any Scottish legal rights in immoveable property. As succession to immoveables is governed by the *lex situs*, this means that immoveable property situated in Scotland is immune from all legal rights or their equivalents, Scottish or foreign. Equally, there are no Scottish rights to attempt to enforce against foreign immoveable property and any

---

[9] (1967) 12 J.L.S. 401.
[10] *Macdonald* v. *Macdonald*, *supra*.

equivalents to Scottish legal rights which may exist will be those granted by that foreign system. It will be noted, however, that the English equivalent under the Inheritance (Provision for Family and Dependants) Act 1975 applies only in cases where the deceased died domiciled in England and Wales.[11] It cannot therefore be invoked by the dependants of a deceased who dies domiciled in Scotland, but who owned immoveable property in England. The (English) Law Commission has so far rejected proposals for rectification of this anomaly.

Free estate

In the distribution of the free estate, the general rules that moveables are governed by the *lex domicilii* of the deceased and immoveables by the *lex situs* of the property operate with full force. The preservation of these rules for this Part of the Succession Act is reinforced by the provision in section 1 (1) that it applies to "estate the succession to which falls to be regulated by the law of Scotland."

The Crown as ultimus haeres

The property of anyone dying without heirs or testate beneficiaries passes to the Crown as *ultimus haeres*. The estate is received and administered by the Queen's and Lord Treasurer's Remembrancer. There are serious doubts about the theoretical nature of this right of the Crown[12] but in practice the Crown claims the moveable property in Scotland of foreign domiciliaries and does not claim moveable property abroad belonging to Scottish domiciliaries.[13]

Testate succession

The questions of capacity to make a will, of formal validity of the will, of essential validity of the will and of construction of the terms used in a will give rise to different considerations of private international law.

In Scotland, capacity to make a will is now attained at the age of 12.[14] Below that age, there is no legal capacity to make a will, and other legal systems impose restrictions on different categories of persons. The rule appears to be that capacity to make a will of moveable estate is referred to the law of the testator's domicile at the date of execution of the will while a will dealing with immoveables would be referred to the *lex situs*. The Scottish Law Commission has recommended that capacity should in all cases be referred to the domestic law of the country of the deceased's domicile at the time of making (or revoking) the will.[15]

Formal validity

Formal validity is now governed primarily by the Wills Act 1963.[16] A will is validly executed if it is properly executed according to the internal

---

[11] s. 1 (1).

[12] Anton, *supra*, pp. 678–680.

[13] As between Scotland and England, see Law Reform (Miscellaneous Provisions) (Scotland) Act 1940 (3 & 4 Geo. 6, c. 42), s. 6.

[14] Age of Legal Capacity (Scotland) Act 1991 (c. 50), s. 2 (2).

[15] *Report on Succession*, recommendation 67.

[16] c. 44.

law of the country of the testator's domicile, nationality or habitual residence either at the date of execution or at the date of death. In addition it is validly executed if it conforms to the law of the place of execution or to the law with which a ship or aeroplane is most closely connected if the testator is travelling in it. A will dealing only with immoveable property may employ the formalities of the *lex situs* of the immoveable property.

Applying this to the Scottish solicitor, he may therefore properly use the Scottish formalities whenever a will is executed in this country, whenever the testator qualifies by reason of domicile, nationality or habitual residence, and whenever the will deals solely with Scottish immoveables. What he must *not* do is to send a will abroad for signature without considering the Wills Act. There are numerous cases in which people with some family connection with Scotland (often an interest in a Scottish trust) seek to make a will dealing only with their Scottish estate although they are no longer domiciled or resident here and have another nationality. Unless the will deals solely with Scottish heritage, the formalities will have to be those pointed out by the Wills Act. It is not the case that the ordinary Scottish attested will, signed before two witnesses, is acceptable everywhere. For example, several of the United States require three witnesses, and South African law requires the witnesses to sign on each page. Several countries simply do not have the concept of the attested will and may require either a holograph will or a formal notarial act. Since domicile, residence and nationality can all be difficult concepts, and may be difficult to prove many years after the relevant date, it will often be wise to ensure that a will sent out from Scotland should be taken to a local lawyer for execution according to the formalities of the place of execution. That place should easily be identified and virtually every legal system will accept the formalities of the place of execution.

When the provisions of the Administration of Justice Act 1982[17] are brought into force, there will be a new form of "international will" which will automatically be accepted as formally valid in all contracting countries if it complies with the formalities specified in the Act, irrespective of any contrary requirements in the local law.

Essential validity of wills is governed by different considerations, as the content of a will may not be acceptable even if the formalities of execution have been properly observed. Questions of public policy may arise, or there may be statutory provisions such as the Scottish rules prohibiting successive liferents, entails or accumulations. For these purposes the governing law is the law of the domicile *at the time of death* for moveable property and the *lex situs* for immoveable property.[18]

Construction of the terms used in wills depends upon the testator's intention, but there is rarely an express statement of intention. In the

---

[17] c. 53, ss. 27 & 28 and Sched. 2.

[18] *Ommanney* v. *Bingham* (1796) 3 Pat. 448; *Brown's Trs.* v. *Gregson*, 1920 S.C. (H.L.) 87.

absence of express intentions or of unambiguous directions there will be some presumption that a will of moveable property will be construed according to the law of the domicile and a will of immoveable property by the law of the *situs*. The domicile in question is probably the domicile at the time of execution of the will.[19]

Administration of estates

Quite apart from questions of beneficial right to the property of a deceased person, many problems may arise in the administration of the property if there is a foreign element. For example, the general rule in Scotland is that the right to be executor is determined by the law of the deceased's domicile so that confirmation will be issued to the foreign executor. Indeed if the deceased was domiciled abroad, a petition for confirmation in Scotland would be rejected if based on Scottish internal law. However, some legal systems (*e.g.* Germany) do not provide for the appointment of executors in our sense, and hold that deceased's property vests directly and immediately in the heirs without any intervention or formality. In these cases, confirmation will be granted on evidence from a qualified person as to who is entitled under the law of the domicile to administer the estate.

A clear distinction is made between the *right* to administer the property and the *title* or authority to do so. As indicated above, the fact that the right to the office of executor is determined by the law of the deceased's domicile does not absolve him from the necessity of further procedure where the property is situated. He must still obtain authority to deal with the property, and for considerations of effectiveness of control, this authority must be conferred by the *lex situs* of the property. Thus a foreign executor must still obtain confirmation from the Scottish courts to be entitled to uplift property here and conversely a Scottish executor of a person dying domiciled in Scotland requires to obtain the appropriate authority under the law of the country where the property is situated. Even a formal grant of powers and title to an executor in one country does not of itself give the executor any authority over property subject to another legal system. Hence in principle it is necessary to obtain a separate grant of authority under each legal system having control over any of the deceased's property. At one time, for example, this meant that a Scottish executor had to obtain a separate grant of probate or letters of administration in England, and vice versa.

The Confirmation of Executors (Scotland) Act 1858 established a more convenient procedure commonly known as "resealing" under which an English grant of representation could be certified, and thus given full effect in Scotland, while comparable provisions permitted the resealing of Scottish confirmations in England (latterly the Supreme Court of Judicature (Consolidation) Act 1925). Despite a strong attachment to the

---

[19] Anton, *supra*, pp. 686–687.

procedure in some quarters, resealing was a rather farcical process over which the courts nominally granting authority could and did exercise little control.

Substantial reform was eventually achieved by the Administration of Estates Act 1971. This Act ended the need for resealing or certification as between the courts of England and Wales, Scotland and Northern Ireland. There is now automatic recognition in each of these jurisdictions of confirmations or grants of representation issued by any of the others, subject to the important proviso that the deceased died domiciled in the jurisdiction issuing the confirmation or grant to be recognised.[20] Oddly enough, there seems not to be any special procedure for grants of representation in the Channel Islands or Isle of Man.

Outwith the United Kingdom jurisdictions, there is not as yet any system of automatic recognition of the title of executors appointed elsewhere. Special reciprocal provisions do exist between Scotland and most other Commonwealth and colonial systems in a special relationship with the United Kingdom under the Colonial Probates Acts of 1892 and 1927.[21]

Where no reciprocal arrangements exist, the basic rule still applies, so that the foreign executor requires confirmation in Scotland and vice versa. However progress is being made in the development of a Hague Convention for the international recognition of the title of executors, and it is to be hoped that this will speedily reach fruition without too many nationalistic obstacles being put in its path.

---

[20] ss. 1 (1), 2 (2) and 3 (1).

[21] Lists of the territories are set out in the Colonial Probates Act Application Orders 1965 (No. 1530) and 1976 (No. 579). See Anton, pp. 658–659. For procedure, see Currie, *Confirmation*, 7th ed., pp. 258–266.

Chapter 10

THE SCOTTISH LAW COMMISSION'S PROPOSALS FOR REFORM

The Scottish Law Commission published three consultative memoranda on the law of succession in 1986.[1] Following on the comments received in response to the memoranda, the Commission has now published its *Report on Succession*.[2] This Report proposes major changes in the law of intestate succession and a number of reforms in other parts of the law of succession, which will make valuable improvements in the law. The detailed consideration of the existing law, and of the need for reform, set out in the Consultative Memoranda will remain valuable sources as well as the final recommendations in the Report. The draft Bill included with the Report is likely to form the basis of the legislation which will replace the Succession (Scotland) Act 1964, although there may well be alteration of particular details. It is not known when the government will find time in the legislative programme for the new Succession Bill, but it is hoped that it will be within the next three or four years and that the history of delay before the passing of the 1964 Act referred to in Chapter 1 will not be repeated with its successor.

This chapter sets out the broad scheme of the reforms proposed by the Scottish Law Commission. It does not purport to be a detailed analysis of the text of the draft Bill, as that is likely to be subject to amendment both before being submitted to Parliament and in the course of its eventual progress through Parliament, but some comment is offered on points where difficulty may arise or where contrary views may be pressed on Parliament.

Private international law

The Commission proposes only relatively small alterations.[3] The existing rules will continue in force subject to two provisions. One is that capacity to make or revoke a will should be determined by the law of the domicile at the time of making or revoking the will, irrespective of whether it deals with moveables or with immoveables.[4] The other is a very valuable attempt to clear up some of the confusion surrounding survivorship destinations. Special destinations create unnecessary problems even in internal Scots law, but these are compounded if more than one system is involved. Particular

---

[1] No. 69—*Intestate Succession and Legal Rights*; No. 70—*The Making and Revocation of Wills*; No. 71—*Some Miscellaneous Topics in the Law of Succession*.

[2] Scot. Law Com. No. 124 (1990).

[3] Draft Bill, cl. 32.

[4] *Supra*, p. 119.

problems have arisen over the working rule of English law that a title taken in the name of two persons automatically implies a survivorship destination, and the cases have not given a clear lead on the system of law to be applied. Hence the Commission proposes that the question of whether the terms of a title to moveable property should pass the property on the owner's death should be determined by the law of the deceased's domicile at his death.

Proof of survivorship

The practical consequences of two members of a family dying within a short time of each other are the same as those when they die in the same incident without it being possible to prove that one survived the other. The present law treats proved survival for one second in the same way as survival for a period of years although it is clearly not appropriate to do so. In addition, the words of a will which purports to deal with the potential problems will be scrutinised and analysed with very precise logic, whether or not that seems sensible in the circumstances.[5]

The Commission therefore proposes a general rule that mere survivorship should not be sufficient to qualify a beneficiary to inherit or to succeed under a special destination.[6] Instead it would be necessary to survive for a period to be specified by Parliament. The Commission suggests five days, counting from the beginning of the day on which the deceased died, but longer periods up to 30 days are often specified in wills and a period longer than five days may eventually be chosen. The general principle is very welcome. Where a problem still arises in which it is uncertain whether either person survived for the five days, the estate of each of them would be distributed as if the other had failed to survive.

A very valuable provision in clause 28 (3) of the proposed Bill would remove the difficulty when the word "predeceasing" is used in a will. At present a third party whose right depends on the predecease of someone else will be unable to prove the *pre*-decease in the event of a common calamity even if the other person cannot be proved to have survived. When the Bill is enacted, anyone who has failed to survive for the requisite period will be regarded for the purposes of the succession rights of other persons as having predeceased the deceased. Thus a destination-over which depends on a beneficiary "predeceasing" will come into effect if he cannot be proved to have survived for the specified period after the deceased's death.

The unworthy heir

The Commission's recommendations appear as clauses 19 and 20 of the proposed Bill. The aim is to rationalise the existing mixture of statutory

---

[5] See *Re Rowland* [1963] 1 Ch. 1 where a provision in the event of the testator's wife's death "coinciding" with his own was held not to include the case where they both perished without proof of survivorship when a ship sank.

[6] cl. 28.

provisions and common law rules of doubtful effect. The Parricide Act 1594 would be repealed and the whole law restated. Unfortunately the Commission proceeded on the assumption that the existing common law was based on the principle that no one can invoke the law to obtain a benefit from his or her own crime. That this is not so is demonstrated by the fact that many crimes exist which would not act as disqualification (*e.g.* death caused in an accident which amounted to only careless driving) and a version of the disqualification does exist even where there is no crime (*e.g.* suicide, which prevents the deceased's estate from receiving the proceeds of his life insurance).

The proposal is that only a specified and limited list of crimes would bring about disqualification. Final conviction of murder, culpable homicide or manslaughter or convictions elsewhere of crimes which would amount to these crimes in Britain would automatically result in forfeiture of rights of succession. The specification of a list of crimes may well make the law clearer, but it is a serious mistake to make the disqualification also depend upon conviction by a court. One of the reasons why the Parricide Act was never invoked was precisely that it required conviction by an assize. If that could not be shown, for example if the killer merely disappeared without conviction, then there was no disqualification.[7] The benefit of certainty in the statutory rule would be offset by the ability to avoid the disqualification by disappearance, and even if the common law rule is, as suggested, to be retained along with the statutory rule, the suicide of a murderer would prevent the disqualification from coming into effect. It is to be hoped that this provision will be improved when the Bill is before Parliament.

The proposal is that any person who has incurred forfeiture would be deemed to have failed to survive the victim, but this may be modified in the light of the decision in *Hunter's Exrs., Petrs.*[8]

The Forfeiture Act 1982 would be repealed and replaced with a more carefully drafted provision in clause 20. Apart from cases where the killer has been convicted of murder, it will be possible to apply to the court for relief, in whole or in part, from the forfeiture.

Special destinations

Special destinations will be defined in the Bill and will be treated as rights of succession for purposes of the new legal share and the surviving spouse's right to have the matrimonial home allocated as part of his or her share. All special destinations except the common survivorship destination will be abolished for deeds executed after the commencement of the new Act.[9]

Although it is unfortunate that the Commission did not find itself able to recommend the total abolition of special destinations (which have been

---

[7] *Yeaman* v. *Oliphant* (1663) Mor. 4773 and *Oliphant* v. *Oliphant* (1674) Mor. 3429.
[8] 1992 S.L.T. 1141.
[9] cl. 29.

unnecessary and a source of continual trouble since 1868) the recommendations do at least go some way towards mitigating their worst effects. In the remaining survivorship destinations, there will no longer be any restriction on either party such as to prevent them from evacuating the destination either *inter vivos* or *mortis causa*. It will not matter which party provided the money for the purchase, as either will be able to confer a good title to his half either by *inter vivos* transfer or by will. Evacuation of the destination by will would still require express reference to the destination and a declared intention to revoke it.

However, if there is a contract not to revoke the destination, there could be a claim for damages against the person who has revoked it, based on the contract. This would not affect the validity of the evacuation. It will also be made clear that anyone succeeding to property by virtue of a destination will be liable for the debts of the deceased. This will remove any effect which the decision in *Barclay's Bank* v. *McGreish*[10] may have had. It will be the person succeeding to the property who will be liable for the debts up to the value of the property, but he may have a right of relief against the executors, and could in any event always renounce the succession.

Intestate succession

The Commission's proposals would produce a major simplification of the law which is greatly to be welcomed, even if teachers of law will thereby lose a fertile source of knotty examination questions. They will also further increase the preference given to the surviving spouse over the deceased's children or other relatives.

The distinction between heritage and moveables will genuinely disappear, apart from the preservation of the old rules of intestate heritable succession for titles of honour.[11] The estate to be divided on death will be treated as a single cash figure, being the total of the values of all the items of the estate, less the debts. It will not be necessary to keep the values of heritage and moveables separate, and neither will it be necessary to calculate apportionments between them.

The present complex method of working through three sets of rules, themselves subdivided, in order to work out the division of an intestate estate will be abolished. In its place there will be a single Part of the new Act, consisting of a mere four sections, which will cover the whole of the rules of intestate succession.

Broadly, the surviving spouse will receive the first £100,000[12] of the net estate. If there are issue of the intestate, they would be entitled to share only when the estate exceeds that figure, when they would be entitled to

---

[10] 1983 S.L.T. 344.

[11] cl. 36 (4).

[12] The figure used in the Act, when passed, would be subject to alteration by the Secretary of State by Statutory Instrument.

one half of the surplus over £100,000. The remaining half of the surplus would go to the spouse.[13] If there are no issue of the intestate, the surviving spouse would take the whole estate, irrespective of its size, in preference to any other relatives. In any circumstances, the spouse would be entitled to require the executor to transfer the matrimonial home as part of his or her share of the estate.[14]

If there is no surviving spouse, the order of succession to the whole estate would be very like the present rules in the Succession (Scotland) Act 1964 for the division of the free estate, except of course that the spouse is not included.[15] However, one significant difference will be that collaterals of the half blood will share equally with collaterals of the full blood instead of being postponed to them as at present.[16]

Representation will apply on the same basis as in sections 5 and 6 of the 1964 Act[17] and the Bill therefore repeats the error made in 1964 of commencing representation only at the level of the nearest class to the deceased in which a survivor is found. Despite the fact that clause 2 states a general principle of representation, this is immediately contradicted by clause 3 and the anomalous variations which arise from the chance of survival of one member of intervening generations will be perpetuated. It is to be hoped that Parliament will rectify this anomaly.

Legal share and legal rights

The time-hallowed legal rights of *jus relictae*, *jus relicti* and legitim, and their various functions, will disappear from the law when the new Act is passed, being expressly abolished by clause 5 (6). Collation *inter liberos* will disappear along with them. In their place will be a new right, to be called legal share, based on an entirely new concept. They will no longer be part of the law of intestate succession and the old authorities will no longer be relevant.

The new legal share will be solely a protection against disinheritance and will be claimable whenever the surviving spouse or the issue of the deceased are dissatisfied with their provisions (or lack of provisions) in the deceased's will. It will be a right to a fixed share and not a mere right to apply to the court for a discretionary award. It will not vest automatically as it will have to be expressly claimed by the beneficiary within two years of the deceased's death.[18] If a spouse or child does not claim legal share within the time limit, there will be no share.

The protection is primarily for a surviving spouse, although the Commission, after some hesitation, does recommend that issue should also have some protection. If one assumes that both spouse and issue are

---

[13] cl. 1 (2).
[14] cl. 23.
[15] cl. 1 (3).
[16] cl. 1 (4).
[17] cll. 2 and 3.
[18] cl. 6 (1).

completely cut out of the deceased's will, the spouse's legal share will be 30 per cent. of the first £200,000 of the net estate, plus 10 per cent. of the estate above £200,000. The slicing principle recognises that above a certain figure, the argument for protection becomes less strong. If there is no surviving spouse, the legal share of the issue will be the same as that of the spouse.

If the deceased was survived by both spouse and by issue, the spouse's share remains the same, but to avoid excessive interference with testamentary freedom (especially as heritage will now be included in the estate subject to legal share) and recognising that the claim of children is less strong, the legal share of issue will be one half of the spouse's share, *i.e.* 15 per cent. and 5 per cent. respectively.[19] However, there is a very opaque provision, the meaning of which should be spelt out more clearly. Clause 5 (3) of the draft Bill states that for the purpose of calculating the amount of any claim by surviving issue under clause 7, the net estate of the deceased will not include the first £100,000 of the net estate to the fee of which the spouse succeeds otherwise than by virtue of a claim for legal share by the spouse. This fairly clearly means that the first £100,000 to which a spouse succeeds by testamentary succession (including special destinations) will be excluded in calculating the legal share of the issue, so that in most such cases the children will have no legal share at all in competition with a bequest to a spouse. Their right would be to 15 per cent. of the estate from £100,000 to £300,000 and 5 per cent. thereafter, but nothing from the estate below £100,000. This means that the spouse will always receive the first £100,000 and the *Kerr, Petr.* problem of intestacy being more profitable than a will should cease to exist.

However, it is not entirely clear whether the right of the issue will still be postponed to the spouse's first £100,000 if both spouse and issue are excluded from benefit under the will. It would seem not, in view of the fact that clause 5 (3) excludes from the issue only property to which the spouse "succeeds otherwise than by virtue of a claim by the spouse under this Part of this Act" but the result might be more clearly expressed. If this is correct, the total legal share when both spouse and issue are ignored in the will would amount to 45 per cent. of the first £200,000 and 15 per cent. thereafter. There are very welcome provisions clarifying the incidence of legal shares and liability for expenses and provision for payment to be made in instalments over 10 years when the estate includes agricultural property[20] and interest will be payable on legal share at 7 per cent.

A very significant provision appears in clause 8. If a claim for legal share is carried through to payment, the claimant is deemed to have failed to survive the deceased and forfeits all rights of succession to the deceased's estate other than the legal share.

---

[19] cl. 7.
[20] cll. 9–11.

Validation of wills

Cases arise in which there is no doubt that a purported will was genuinely intended to operate as a will, but where the will has to be declared invalid through failure to comply with the appropriate formalities. This is especially true when several different legal systems might possibly be involved and the formalities in fact employed do not meet the requirements of the system or systems pointed out by private international law. However other problems can arise, such as the one pointed out by the Law Commission of both husband and wife having mirror-image wills but signing each other's will by mistake. Clause 12 of the draft Bill would give the court power to declare the will to be genuine, whereupon it would receive effect as if it were formally valid. This is an important power for the limited number of cases which are likely to arise, and may indeed help to reduce litigation, for anyone who might now present a purely technical objection to the validity of the execution of a will in order to benefit on intestacy would realise that the court would probably uphold the will.

Rectification of wills

The Commission proposes in clause 13 that the court (including both the Court of Session and the sheriff court) should be given power to rectify errors in the expression of a will, but only where the will was drawn up by someone other than the testator, and the will as signed did not in fact carry out the testator's instructions. This means that there would have to have been instructions, the existence of which can be proved, which the person preparing the will failed to implement. Applications for rectification would have to be presented within six months of the granting of confirmation to the deceased's estate. There is some opposition to this power being created, but the vast majority of consultees supported it, and it will in any event be of rare occurrence.

Revocation of wills

The Commission proposes that on divorce, the former spouse of the testator should be treated as having failed to survive the testator for the purposes of the testator's will. The effect will be a revocation of the provisions in favour of the spouse. It is not recommended that wills should be automatically revoked by the subsequent marriage of the testator. The *conditio si testator sine liberis decesserit*, which permits a will to be revoked at the instance of an after-born child who is not provided for in the will, is to be abolished.[21]

The confused state of the law on the revival of wills which have been revoked is much improved by clause 16. A will which has been *expressly*

---

[21] cll. 14 and 15.

revoked by a later will (but not one which was merely impliedly revoked by it) will no longer be revived by the revocation of the later will. The unsatisfactory decisions in *Bruce's J.F.* v. *Lord Advocate*[22] and *Scott's J.F.* v. *Johnston*[23] will be reversed and the law will return to the distinction proposed in *Nicolson* v. *Nicolson's Tutrix*.[24]

Conditio si institutus sine liberis decesserit

Clause 17 of the proposed Bill would retain the substance of this doctrine, but in a modified form and under the description of "Beneficiary predeceasing leaving issue." It will be interesting to see if the old name remains in general use or whether the more bland terminology of the Bill is adopted. Effectively the doctrine remains in force for gifts to direct descendants. Any such gift will impliedly include a provision in favour of the beneficiary's issue in the event of the beneficiary predeceasing the testator. However the doctrine will no longer apply to gifts to nephews and nieces. The present law has the anomalous result that a gift to brothers or sisters does not include an implied benefit for nephews and nieces in the event of the predecease of the brother or sister, but does impliedly include the beneficiary's issue if the gift is directly to a nephew or niece. This clearly had to be tidied up in one direction or the other, and the Commission has recommended that it be done by complete removal of the implied provision in the case of collaterals and their issue. It may be that this will not meet with general approval.

Administration of estates

A number of provisions affecting the administration of estates is included in Part V of the proposed Bill. These are mainly minor matters of tidying up the procedure and powers of executors, such as the provision removing the provision of the common law preventing an executor from transferring to himself the deceased's interest in a lease.[25] There are provisions for the valuation of the estate of a deceased person, and some long-standing rules of little practical importance, such as the right to aliment and temporary aliment from the estate will be abolished.

---

[22] 1969 S.L.T. 337.
[23] 1971 S.L.T. (Notes) 41.
[24] 1922 S.C. 649.
[25] *Inglis* v. *Inglis*, 1983 S.L.T. 437.

Appendix 1

RULES OF DIVISION, ACCORDING TO THE LAW OF SCOTLAND

Rules of Division, according to the Law of Scotland, of the Estate of a Person who has Died Intestate on or after September 10, 1964

References to a section are to that section of the Succession (Scotland) Act 1964. There being three different sets of rules, any or all of which may be called into play in a given succession; those applied are indicated against each entry by the following abbreviations:

PR—Prior rights to a house, furniture and a monetary provision under sections 8 and 9.

LR—Legal rights of *jus relicti*, *jus relictae* and legitim under common law as amended by the 1964 Act and other statutes.

FE—Succession to the free estate, heritable and moveable, under Part I of the 1964 Act.

I. Succession by a Surviving Spouse

If the person dies, leaving	*Rules Applicable*	*The estate is divided thus*
1. Spouse only.	PR LR FE	Whole to spouse. Comprising (1) prior right under section 8 to deceased's interest in the house in which surviving spouse was ordinarily resident (maximum £65,000), and to the deceased's interest in the furniture and plenishings of that house (maximum £12,000); (2) prior right under section 9 to £35,000; (3) *jus relicti* or *relictae* (½ from balance of moveables), and (4) whole free estate under section 2 (1) (e). (See note 8.)
2. Spouse and the deceased's child whether by marriage to the surviving spouse or not, and whether legitimate or not.	PR LR FE	Spouse has (1) prior right under section 8 to deceased's interest in the house in which the surviving spouse was ordinarily resident (maximum £65,000) and to the deceased's interest in the furniture and plenishings of that house (maximum £12,000); (2) if net balance of the estate is less than £21,000, prior right under section 9 to whole balance; if balance is over £21,000, prior right to £21,000 therefrom, taken rateably from heritage and moveables; and (3) legal right of *jus relicti* or *jus relictae* to one-third of the moveable estate remaining after the prior rights under sections 8 and 9 have been met. Child (or children equally among them) receive the whole remainder of the estate, comprising (a) legitim—a further one-third of the moveable estate remaining after the spouse's prior rights under sections 8 and 9, and (b) free estate—the remaining one-third of the moveables plus the heritage not required for prior rights. (See note 5 and note 8.)

I. SUCCESSION BY A SURVIVING SPOUSE—*cont.*

If the person dies, leaving	*Rules Applicable*	*The estate is divided thus*
3. Spouse and that spouse's children by marriage to deceased and prior marriages.	PR LR FE	Spouse entitled to rights as in No. 2. Remainder (legitim and free estate as above) to deceased's children equally.
4. Spouse and children and issue of predeceasing children.	PR LR FE	Spouse entitled to rights as in No. 2. Remainder (legitim and free estate) to surviving children *per capita* and issue of predeceasing children *per stirpes*.
5. Spouse and grandchild or grandchildren.	PR LR FE	Spouse entitled to rights as in No. 2. Remainder (legitim and free estate) to grandchild or among grandchildren equally. (See note 5.)
6. Spouse and remoter issue.	PR LR FE	Spouse entitled to rights as in No. 2. Remainder (legitim and free estate) to members of the nearest class of issue of which there are survivors, *per capita*, and to issue of predeceasing members of that class, *per stirpes*. (See note 5.)
7. Spouse and brothers and sisters. (See note 3 at end.)	PR LR FE	Spouse has (1) prior right under section 8 to deceased's interest in the house in which the surviving spouse was ordinarily resident (maximum £65,000) and to the deceased's interest in the furniture and plenishings of that house (maximum £12,000); (2) If the net balance of the estate is less than £35,000, prior right under section 9 to the whole balance: if the balance is over £35,000, prior right to £35,000 therefrom, rateably from heritage and moveables; and (3) legal right of *jus relicti* or *jus relictae* to one-half of the moveable estate remaining after the prior rights under sections 8 and 9 have been met. Brothers and sisters share the whole remainder of the estate equally between them as free estate. (See note 8.)
8. Spouse and brothers and sisters and/or issue of predeceasing brothers and sisters	PR LR FE	Spouse entitled to rights as in No. 7. Remainder to surviving brothers and sisters *per capita* and issue of predeceasing brothers and sisters *per stirpes*. If all brothers and sisters have predeceased, and there is issue of some or all of them, the remainder to members of the nearest class of issue of which there are survivors, *per capita*, and to issue of predeceasing members of that class, *per stirpes*.
9. Spouse and parent or parents, and brothers and sisters and/or issue of predeceasing brothers and sisters.	PR LR FE	Spouse entitled to rights as in No. 7. Remainder, one-half to surviving parent or to both parents equally between them, and one-half to brothers and sisters equally (or to their issue on principles noted in No. 8).
10. Spouse and parent or parents.	PR LR FE	Spouse entitled to rights as in No. 7. Remainder to surviving parent or to both parents equally between them.
11. Spouse and uncles and aunts (or issue thereof) and/or grandparents or remoter ancestors.	PR LR FE	Whole to spouse (as in No. 1).

II. SUCCESSION BY DESCENDANTS
(Illegitimate Persons—see Note 5)

If the person dies, leaving	*Rules Applicable*	*The estate is divided thus*
12. Children only.	LR FE	Whole estate to children equally. (One-half of moveable estate as legitim, whole balance of estate as free estate.)
13. Children and issue of predeceasing children.	LR FE	Whole estate to surviving children *per capita* and issue of predeceasing children *per stirpes*. (Legitim and free estate as in No. 12.)
14. Grandchildren.	LR FE	Whole estate (being legitim and free estate as in No. 12) to grandchildren equally.
15. Remoter issue.	LR FE	Whole estate (being legitim and free estate as in No. 12) to members of the nearest class of issue of which there are survivors, *per capita*, and to issue of predeceasing members of that class, *per stirpes*.
16. Issue and spouse.	PR LR FE	See Nos. 2 to 6.
17. Issue and collaterals.	LR FE	Whole to issue as in Nos. 12 to 15.
18. Issue of ascendants.	LR FE	Whole to issue as in Nos. 12 to 15.

III. SUCCESSION BY COLLATERALS

If the person dies, leaving	*Rules Applicable*	*The estate is divided thus*
19. Brothers and sisters.	FE	Whole estate equally among them.
20. Brothers and sisters and nephews and nieces, being issue of predeceasing brothers and sisters.	FE	Whole estate to brothers and sisters *per capita* and nephews and nieces *per stirpes*.
21. Nephews and nieces.	FE	Whole estate equally among them.
22. Remoter issue of brothers and sisters.	FE	Whole estate to members of the nearest class of issue of which there are survivors, *per capita*, and to issue of predeceasing members of that class, *per stirpes*.
23. Brothers and sisters (or their issue) and issue of the intestate.	LR FE	Brothers and sisters (or their issue) are excluded: whole to issue. (See No. 17 and Nos. 12–15.)
24. Brothers and sisters (or their issue) and spouse.	PR LR FE	See Nos. 7 and 8.
25. Brothers and sisters (or their issue), spouse and parent or parents.	PR LR FE	See No. 9.
26. Brothers and sisters and parent or parents.	FE	One-half of the estate to brothers and sisters equally; one-half to surviving parent or to both parents equally.

III. SUCCESSION BY COLLATERALS—*cont.*

If the person dies, leaving	*Rules Applicable*	*The estate is divided thus*
27. Brothers and sisters, nephews and nieces who are issue of predeceasing brothers and sisters, and parent or parents.	FE	One-half of the estate to brothers and sisters *per capita* and nephews and nieces *per stirpes*; one-half to surviving parent or to both parents equally.
28. Remoter issue of brothers and sisters, and parent or parents.	FE	One-half of the estate to members of the nearest class of issue of bothers and sisters of which there are survivors, *per capita*, and to issue of predeceasing members of that class, *per stirpes*; one-half to surviving parent or to both parents equally.
29. Brothers and sisters (or their issue), and uncles and aunts or remoter ascendants.	FE	Whole estate to brothers and sisters or their issue, the division being to members of the class nearest to the intestate of which there are survivors, *per capita*, and to issue of predeceasing members of that class, *per stirpes*.
30. Brothers and sisters, full blood, and brothers and sisters of half blood (consanguinean and uterine).	FE	Whole estate to brothers and sisters of full blood equally among them.
31. Brothers and sisters of half blood (consanguinean and uterine).	FE	Whole estate equally among them, with no distinction between consanguinean and uterine.
32. Brothers and sisters of half blood (consanguinean or uterine) and/or issue of same.	FE	As for full blood. See Nos. 19 to 22.
33. Brothers and sisters of half blood (consanguinean or uterine) spouse and other relations of intestate.	PR LR FE	As for full blood. See Nos. 23 to 29.

IV. SUCCESSION BY ASCENDANTS

34. Father only.	FE	Whole estate to father.
35. Mother only.	FE	Whole estate to mother.
36. Father and mother.	FE	Whole estate equally between father and mother.
37. Parent or parents, uncles and aunts (paternal and maternal) and their descendants.	FE	Whole estate to the surviving parent or to both parents equally as in Nos. 34 to 36.
38. Parent or parents and grandparents (paternal and maternal) or remoter ancestors.	FE	Whole estate to the surviving parent or to both parents equally as in Nos. 34 to 36.
39. Paternal and maternal uncles and aunts, and issue of predeceasing uncles and aunts.	FE	Whole estate to uncles and aunts (paternal and maternal) *per capita* and to cousins *per stirpes*.

IV. SUCCESSION BY ASCENDANTS—*cont.*

If the person dies, leaving	*Rules Applicable*	*The estate is divided thus*
40. Cousins only (on paternal or maternal sides), or their issue.	FE	Whole estate to cousins (paternal and maternal) or their issue, the division being to members of the class nearest to the intestate of which there are survivors, *per capita*, and to issue of predeceasing members of that class, *per stirpes*.
41. Paternal and maternal uncles and aunts, or their issue and paternal and maternal grandparents or remoter ancestors.	FE	Whole estate to uncles and aunts (paternal and maternal) *per capita* and to cousins *per stirpes*.
42. Paternal and maternal grandparents, great-uncles and great-aunts.	FE	Whole estate to grandparents (paternal and maternal) equally among them.
43. Paternal and maternal great-uncles and great-aunts (or issue of such) and great-grandparents or remoter ancestors (or issue of collaterals of such).	FE	Whole estate to great-uncles and great-aunts (paternal and maternal) or their issue, the division being to members of the class nearest to the intestate of which there are survivors, *per capita*, and to issue of predeceasing members of that class, *per stirpes*.
44. Great-grandparents or remoter ancestors and issue of collaterals of such.	FE	Infinite search, with division on the principles illustrated in Nos. 34 to 43; lineal ancestors on paternal or maternal sides succeeding before their collaterals and division among such collaterals and their issue being to members of the class nearest to the intestate of which there are survivors, *per capita*, and to issue of predeceasing members of that class, *per stirpes*.
45. Parent or parents and spouse.	PR LR FE	See No. 10.
46. Remoter ascendants and spouse.	PR LR FE	See No. 11.
47. Ascendants and issue of intestate.	LR FE	See No. 18 and Nos. 12 to 15.
48. Parent or parents and collaterals.	FE	See Nos. 26 to 28.
49. Remoter ascendants and collaterals.	FE	See No. 29.

V. CROWN

50. No other successor.	FE	Whole to Crown as *ultimus haeres*.

Notes

1. *Estate affected*

This table applies to the whole of the intestate estate, both heritable and moveable, of a deceased person so far as it is estate the succession to which falls to be regulated by the law of Scotland. There are, however, certain specialties.

(a) *Tenancies of crofts*. Crofting tenancies were originally excluded from the operation of the Succession Act, but in respect of the estates of persons dying on or after November 25, 1968, they now fall to be dealt with under the Act (Law Reform (Miscellaneous Provisions) (Scotland) Act 1968, s. 22 (3)).

(b) *Titles, coats of arms, etc.* The 1964 Act does not apply to the succession to any title, coat of arms, honour or dignity transmissible on the death of the holder thereof. Accordingly these items fall to be regulated by the pre-existing law (section 37 (1) (*a*)).

2. *Private international law*

Briefly, this table applies to the devolution of the moveable estate of persons who die domiciled in Scotland and to the devolution of all immoveable property in Scotland, whatever the domicile of the deceased. The pre-existing rules for choice of law are preserved by section 37 (2).

3. *Collaterals of the half blood*

The previous differentiation between collaterals of the half blood consanguinean and those of the half blood uterine has been removed by the 1964 Act. Accordingly, where brothers and sisters of an intestate, or of a parent or other ancestor of an intestate, have right to the whole, or one-half as the case may be, of the free intestate estate, collaterals of the whole blood are entitled to succeed thereto in preference to collaterals of the half blood, but where collaterals of the half blood are entitled to succeed they rank without distinction as between the half blood consanguinean and the half blood uterine (section 3).

4. *Representation*

Prior to the 1964 Act, representation was unlimited in intestate heritable succession but was severely limited in moveable succession. The effect of the Act is to apply a modified version of the previous rules of intestate moveable succession to the total free estate, heritable and moveable, of an intestate.

Accordingly, infinite representation has been introduced in legitim (section 11) and also in the distribution of the free estate (sections 5 and 6). There is no representation in a surviving spouse's prior rights, nor in *jus relicti* and *jus relictae*. A class (*e.g.* children) through which representation would otherwise apply is ignored if all members have predeceased (sections 6 and 11).

5. *Illegitimate children*

Substantial changes in the succession rights of illegitimate children were effected by the Law Reform (Miscellaneous Provisions) (Scotland) Act 1968 in respect of the estates of persons dying on or after November 25, 1968 and the Law Reform (Parent and Child) (Scotland) Act 1986 in respect of persons dying on or after December 8, 1986.

Briefly, from 1968 to 1986 illegitimate children were on a basis of formal equality with legitimate children in the succession to both parents, but could not represent a predeceasing parent and had no collaterals.

From December 8, 1986 the status of illegitimacy is abolished in succession and all rights of succession are determined by biological blood relationship rather than by marriage of the parents. The child formerly classed as illegitimate now has complete rights of succession, including representation, and has collaterals like any other child.

6. *Adopted children*

While the previous position was that an adopted child had no rights on the intestacy of the adopting parents and retained any rights which it had in the estates of its natural parents, the 1964 Act sets out to ensure that for the purposes of succession, or of the disposal of property by deed *inter vivos*, any adopted person is to be treated as the lawful child of the adopter and that rights in the estates of its natural parents are cut off. The detailed provisions for achieving this appear in Part IV of the Act.

7. *Interest*

Interest is payable on the ascertained amounts of the legal rights of *jus relicti*, *jus relictae* and legitim from the date of death until paid, usually at the rate earned by the estate. No interest is payable on the value of a surviving spouse's prior right to the deceased's dwelling-house and its furniture and plenishings under section 8 of the 1964 Act. Interest is, however, payable on the £21,000 or £35,000 available to a surviving spouse as a prior right under section 9 at a rate which was fixed at 4 per cent. for deaths before August 1, 1981 but is now variable and is 7 per cent. (S.I. 1981 No. 805.) This interest runs for the period from the date of death until payment. There is, of course, no interest on the value of the rights of succession to the free estate.

8. *Prior rights to a house and its furniture and plenishings*

A house to which section 8 applies is any one dwelling-house in which the surviving spouse of the intestate was ordinarily resident at the date of death of the intestate (section 8 (4)). The deceased's "relevant interest" therein which may pass to the surviving spouse is the interest of an owner or of a tenant, other than one whose tenancy is subject to the Rent Acts, and is subject to any heritable debt secured over the interest. The right is applicable to only one house even if the survivor was ordinarily resident in more than one, and the maximum benefit which the surviving spouse may receive under this head is £65,000. If the value of the deceased's interest in the house is greater, the survivor receives that sum and not the house itself (section 8 (1) (*b*)). Even if the value does not exceed the limit, in the cases specified in section 8 (2) the survivor receives not the house itself, but the substituted value thereof.

The survivor is also entitled to the deceased's interest in the furniture and plenishings (excluding heirlooms—section 8 (6) (*b*) and (*c*)) of any one house in which the survivor was ordinarily resident. A maximum limit of £12,000 is placed on the value of the furniture and plenishings to be transferred under this head. Should the value be greater, the surviving spouse may choose items to a value not exceeding that sum.

APPENDIX 2

EXAMPLES OF THE DIVISION OF INTESTATE ESTATES

Some simplified examples are given of the division of typical estates to illustrate points which arise in practice. Unless otherwise stated, the values shown are the net values of the estate after taxation, payment of debts and expenses of administration. In addition the examples are worked out as if the distribution of the estate occurred on the day of death, so that no account is taken of the interest payable on prior and legal rights from the date of death until payment, nor of any income arising after the date of death. The distinction between heritage and moveables is preserved where it is still relevant, *i.e.* in prior and legal rights.

X is the intestate. Square brackets indicate that the person concerned predeceased the intestate. The deceased was domiciled in Scotland and all the assets are situated in Scotland.

Example 1. Surviving spouse's prior rights exhaust the estate.

Family [X] = W

S D

Estate (Net values after debts, etc.)

	Heritage £	*Moveables* £
Deceased's house (widow ordinarily resident therein)	60,000	
Furniture and plenishings thereof . .		8,000
Other moveable estate		20,000
	60,000	28,000

(1) *Prior rights (section 8)*		
Widow—house (she being ordinarily resident therein and value being under £65,000)	60,000	
Widow—its furniture and plenishings (subject to £12,000 limit on value)		8,000
Balance	—	20,000

	Heritage £	*Moveables* £
(2) *Prior rights (section 9)*		
Widow—preferential right to £21,000 (there being issue of the deceased), if so much is available		20,000
Balance	—	—

The estate is not large enough for there to be a surplus after the spouse's prior rights and thus the widow takes the whole estate and the children receive nothing. Their rights are postponed to those of the deceased's spouse (s. 9 (2)). If there had been a will in favour of the widow, there would have been no prior rights and the children would have been entitled to legitim of one-third of the total moveable estate, but if there was no destination-over of the gift to the wife, she might have been able to create an intestacy by renouncing her benefit under the will (*Kerr, Petr.*, 1968 S.L.T. (Sh.Ct.) 61).

Example 2. All rules of intestate succession operate.

Family

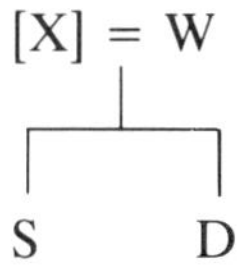

Estate

	Heritage £	*Moveables* £
Deceased's house (widow ordinarily resident therein)	75,000	
Furniture and plenishings thereof . .		9,000
Holiday house	10,000	
Other estate (bank A/cs; shares, etc.) .		21,000
Gross estate	85,000	30,000
Less Debts		
Loan secured over matrimonial home .	10,000	
Suppliers' accounts		1,000
Net estate	75,000	29,000

(1) *Prior rights (section 8)*		
Widow—deceased's interest in house. (Value £65,000 after heritable debt: s.(8)(6)(*d*))	65,000	
Widow—furniture and plenishings . .		9,000
Net after s. 8	10,000	20,000

		Heritage £	*Moveables* £
(2) *Prior rights (section 9)*			
Widow—right to £21,000, rateably from heritage and moveables.			
Total estate available 30,000			
Of which heritage is 1/3 and bears 1/3		7,000	
Of which moveables are 2/3 and bear 2/3			14,000
Net after prior rights		3,000	6,000
(3) *Legal rights*			
Widow—*jus relictae* (1/3rd of moveables)	2,000		
Children—Legitim 1/3 moveables—equally	2,000		
			4,000
Net after legal rights		3,000	2,000
(4) *Free estate*			
Heritage and moveable assimilated .			5,000
S receives 1/2 (s.2)		2,500	
D receives 1/2 (s.2)		2,500	5,000
			£ —
Scheme of Division			
Widow			
Prior rights	£		
Section 8(1)	65,000		
Section 8	9,000		
Section 9	21,000		
		95,000	
Jus relictae		2,000	97,000
Son			
Legitim		1,000	
Free estate (s.2)		2,500	3,500
Daughter			
Legitim		1,000	
Free estate		2,500	3,500
			104,000

Example 3. Collation *inter liberos* when there is representation in legitim.

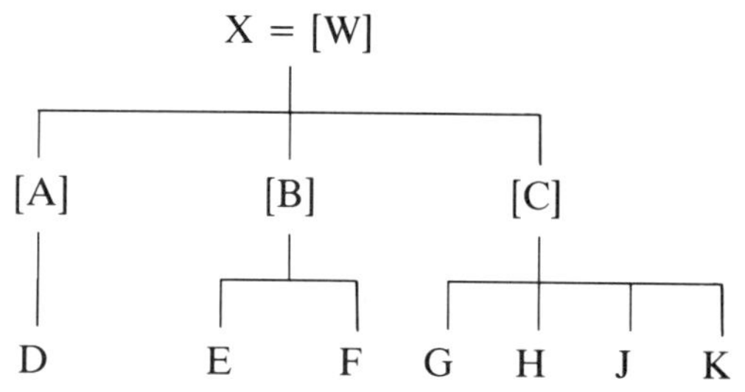

The intestate has died, predeceased by his spouse and all three of his children, but is survived by seven grandchildren, in families of one, two and four respectively. During his lifetime, X had made an advance of £3,000 to A. The legitim fund derived from the estate owned by X at the date of his death amounts to £18,000. Although only £18,000 is available for distribution as legitim at the date of death, the total after collation *inter liberos* is £21,000.

The existence of collation demonstrates that the right to legitim is not necessarily co-extensive with the right to share in the free estate and that it is not appropriate to lump together the legitim fund and the free estate and then to divide the total.

If A had survived his father, he would have been entitled to 1/3 of £21,000 = £7,000 less the £3,000 advance, *i.e.* £4,000 and this might have passed down to his only child D.

As A has predeceased his father, along with all the other children of X, the effect of section 11 (2) is that there is not true representation by division into thirds, one part going to each of the families of A, B and C. Instead there is equal division into 1/7 shares among the seven grandchildren.

In these circumstances, D is entitled to only 1/7 of the combined fund of legitim plus advance (£21,000) or £3,000. However, as a condition of that entitlement, section 11 (3) requires him to collate "the proportion appropriate to him" of any advances to his ancestor A. The advance to A was of exactly the amount to which D would be entitled from the combined fund. If the "appropriate" proportion which D must collate is the whole of the advance (as seems likely despite the unfairness) then D receives nothing, although he would have received £4,000 if his father had not been inconsiderate enough to die before the grandfather.

Example 4. Heritable securities in the calculation of legal rights.

Family

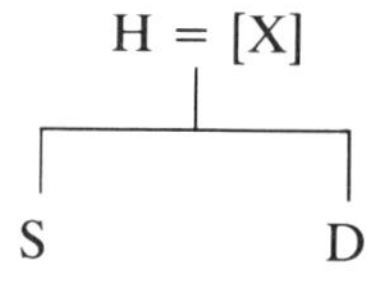

X dies intestate leaving a net estate consisting of a debt of £21,000 due to the deceased, secured by a standard security and of moveable assets also worth £21,000, making a total of £42,000. There being no house or furniture owned by the intestate, her husband is entitled to a section 9 prior right of £21,000 plus *jus relicti* of one-third of the remaining moveables.

The heritable security is heritable for the purposes of *jus relicti* and legitim, but is moveable for all other purposes of succession. This leaves the executor with an insoluble problem when allocating funds to meet the husband's prior right, as his possible courses of action lead to different total shares for the husband. The problem is that the heritable security is moveable for the purposes of prior rights. Three possible courses of action may be envisaged.

I. *The heritable security is allocated to the prior right*

Prior right s.9 (the security is allocated to this right, and there remains £21,000 of moveables)	£21,000
Jus relicti (1/3 of remainder)	£ 7,000
Total for husband	£28,000

II. *Moveables other than the security allocated to the prior right*

Prior right s.9 (the moveables other than the security are allocated to this right, and there remains the heritable security of £21,000)	21,000
Jus relicti (security not subject to legal rights)	—
Total for husband	£21,000

III. *Security treated as if it were heritable at all stages*

	Heritage (debt)	*Moveables* (balance)	*Husband*
	£	£	£
	21,000	21,000	
Prior right s. 9 apportioned	10,500	10,500	21,000
	10,500	10,500	
Jus relicti		3,500	3,500
Total for husband			24,500

Situation I gives the husband £28,000, Situation II gives him only £21,000 and Situation III gives him £24,500. Although there is nothing to require an executor to make one choice rather than another, the only rational answer seems to be the third course, treating the heritable security as a heritable asset at all stages.

APPENDIX 3

TEXT OF RELEVANT STATUTES

Contents

Wills Act 1963

(1963 c. 44)

An Act to repeal the Wills Act 1861, and make new provision in lieu thereof; and to provide that certain testamentary instruments shall be probative for the purpose of the conveyance of heritable property in Scotland. [31st July 1963]

General rule as to formal validity

1. A will shall be treated as properly executed if its execution conformed to the internal law in force in the territory where it was executed, or in the territory where, at the time of its execution or of the testator's death, he was domiciled or had his habitual residence, or in a state of which, at either of those times, he was a national.

Additional rules

2.—(1) Without prejudice to the preceding section, the following shall be treated as properly executed—

(*a*) a will executed on board a vessel or aircraft of any description, if the execution of the will conformed to the internal law in force in the territory with which, having regard to its registration (if any) and other relevant circumstances, the vessel or aircraft may be taken to have been most closely connected;

(*b*) a will so far as it disposes of immovable property, if its execution conformed to the internal law in force in the territory where the property was situated;

(*c*) a will so far as it revokes a will which under this Act would be treated as properly executed or revokes a provision which under this Act would be treated as comprised in a properly executed will, if the execution of the later will conformed to any law by reference to which the revoked will or provision would be so treated;

(*d*) a will so far as it exercises a power of appointment, if the execution of the will conformed to the law governing the essential validity of the power.

(2) A will so far as it exercises a power of appointment shall not be treated as improperly executed by reason only that its execution was not in accordance with any formal requirements contained in the instrument creating the power.

Certain requirements to be treated as formal

3. Where (whether in pursuance of this Act or not) a law in force outside the United Kingdom falls to be applied in relation to a will, any requirement of that law whereby special formalities are to be observed by testators answering a particular description, or witnesses to the execution of a will are to possess certain qualifications, shall be treated, notwithstanding any rule of that law to the contrary, as a formal requirement only.

Construction of wills

4. The construction of a will shall not be altered by reason of any change in the testator's domicile after the execution of the will.

5. [Repealed by the Succession (Scotland) Act 1964, Sched. 3.]

Interpretation

6.—(1) In this Act—

"internal law" in relation to any territory or state means the law which would apply in a case where no question of the law in force in any other territory or state arose;

"state" means a territory or group of territories having its own law of nationality;

"will" includes any testamentary instrument or act, and "testator" shall be construed accordingly.

(2) Where under this Act the internal law in force in any territory or state is to be applied in the case of a will, but there are in force in that territory or state two or more systems of internal law relating to the formal validity of wills, the system to be applied shall be ascertained as follows—

(*a*) If there is in force throughout the territory or state a rule indicating which of those systems can properly be applied in the case in question, that rule shall be followed; or

(*b*) If there is no such rule, the system shall be that with which the testator was most closely connected at the relevant time, and for this purpose the relevant time is the time of the testator's death where the matter is to be determined by reference to circumstances prevailing at his death, and the time of execution of the will in any other case.

(3) In determining for the purposes of this Act whether or not the execution of a will conformed to a particular law, regard shall be had to the formal requirements of that law at the time of execution, but this shall not prevent account being taken of an alteration of law affecting wills

executed at that time if the alteration enables the will to be treated as properly executed.

Short title, commencement, repeal and extent

7.—(1) This Act may be cited as the Wills Act 1963.

(2) This Act shall come into operation on 1st January 1964.

(3) The Wills Act 1861, is hereby repealed.

(4) This Act shall not apply to a will of a testator who died before the time of the commencement of this Act and shall apply to a will of a testator who dies after that time whether the will was executed before or after that time, but so that the repeal of the Wills Act 1861, shall not invalidate a will executed before that time.

[1] (5) It is hereby declared that this Act extends to Northern Ireland.

NOTE

[1] As amended by the Northern Ireland Constitution Act 1973, Sched. 6, Pt. I.

Succession (Scotland) Act 1964

(1964 c. 41)

An Act to assimilate and amend the law of Scotland with respect to the succession to the heritable and moveable property of deceased persons; to amend the law in relation to the legal and other prior rights exigible out of such property, to the administration of deceased persons' estates and other property passing on death, to the capacity of minors to test, and to the presumption of survivorship; to provide for certain testamentary dispositions to be probative; to provide for adopted persons to be treated for certain purposes as children of their adopters; to make new provision as to the financial rights and obligations of the parties on the dissolution of a marriage; and for purposes connected with the matters aforesaid [10th June 1964]

Part I

Intestate Succession

Assimilation of heritage to moveables for purpose of devolution on intestacy

1.—(1) The whole of the intestate estate of any person dying after the commencement of this Act (so far as it is estate the succession to which falls to be regulated by the law of Scotland) shall devolve, without distinction as between heritable and moveable property, in accordance with—

(*a*) the provisions of this Part in this Act; and

(*b*) any enactment or rule of law in force immediately before the commencement of this Act which is not inconsistent with those provisions and which, apart from this section, would apply to that person's moveable intestate estate, if any;

and, subject to section 37 of this Act, any enactment or rule of law in force immediately before the commencement of this Act with respect to the succession to intestate estates shall, in so far as it is inconsistent with the provisions of this Part of this Act, cease to have effect.

(2) Nothing in this Part of this Act shall affect legal rights or the prior rights of a surviving spouse; and accordingly any reference in this Part of this Act to an intestate estate shall be construed as a reference to so much of the net intestate estate as remains after the satisfaction of those rights, or the proportion thereof properly attributable to the intestate estate.

Rights of succession to intestate estate

2.—(1) Subject to the following provisions of this Part of this Act—

(*a*) where an intestate is survived by children, they shall have right to the whole of the intestate estate;

(*b*) where an intestate is survived by either of, or both, his parents and is also survived by brothers or sisters, but is not survived by any prior relative, the surviving parent or parents shall have right to one half of the intestate estate and the surviving brothers and sisters to the other half thereof;

(*c*) where an intestate is survived by brothers or sisters, but is not survived by any prior relative, the surviving brothers and sisters shall have right to the whole of the intestate estate;

(*d*) where an intestate is survived by either of, or both, his parents, but is not survived by any prior relative, the surviving parent or parents shall have right to the whole of the intestate estate;

(*e*) where an intestate is survived by a husband or a wife, but is not survived by any prior relative, the surviving spouse shall have right to the whole of the intestate estate;

(*f*) where an intestate is survived by uncles or aunts (being brothers or sisters of either parent of the intestate), but is not survived by any prior relative, the surviving uncles and aunts shall have right to the whole of the intestate estate;

(*g*) where an intestate is survived by a grandparent or grandparents (being a parent or parents of either parent of the intestate), but is not survived by any prior relative, the surviving grandparent or grandparents shall have right to the whole of the intestate estate;

(*h*) where an intestate is survived by brothers or sisters of any of his grandparents (being a parent or parents of either parent of the intestate), but is not survived by any prior relative, those surviving brothers and sisters shall have right to the whole of the intestate estate;

(*i*) where an intestate is not survived by any prior relative, the ancestors of the intestate (being remoter than grandparents) generation by generation successively, without distinction between the paternal and maternal lines, shall have right to the whole of the intestate estate; so however that, failing ancestors of any generation, the brothers and sisters of any of those ancestors shall have right thereto before ancestors of the next more remote generation.

(2) References in the foregoing subsection to brothers or sisters include respectively brothers and sisters of the half blood as well as of the whole blood; and in the said subsection "prior relative", in relation to any class of person mentioned in any paragraph of that subsection, means a person of any other class who, if he had survived the intestate, would have had right to the intestate estate or any of it by virtue of an earlier paragraph of that subsection or by virtue of any such paragraph and section 5 of this Act.

Succession of collaterals

3. Subject to section 5 of this Act, where brothers and sisters of an intestate or of an ancestor of an intestate (in this section referred to as "collaterals") have right to the whole, or, in a case to which subsection (1) (*b*) of the last foregoing section applies, to a half, of the intestate estate, the collaterals of the whole blood shall be entitled to succeed thereto in preference to the collaterals of the half blood; but where the collaterals of the half blood have right as aforesaid they shall rank without distinction as between those related to the intestate, or, as the case may be, the ancestor, through their father and those so related through their mother.

4. [Repealed by the Law Reform (Parent and Child) (Scotland) Act 1986, Sched. 2, with effect from 8th December 1986.]

Representation

5.—(1) Subject to section 6 of this Act, where a person who, if he had survived an intestate, would, by virtue of any of the foregoing provisions of this Part of this Act, have had right (otherwise than as a parent or spouse of the intestate) to the whole or to any part of the intestate estate has predeceased the intestate, but has left issue who survive the intestate, such issue shall have the like right to the whole or to that part of the intestate estate as the said person would have had if he had survived the intestate.

(2) The right of any issue entitled to share in an intestate estate by virtue of the foregoing subsection to be appointed to the office of executor on the intestate estate shall be postponed to the right thereto of any person who succeeds to the whole or part of the intestate estate by virtue of the foregoing provisions of this Act apart from this section and who applies for appointment to that office.

Division of intestate estate among those having right thereto

6. If, by virtue of the foregoing provisions of this Part of this Act, there are two or more persons having right among them to the whole, or, in a case to which section 2 (1) (*b*) of this Act relates, to a half, of an intestate estate, then the said estate, or, as the case may be, that half thereof, shall—

(*a*) if all of those persons are in the same degree of relationship to the intestate, be divided among them equally; and (*b*) in any other case, be divided equally into a number of parts equal to the aggregate of—

(i) those of the said persons who are nearest in degree of relationship to the intestate (in this section referred to as "the nearest surviving relatives"), and

(ii) any other persons who were related to the intestate in that degree, but who have predeceased him leaving issue who survive him;

and, of those parts, one shall be taken by each of the nearest surviving relatives, and one shall be taken *per stirpes* by the issue of each of the said predeceased persons.[1]

NOTE

[1] Further sentence added by the Law Reform (Miscellaneous Provisions) (Scotland) Act 1968, Sched. 1 (estate of any person dying after the commencement of that Act), and repealed by the Law Reform (Parent and Child) (Scotland) Act 1986, Sched. 2, with effect from December 8, 1986.

Saving of right of Crown as *ultimus haeres*

7. Nothing in this Part of this Act shall be held to affect the right of the Crown as *ultimus haeres* to any estate to which no person is entitled by virtue of this Act to succeed.

PART II

[1] LEGAL AND OTHER PRIOR RIGHTS IN ESTATES OF DECEASED PERSONS

NOTE

[1] See the Finance Act 1985, s. 84 (5) and (6).

Prior rights of surviving spouse, on intestacy, in dwelling house and furniture

[1] **8.**—(1) Where a person dies intestate leaving a spouse, and the intestate estate includes a relevant interest in a dwelling house to which this section applies, the surviving spouse shall be entitled to receive out of the intestate estate—

(*a*) where the value of the relevant interest does not exceed £65,000[2] or such larger amount as may from time to time be fixed by order of the Secretary of State—

(i) if subsection (2) of this section does not apply, the relevant interest;

(ii) if the said subsection (2) applies, a sum equal to the value of the relevant interest;

(*b*) in any other case, the sum of £65,000[2] or such larger amount as may from time to time be fixed by order of the Secretary of State:

Provided that, if the intestate estate comprises a relevant interest in two or more dwelling houses to which this section applies, this subsection shall have effect only in relation to such one of them as the surviving spouse may elect for the purposes of this subsection within six months of the date of death of the intestate.

(2) This subsection shall apply for the purposes of paragraph (*a*) of the foregoing subsection if—

(*a*) the dwelling house forms part only of the subjects comprised in one tenancy or lease under which the intestate was the tenant; or

(*b*) the dwelling house forms the whole or part of subjects an interest in which is comprised in the intestate estate and which were used by the intestate for carrying on a trade, profession or occupation, and the value of the estate as a whole would be likely to be substantially diminished if the dwelling house were disposed of otherwise than with the assets of the trade, profession or occupation.

(3) Where a person dies intestate leaving a spouse, and the intestate estate includes the furniture and plenishings of a dwelling house to which this section applies (whether or not the dwelling house is comprised in the intestate estate), the surviving spouse shall be entitled to receive out of the intestate estate—

(*a*) where the value of the furniture and plenishings does not exceed £12,000[3] or such larger amount as may from time to time be fixed by order of the Secretary of State, the whole thereof;

(*b*) in any other case, such part of the furniture and plenishings, to a value not exceeding £12,000[3] or such larger amount as may from time to time be fixed by order of the Secretary of State, as may be chosen by the surviving spouse:

Provided that, if the intestate estate comprises the furniture and plenishings of two or more such dwelling houses, this subsection shall have effect only in relation to the furniture and plenishings of such one of them as the surviving spouse may elect for the purposes of this subsection within six months of the date of death of the intestate.

(4) This section applies, in the case of any intestate, to any dwelling house in which the surviving spouse of the intestate was ordinarily resident at the date of death of the intestate.

[4] (5) Where any question arises as to the value of any furniture or plenishings, or of any interest in a dwelling house, for the purposes of any provision of this section the question shall be determined by arbitration by a single arbiter appointed, in default of agreement, by the sheriff of the sheriffdom in which the intestate was domiciled at the date of his death or, if that sheriffdom is uncertain or the intestate was domiciled furth of Scotland, the sheriff of Lothian and Peebles at Edinburgh.

(6) In this section—

(*a*) "dwelling house" includes a part of a building occupied (at the date of death of the intestate) as a separate dwelling; and any reference to a dwelling house shall be construed as including any garden or portion of ground attached to, and usually occupied with, the dwelling house or otherwise required for the amenity or convenience of the dwelling house;

(*b*) "furniture and plenishings" includes garden effects, domestic animals, plate, plated articles, linen, china, glass, books, pictures, prints, articles of household use and consumable stores; but does not include any article or animal used at the date of death of the intestate for business purposes, or money or securities for money, or any heirloom;

(*c*) "heirloom", in relation to an intestate estate, means any article which has associations with the intestate's family of such nature and extent that it ought to pass to some member of that family other than the surviving spouse of the intestate;

(*d*) "relevant interest", in relation to a dwelling house, means the interest therein of an owner, or the interest therein of a tenant, subject in either case to any heritable debt secured over the interest; and for the purposes of this definition "tenant" means a tenant under a tenancy or lease (whether of the dwelling house alone or of the dwelling house together with other subjects) which is not a tenancy to which the Rent Acts 1971–74 apply.

NOTES

[1] As amended by the Succession (Scotland) Act 1973, s. 1 (1) (*a*), in the case of a person dying on or after May 23, 1973. As amended by S.I. 1988 No. 633, in the case of a person dying on or after May 1, 1988. Saved by the Prescription and Limitation (Scotland) Act 1973, Sched. 1, para. 2 (*f*).

[2] Earlier values: September 10, 1964 to May 22, 1973—£15,000: May 22, 1973 to July 31, 1981—£30,000; August 1, 1981 to April 30, 1988—£50,000.

[3] Earlier values: September 10, 1964 to May 22, 1973—£5,000; May 22, 1973 to July 31, 1981—£8,000; August 1, 1981 to April 30, 1988—£10,000.

[4] Amended by the Sheriff Courts (Scotland) Act 1971, Sched. 1, para. 1. For interpretation of the term "sheriff," see *ibid.* s. 4 (2) and the Interpretation Act 1978, Sched. 1.

Prior right of surviving spouse to financial provision on intestacy

[1] **9.**—[2] (1) Where a person dies intestate and is survived by a husband or wife, the surviving spouse shall be entitled to receive out of the intestate estate—

(*a*) if the intestate is survived by issue, the sum of £21,000[3] or such larger amount as may from time to time be fixed by order of the Secretary of State, or

(*b*) if the intestate is not survived by issue, the sum of £35,000[4] or such larger amount as may from time to time be fixed by order of the Secretary of State,

together with, in either case, interest at the rate of 7 per cent[5] per annum or at such rate as may from time to time be fixed by order of the Secretary of State on such sum from the date of the intestate's death until payment:

Provided that where the surviving spouse is entitled to receive a legacy out of the estate of the intestate (other than a legacy of any dwelling house to which the last foregoing section applies or of any furniture and plenishings of any such dwelling house), he or she shall, unless he or she renounces the legacy, be entitled under this subsection to receive only such sum, if any, as remains after deducting from the sum fixed by virtue of paragraph (*a*) of this subsection or the sum fixed by virtue of paragraph (*b*) of this subsection, as the case may be, the amount or value of the legacy.

(2) Where the intestate estate is less than the amount which the surviving spouse is entitled to receive by virtue of subsection (1) of this

section the right conferred by the said subsection on the surviving spouse shall be satisfied by the transfer to him or her of the whole of the intestate estate.

(3) The amount which the surviving spouse is entitled to receive by virtue of subsection (1) of this section shall be borne by, and paid out of, the parts of the intestate estate consisting of heritable and moveable property respectively in proportion to the respective amounts of those parts.

(4) Where by virtue of subsection (2) of this section a surviving spouse has right to the whole of the intestate estate, he or she shall have the right to be appointed executor.

(5) The rights conferred by the Intestate Husband's Estate (Scotland) Acts 1911 to 1959 on a surviving spouse in his or her deceased spouse's estate shall not be exigible out of the estate of any person dying after the commencement of this Act.

(6) For the purposes of this section—

(*a*) the expression "intestate estate" means so much of the net intestate estate as remains after the satisfaction of any claims under the last foregoing section; and

(*b*) the expression "legacy" includes any payment or benefit to which a surviving spouse becomes entitled by virtue of any testamentary disposition; and the amount or value of any legacy shall be ascertained as as the date of the intestate's death.

NOTES

[1] As amended by the Law Reform (Miscellaneous Provisions) (Scotland) Act 1980, s. 4 and S.I. 1988 No. 633, in the case of a person dying on or after May 1, 1988. Saved by the Prescription and Limitation (Scotland) Act 1973, s. 6 (2), Sched. 1, para. 2 (*f*).

[2] Amended by the Law Reform (Miscellaneous Provisions) (Scotland) Act 1968, Sched. 1 (estate of any person dying on or after November 25, 1968); the Succession (Scotland) Act 1973, s. 1 (1) (*b*), in the case of a person dying on or after May 23, 1973, and by the Law Reform (Parent and Child) (Scotland) Act 1986, Sched. 2, with effect from December 8, 1986.

[3] Earlier values: September 10, 1964 to May 22, 1973—£2,500; May 23, 1973 to December 30, 1977—£4,000; December 31, 1977 to July 31, 1981—£8,000 (S.I. 1977 No. 2110); August 1, 1981 to April 30, 1988—£15,000 (S.I. 1981 No. 806).

[4] Earlier values: September 10, 1964 to May 22, 1973—£5,000; May 23, 1973 to December 30, 1977—£8,000; December 31, 1977 to July 31, 1981—£16,000 (S.I. 1977 No. 2110); August 1, 1981 to April 30, 1988—£25,000 (S.I. 1981 No. 806).

[5] As from August 1, 1981 the rate of interest is fixed at 7 per cent.: see S.I. 1981 No. 805. (Earlier rate (1964–81) 4 per cent.).

Provisions supplementary to sections 8 and 9

[1] **9A.** Any order of the Secretary of State, under section 8 or 9 of this Act, fixing an amount or rate—

(*a*) shall be made by statutory instrument which shall be subject to annulment in pursuance of a resolution of either House of Parliament; and

(*b*) shall have effect in relation to the estate of any person dying after the coming into force of the order.

NOTE

[1] Added by the Law Reform (Miscellaneous Provisions) (Scotland) Act 1980, s. 4.

Abolition of terce and courtesy, and calculation of legal rights

10.—(1) The right of courtesy of a surviving husband in his deceased wife's estate and the right of terce of a surviving wife in her deceased husband's estate shall not be exigible out of the estate of a person dying after the commencement of this Act.

(2) The amount of any claim to *jus relicti*, *jus relictae* or legitim out of an estate shall be calculated by reference to so much of the net moveable estate as remains after the satisfaction of any claims thereon under the two last foregoing sections.

10A. [Added by the Law Reform (Miscellaneous Provisions) (Scotland) Act 1968, s. 2, in respect of estates of persons dying on or after November 25, 1968, and repealed by the Law Reform (Parent and Child) (Scotland) Act 1986, Sched. 2, with effect from December 8, 1986.]

Representation in, and division of, legitim

[1] **11.**—(1) Subject to the next following subsection, where a person (hereinafter in this section referred to as "the deceased") dies predeceased by a child who has left issue who survive the deceased, and the child would, if he had survived the deceased, have been entitled to legitim out of the deceased's estate, such issue shall have the like right to legitim as the child would have had if he had survived the deceased.

(2) If, by virtue of the foregoing subsection or otherwise, there are two or more persons having right among them to legitim, then the legitim shall—

(*a*) if all of those persons are in the same degree of relationship to the deceased, be divided among them equally, and

(*b*) in any other case, be divided equally into a number of parts equal to the aggregate of—

(i) those of the said persons who are nearest in degree of relationship to the deceased (in this paragraph referred to as "the nearest surviving relatives") and

(ii) any other persons who were related to the deceased in that degree and who (if they had survived him) would have been entitled to legitim out of his estate, but who have predeceased him leaving issue who survive him and are entitled to legitim out of his estate;

and, of those parts, one shall be taken by each of the nearest surviving relatives, and one shall be taken *per stirpes* by the issue of each of the said predeceased persons, being issue who are entitled as aforesaid.

(3) Nothing in the last foregoing subsection shall be construed as altering any rule of law as to collation of advances; and where any person is entitled to claim legitim out of the estate of a deceased person by virtue of subsection (1) of this section he shall be under the like duty to collate any advances made by the deceased to him, and the proportion appropriate to him of any advances so made to any person through whom he derives such entitlement, as if he had been entitled to claim such legitim otherwise than by virtue of the said subsection (1).

(4) For the avoidance of doubt it is hereby declared that where any person is entitled by virtue of subsection (1) of this section to legitim out of the estate of the deceased, and the deceased is not survived by any child, the proportion of the estate due to any surviving spouse in respect of *jus relicti* or *jus relictae* shall be ascertained as if the deceased had been survived by a child.

NOTE

[1] As amended by the Law Reform (Miscellaneous Provisions) (Scotland) Act 1968, Sched. 1, in respect of estate of any person dying on or after November 25, 1968, and by the Law Reform (Parent and Child) (Scotland) Act 1986, Sched. 2, with effect from December 8, 1986.

Legitim not to be discharged by ante-nuptial marriage contract

12. Nothing in any ante-nuptial contract of marriage executed after the commencement of this Act shall operate so as to exclude, on the occurrence of the death of either party to the marriage, the right of any child of the marriage (or of any issue of his coming in his place by virtue of the last foregoing section) to legitim out of the estate of that party unless such child or issue shall elect to accept in lieu of legitim the provision made in his favour under the contract.

Equitable compensation

[1] **13.** Every testamentary disposition executed after the commencement of this Act by which provision is made in favour of the spouse or of any issue of the testator and which does not contain a declaration that the provision so made is in full and final satisfaction of the right to any share in the testator's estate to which the spouse or the issue, as the case may be, is entitled by virtue of *jus relicti*, *jus relictae* or legitim, shall (unless the disposition contains an express provision to the contrary) have effect as if it contained such a declaration.

NOTE

[1] As amended by the Law Reform (Miscellaneous Provisions) (Scotland) Act 1968, Sched. 1, in respect of estate of any person dying on or after November 25, 1968, and by the Law Reform (Parent and Child) (Scotland) Act 1986, Sched. 2, with effect from December 8, 1986.

PART III

ADMINISTRATION AND WINDING UP OF ESTATES

Assimilation for purposes of administration, etc., of heritage to moveables

14.—(1) Subject to subsection (3) of this section the enactments and rules of law in force immediately before the commencement of this Act with respect to the administration and winding up of the estate of a deceased person so far as consisting of moveable property shall have effect (as modified by the provisions of this Act) in relation to the whole of the estate without distinction between moveable property and heritable property; and accordingly on the death of any person (whether testate or intestate) every part of his estate (whether consisting of moveable property or heritable property) falling to be administered under the law of Scotland shall, by virtue of confirmation thereto, vest for the purposes of administration in the executor thereby confirmed and shall be administered and disposed of according to law by such executor.

[1] (2) Provision shall be made by the Court of Session by act of sederunt made under the enactments mentioned in section 22 of this Act (as extended by that section) for the inclusion in the confirmation of an executor, by reference to an appended inventory or otherwise, of a description, in such form as may be so provided, of any heritable property forming part of the estate.

(3) Nothing in this section shall be taken to alter any rule of law whereby any particular debt of a deceased person falls to be paid out of any particular part of his estate.

NOTE

[1] The Administration of Estates Act 1971, s. 6, provides: "6.—(1) It shall be competent to include in the inventory of the estate of any person who dies domiciled in Scotland any real estate of the deceased situated in England and Wales or Northern Ireland, and accordingly in section 9 of the Confirmation of Executors (Scotland) Act 1858 the word 'personal' wherever it occurs is hereby repealed.

(2) Section 14 (2) of the Succession (Scotland) Act 1964 (act of sederunt to provide for description of heritable property) shall apply in relation to such real estate as aforesaid as it applies in relation to heritable property in Scotland."

Provisions as to transfer of heritage

15.—(1) Section 5 (2) of the Conveyancing (Scotland) Act 1924 (which provides that a confirmation which includes a heritable security shall be a valid title to the debt thereby secured) shall have effect as if any reference therein to a heritable security, or to a debt secured by a heritable security, included a reference to any interest in heritable property which has vested in an executor in pursuance of the last foregoing section by virtue of a confirmation:

[1] Provided that a confirmation (other than an implied confirmation within the meaning of the said section 5 (2)) shall not be deemed for the purposes of the said section 5 (2) to include any such interest unless a description of the property, in accordance with any act of sederunt such as is mentioned in subsection (2) of the last foregoing section, is included or referred to in the confirmation.

(2) Where in pursuance of the last foregoing section any heritable property has vested in an executor by virtue of a confirmation, and it is necessary for him in distributing the estate to transfer that property—

(*a*) to any person in satisfaction of a claim to legal rights or the prior rights of a surviving spouse out of the estate, or

(*b*) to any person entitled to share in the estate by virtue of this Act, or

(*c*) to any person entitled to take the said property under any testamentary disposition of the deceased,

the executor may effect such transfer by endorsing on the confirmation (or where a certificate of confirmation relating to the property has been issued in pursuance of any act of sederunt, on the certificate) a docket in favour of that person in the form set out in Schedule 1 to this Act, or in a form as nearly as may be to the like effect, and any such docket may be specified as a midcouple or link in title in any deduction of title; but this section shall not be construed as prejudicing the competence of any other mode of transfer.

NOTE

[1] As amended by the Law Reform (Miscellaneous Provisions) (Scotland) Act 1968, s. 19.

Provisions relating to leases

[1] **16.**—(1) This section applies to any interest, being the interest of a tenant under a lease, which is comprised in the estate of a deceased person and has accordingly vested in the deceased's executor by virtue of section 14 of this Act; and in the following provisions of this section "interest" means an interest to which this section applies.

(2) Where an interest—

(*a*) is not the subject of a valid bequest by the deceased, or

(*b*) is the subject of such a bequest, but the bequest is not accepted by the legatee, or

[2] (*c*) being an interest under an agricultural lease, is the subject of such a bequest, but the bequest is declared null and void in pursuance of section 16 of the Act of 1886 or section 11 of the 1991 Act, or becomes null and void under section 10 of the Act of 1955,

and there is among the conditions of the lease (whether expressly or by implication) a condition prohibiting assignation of the interest, the executor shall be entitled, notwithstanding that condition, to transfer the interest to any one of the persons entitled to succeed to the deceased's intestate estate, or to claim legal rights or the prior rights of a surviving spouse out of the estate, in or towards satisfaction of that person's entitlement or claim; but shall not be entitled to transfer the interest to any other person without the consent—

(i) in the case of an interest under an agricultural lease, being a lease of a croft within the meaning of section 3 (1) of the Act of 1955, of the Crofters Commission;

(ii) in any other case, of the landlord.

(3) If in the case of any interest—

(*a*) at any time the executor is satisfied that the interest cannot be disposed of according to law and so informs the landlord, or

(*b*) the interest is not so disposed of within a period of one year or such longer period as may be fixed by agreement between the landlord and the executor or, failing agreement, by the sheriff on summary application by the executor—

[2] (i) in the case of an interest under an agricultural lease which is the subject of a petition to the Land Court under section 16 of the Act of 1886 or an application to that court under section 11 of the 1991 Act, from the date of the determination or withdrawal of the petition or, as the case may be, the application,

(ia) in the case of an interest under an agricultural lease which is the subject of an application by the legatee to the Crofters Commission under section 10 (1) of the Act of 1955, from the date of any refusal by the Commission to determine that the bequest shall not be null and void, (ib) in the case of an interest under an agricultural lease which is the subject of an intimation of objection by the landlord to the legatee and the Crofters Commission under section 10 (3) of the Act of 1955, from the date of any decision of the Commission upholding the objection,

(ii) in any other case, from the date of death of the deceased,

either the landlord or the executor may, on giving notice in accordance with the next following subsection to the other, terminate the lease (in so far as it relates to the interest) notwithstanding any provision therein, or any enactment or rule of law, to the contrary effect.

(4) The period of notice given under the last foregoing subsection shall be—

(*a*) in the case of an agricultural lease, such period as may be agreed, or, failing agreement, a period of not less than one year and not more than two years ending with such term of Whitsunday or Martinmas as may be specified in the notice; and

(*b*) in the case of any other lease, a period of six months:

Provided that paragraph (*b*) of this subsection shall be without prejudice to any enactment prescribing a shorter period of notice in relation to the lease in question.

(5) Subsection (3) of this section shall not prejudice any claim by any party to the lease for compensation or damages in respect of the termination of the lease (or any rights under it) in pursuance of that subsection; but any award of compensation or damages in respect of such termination at the instance of the executor shall be enforceable only against the estate of the deceased and not against the executor personally.

(6) Where an interest is an interest under an agricultural lease, and—

(*a*) an application is made under section 3 of the Act of 1931 or section 13 of the Act of 1955 to the Land Court for an order for removal, or

[2] (*b*) a reference is made under section 23 (2) and (3) of the 1991 Act to an arbiter to determine any question which has arisen under section 22 (2) (*e*) of that Act in connection with a notice to quit,

the Land Court shall not make the order, or, as the case may be, the arbiter shall not make an award in favour of the landlord, unless the court or the arbiter is satisfied that it is reasonable having regard to the fact that the interest is vested in the executor in his capacity as executor, that it should be made.

(7) Where an interest is not an interest under an agricultural lease, and the landlord brings an action of removing against the executor in respect of a breach of a condition of the lease, the court shall not grant decree in the action unless it is satisfied that the condition alleged to have been breached is one which it is reasonable to expect the executor to have observed, having regard to the fact that the interest is vested in him in his capacity as an executor.

[2] (8) Where an interest is an interest under an agricultural lease and is the subject of a valid bequest by the deceased, the fact that the interest is vested in the executor under the said section 14 shall not prevent the

operation, in relation to the legatee, of paragraphs (*a*) to (*h*) of section 16 of the Act of 1886, or, as the case may be, section 11 (2) to (8) of the 1991 Act, or, as the case may be, subsections (2) to (7) of section 10 of the Act of 1955.

[2] (9) In this section—

"agricultural lease" means a lease of a holding within the meaning of the Small Landholders (Scotland) Acts 1886 to 1931 or of the 1991 Act or a lease of a croft within the meaning of section 3 (1) of the Act of 1955;

"the Act of 1886" means the Crofters Holdings (Scotland) Act 1886;

"the Act of 1931" means the Small Landholders and Agricultural Holdings (Scotland) Act 1931;

"the 1991 Act" means the Agricultural Holdings (Scotland) Act 1991;

"the Act of 1955" means the Crofters (Scotland) Act 1955;

"lease" includes tenancy.

NOTES

[1] As amended by the Law Reform (Miscellaneous Provisions) (Scotland) Act 1968, Sched. 2 (estates of any person dying on or after November 25, 1968). See the Agriculture Act 1986, Sched. 2, para. 3. As regards notices to quit, see the Agricultural Holdings (Scotland) Act 1991, s. 25.

[2] As amended by the Agricultural Holdings (Scotland) Act 1991, Sched. 11, para. 24.

Protection of persons acquiring title

[1] **17.** Where any person has in good faith and for value acquired title to any interest in or security over heritable property which has vested in an executor as aforesaid directly or indirectly from—

(*a*) the executor, or

(*b*) a person deriving title directly from the executor,

the title so acquired shall not be challengeable on the ground that the confirmation was reducible or has in fact been reduced, or, in a case falling under paragraph (*b*) above, that the title should not have been transferred to the person mentioned in that paragraph.

NOTE

[1] Saved by the Law Reform (Miscellaneous Provisions) (Scotland) Act 1968, s. 7.

Provisions as to entails and special destinations

18.—[1] (1) On the death of the heir of entail in possession of any property subject to an entail, the entailed property shall, if the executor of the deceased is confirmed thereto, vest in the executor for the purpose of enabling it to be conveyed to the heir of entail next entitled thereto under the entail (if such conveyance is necessary) and for that purpose only.

[1] (2) On the death of a person entitled to any heritable property subject to a special destination in favour of some other person, being a destination which the deceased could not competently have, or in fact has not, evacuated by testamentary disposition or otherwise, the property shall, if the executor of the deceased is confirmed thereto, vest in the executor for the purpose of enabling it to be conveyed to the person next entitled thereto under the destination (if such conveyance is necessary) and for that purpose only.

(3) Section 14 (2) of this Act shall apply in relation to property to which this section refers as it applies to property to which the said section 14 (2) refers.

(4) Sections 15 and 17 of this Act shall apply to property which has vested in an executor by virtue of this section as they apply to property which has vested in an executor by virtue of section 14 of this Act, as if the person next entitled to the first mentioned property were a person entitled to share in the estate of the deceased.

NOTE

[1] See the Inheritance Tax Act 1984, s. 209 (1).

19. [Repealed by the Finance Act 1975, Sched. 13.]

Executor dative to have powers of a trustee

20. An executor dative appointed to administer the estate of a deceased person shall have in his administration of such estate the whole powers, privileges and immunities, and be subject to the same obligations, limitations and restrictions, which gratuitous trustees have, or are subject to, under any enactment or under common law, and the Trusts (Scotland) Acts 1921 and 1961 shall have effect as if any reference therein to a trustee included a reference to such an executor dative:

Provided that nothing in this section shall exempt an executor dative from finding caution for his intromissions or confer upon him any power to resign or to assume new trustees.

Evidence as to holograph wills in commissary proceedings

21. Notwithstanding any rule of law or practice to the contrary, confirmation of an executor to property disposed of in a holograph testamentary disposition shall not be granted unless the court is satisfied by evidence consisting at least of an affidavit by each of two persons that the writing and signature of the disposition are in the handwriting of the testator.

Court of Session may regulate procedure in commissary proceedings

[1] **22.**—(1) The powers exercisable by the Court of Session by act of sederunt under section 18 of the Confirmation of Executors (Scotland) Act 1858, section 16 of the Sheriff Courts and Legal Officers (Scotland) Act 1927 and section 34 of the Administration of Justice (Scotland) Act 1933 (which empower the court to regulate *inter alia* procedure in proceedings in the sheriff court and in proceedings for the confirmation of executors) shall include power to regulate the procedure to be followed, and to prescribe the form and content of any petition, writ or other document to be used, in connection with the confirmation of executors in cases where, by virtue of this Act, heritable property devolves upon the executor.

(2) Without prejudice to the generality of the powers conferred on the court by the said sections and by this section, the power conferred by the said section 34 to modify, amend or repeal by act of sederunt enactments relating to certain matters shall include power so to modify, amend or repeal any enactment relating to the procedure to be followed in proceedings for the confirmation of executors in such cases as aforesaid.

(3) [Repealed by the Law Reform (Miscellaneous Provisions) (Scotland) Act 1966, Sched., Part I.]

(4) [Repealed by the Finance Act 1975, Sched. 13.]

NOTE

[1] See S.I. 1964 No. 1143 and S.I. 1971 No. 1165.

PART IV

ADOPTED PERSONS

Adopted person to be treated for purposes of succession, etc., as child of adopter

[1] **23.**—(1) For all purposes relating to—

(*a*) the succession to a deceased person (whether testate or intestate), and

(*b*) the disposal of property by virtue of any *inter vivos* deed,

an adopted person shall be treated as the child of the adopter and not as the child of any other person.

In this subsection and in the following provisions of this Part of this Act any reference to succession to a deceased person shall be construed as including a reference to the distribution of any property in consequence of the death of the deceased person and any claim to legal rights or the prior rights of a surviving spouse out of his estate.

(2) In any deed whereby property is conveyed or under which a succession arises, being a deed executed after the making of an adoption order, unless the contrary intention appears, any reference (whether express or implied)—

(*a*) to the child or children of the adopter shall be construed as, or as including, a reference to the adopted person;

(*b*) to the child or children of the adopted person's natural parents or either of them shall be construed as not being, or as not including, a reference to the adopted person; and

(*c*) to a person related to the adopted person in any particular degree shall be construed as a reference to the person who would be related to him in that degree if he were the child of the adopter and were not the child of any other person:

Provided that for the purposes of this subsection a deed containing a provision taking effect on the death of any person shall be deemed to have been executed on the date of death of that person.

[2] (3) Where the terms of any deed provide that any property or interest in property shall devolve along with a title, honour or dignity, nothing in this section or in the Children Act 1975 or in the Adoption (Scotland) Act 1978 shall prevent that property or interest from so devolving.

(4) Nothing in this section shall affect any deed executed, or the devolution of any property on, or in consequence of, the death of a person who dies, before the commencement of this Act.

(5) In this Part of this Act the expression "adoption order" has the same meaning as in section 38 of the Adoption (Scotland) Act 1978

(whether the order took effect before or after the commencement of this Act); and "adopted" means adopted in pursuance of an adoption order.

NOTE
[1] As amended by the Adoption (Scotland) Act 1978, Sched. 3, para. 4. See also the Legitimation (Scotland) Act 1968, ss. 2 (6), 6 (2). Excluded by the Law Reform (Miscellaneous Provisions) (Scotland) Act 1966, s. 5.

Provisions supplementary to section 23

[1] **24.**—(1) For the purposes of the law regulating the succession to any property and for the purposes of the construction of any such deed as is mentioned in the last foregoing section, an adopted person shall be deemed to be related to any other person, being the child or the adopted child of the adopter or (in the case of a joint adoption) of either of the adopters.

(*a*) where he or she was adopted by two spouses jointly and that other person is the child or adopted child of both of them, as a brother or sister of the whole blood;

(*b*) in any other case, as a brother or sister of the half blood.

[2] (1A) Where, in relation to any purpose specified in section 23 (1) of this Act, any right is conferred or any obligation is imposed, whether by operation of law or under any deed coming into operation after the commencement of the Children Act 1975, by reference to the relative seniority of the members of a class of persons, then, without prejudice to any entitlement under Part I of the Law Reform (Miscellaneous Provisions) (Scotland) Act 1968 of an illegitimate child who is adopted by one of his parents.

(*a*) any member of that class who is an adopted person shall rank as if he had been born on the date of his adoption, and

(*b*) if two or more members of the class are adopted persons whose dates of adoption are the same, they shall rank as between themselves in accordance with their respective times of birth.

[3] (2) Notwithstanding anything in the last foregoing section, a trustee or an executor may distribute any property for the distribution of which he is responsible without having ascertained that no adoption order has been made by virtue of which any person is or may be entitled to any interest therein, and shall not be liable to any such person of whose claim he has not had notice at the time of the distribution; but (without prejudice to section 17 of this Act) nothing in this subsection shall affect any right of any such person to recover the property, or any property representing it, from any person who may have received it.

(3) Where an adoption order is made in respect of a person who has been previously adopted, the previous adoption shall be disregarded for the purposes of the last foregoing section in relation to the devolution of any property on the death of any person dying after the date of the subsequent adoption order, and in relation to any deed executed after that date whereby property is conveyed or under which a succession arises.

(4) [Repealed by the Adoption (Scotland) Act 1978, Sched. 4.]

NOTES
[1] Saved by the Legitimation (Scotland) Act 1968, ss. 2 (6), 6 (2).
[2] Added by the Children Act 1975, Sched. 2, para. 5.
[3] Amended by the Adoption Act 1964, s. 1 (1).

PART V

FINANCIAL PROVISIONS ON DIVORCE

25–27. [Repealed by the Divorce (Scotland) Act 1976, Sched. 2.]

PART VI

MISCELLANEOUS AND SUPPLEMENTARY

28. [Repealed by the Age of Legal Capacity (Scotland) Act 1991, Sched. 2.]

Right of tenant to bequeath interest under lease

29.—(1) A bequest by a tenant of his interest under a tenancy or lease to any one of the persons who, if the tenant had died intestate, would be, or would in any circumstances have been, entitled to succeed to his intestate estate by virtue of this Act shall not be treated as invalid by reason only that there is among the conditions of the tenancy or lease an implied condition prohibiting assignation.

[1] (2) This section shall not prejudice the operation of section 16 of the Crofters Holdings (Scotland) Act 1886, or section 11 of the Agricultural Holdings (Scotland) Act 1991 (which relate to bequests in the case of agricultural leases), or of section 10 of the Crofters (Scotland) Act 1955 (which makes similar provision in relation to crofts).

NOTE
[1] As amended by the Law Reform (Miscellaneous Provisions) (Scotland) Act 1968, Sched. 2 (estate of persons dying after the commencement of that Act), and the Agricultural Holdings (Scotland) Act 1991, Sched. 11, para. 25.

Effect of testamentary dispositions on special destinations

30. A testamentary disposition executed after the commencement of this Act shall not have effect so as to evacuate a special destination (being a destination which could competently be evacuated by the testamentary disposition) unless it contains a specific reference to the destination and a declared intention on the part of the testator to evacuate it.

Presumption of survivorship in respect of claims to property

31.—(1) Where two persons have died in circumstances indicating that they died simultaneously or rendering it uncertain which, if either, of them survived the other, then, for all purposes affecting title or succession to property or claims to legal rights or the prior rights of a surviving spouse, (*a*) where the persons were husband and wife, it shall be presumed that neither survived the other; and

(*b*) in any other case, it shall be presumed that the younger person survived the elder unless the next following subsection applies.

(2) If, in a case to which paragraph (*b*) of the foregoing subsection would (apart from this subsection) apply, the elder person has left a testamentary disposition containing a provision, however expressed, in favour of the younger if he survives the elder and, failing the younger, in favour of a third person, and the younger person has died intestate, then it shall be presumed for the purposes of that provision that the elder person survived the younger.

Certain testamentary dispositions to be probative

[1] **32.**—(1) For the purpose of any question arising as to entitlement to any property by virtue of a testamentary disposition to which this section applies, the testamentary disposition shall (notwithstanding anything in any Act passed before this Act) be treated as probative.

(2) This section applies to any testamentary disposition (not being a testamentary disposition which would be treated as probative apart from this section) if—

(*a*) confirmation of an executor to property disposed of in the disposition has been granted in Scotland, or

(*b*) probate, letters of administration or other grant of representation has been issued in England and Wales or Northern Ireland in respect of property disposed of in the disposition and notes the domicile of the deceased in England and Wales or in Northern Ireland, as the case may be, or probate, letters of administration or other grant of representation issued outwith the United Kingdom in respect of such property has been sealed in Scotland under section 2 of the Colonial Probates Act 1892.

NOTE

[1] As amended by the Administration of Estates Act 1971, Sched. 1.

Construction of existing deeds

[1] **33.**—[1a] (1) Subject to subsection (2) of this section, any reference in any deed taking effect after the commencement of this Act to *jus relicti*, *jus relictae* or legitim shall be construed as a reference to the right to *jus relicti*, *jus relictae* or legitim, as the case may be, as modified by Part II of this Act; and any reference in any such deed to courtesy or terce shall be of no effect.

[2] (2) Any reference to legal rights in a marriage contract made before the commencement of this Act and taking effect in consequence of a decree of divorce granted in an action commenced after the commencement of this Act shall be construed as a reference to any right which the husband or the wife, as the case may be, might obtain by virtue of the provisions of section 26 of this Act or section 5 of the Divorce (Scotland) Act 1976 or section 29 of the Matrimonial and Family Proceedings Act 1984 or section 8 of the Family Law (Scotland) Act 1985.

NOTES

[1] As amended by the Law Reform (Miscellaneous Provisions) (Scotland) Act 1968, Sched. 1, in respect of estate of any person dying on or after November 25, 1968.

[1a] As amended by the Law Reform (Parent and Child) (Scotland) Act 1986, Sched. 1, para. 7 (1) and Sched. 2, with effect from December 8, 1986.

[2] As amended by the Divorce (Scotland) Act 1976, Sched. 1, para. 2, the Matrimonial and Family Proceedings Act 1984, Sched. 1, para. 6, and the Family Law (Scotland) Act 1985, Sched. 1, para. 4.

Modification of enactments and repeals

34.—(1) Subject to the provisions of section 37 of this Act, the enactment mentioned in Schedule 2 to this Act shall have effect subject to the modifications specified in that Schedule, being modifications consequential on the provisions of this Act.

(2) [Repealed by the Statute Law (Repeals) Act 1974.]

Transfer of certain jurisdiction to Sheriff of Chancery

35.—(1) If at any time it appears to the Secretary of State expedient to do so he may by order transfer to the Sheriff of Chancery the jurisdiction of any other sheriff in relation to the service of heirs.

(2) An order made under this section may contain such consequential provisions as appears to the Secretary of State to be necessary, including provisions for the consequential repeal or consequential modification of any enactment relating to the matters dealt with in the order.

(3) Any order made under this section shall be made by statutory instrument.

Interpretation

36.—(1) In this Act the following expressions shall, unless the context otherwise requires, have the meanings hereby respectively assigned to them, that is to say—

"deed" includes any disposition, contract, instrument or writing, whether *inter vivos* or *mortis causa*;

"an intestate" means a person who has died leaving undisposed of by testamentary disposition the whole or any part of his estate, and "intestate" shall be construed accordingly;

"intestate estate", in relation to an intestate, means (subject to sections 1 (2) and 9 (6) (*a*) of this Act) so much of his estate as is undisposed of by testamentary disposition;

[0] "issue" means issue however remote;

"Land Court" means the Scottish Land Court;

"lease" and "tenancy" include sub-lease and sub-tenancy, and tenant shall be construed accordingly;

"legal rights" means *jus relicti*, *jus relictae*, and legitim;

"net estate" and "net intestate estate" means respectively so much of an estate or an intestate estate as remains after provision for the satisfaction of[1] estate duty and other liabilities of the estate having priority over legal rights, the prior rights of a surviving spouse and rights of succession, or, as the case may be, the proportion thereof properly attributable to the intestate estate;

"owner" in relation to any heritable property means the person entitled to receive the rents thereof (other than rents under a sub-lease or sub-tenancy);

"prior rights", in relation to a surviving spouse, means the rights conferred by sections 8 and 9 of this Act;

"testamentary disposition" in relation to a deceased, includes any deed taking effect on his death whereby any part of his estate is disposed of or under which a succession thereto arises.

(2) Any reference in this Act to the estate of a deceased person shall, unless the context otherwise requires, be construed as a reference to the whole estate, whether heritable or moveable, or partly heritable and partly moveable, belonging to the deceased at the time of his death or over which the deceased had a power of appointment and, where the deceased immediately before his death held the interest of a tenant under a tenancy or lease which was not expressed to expire on his death, includes that interest:

Provided that—

(*a*) where any heritable property belonging to a deceased person at the date of his death is subject to a special destination in favour of any person, the property shall not be treated for the purposes of this Act as part of the estate of the deceased unless the destination is one which could competently be, and has in fact been, evacuated by the deceased by testamentary disposition or otherwise; and in that case the property shall be treated for the purposes of this Act as if it were part of the deceased's estate on which he has tested; and

(*b*) where any heritable property over which a deceased person had a power of appointment has not been disposed of in exercise of that power and is in those circumstances subject to a power of appointment by some other person, that property shall not be treated for the purposes of this Act as part of the estate of the deceased.

(3) Without prejudice to the proviso to section 23 (2) of this Act, references in this Act to the date of execution of a testamentary disposition shall be construed as references to the date on which the disposition was actually executed and not to the date of death of the testator.

(4) References in this Act to any enactment shall, except where the context otherwise requires, be construed as references to that enactment as amended by or under any other enactment, including this Act.

[2] (5) Section 1 (1) (legal equality of children) of the Law Reform (Parent and Child) (Scotland) Act 1986 shall apply to this Act; and any reference (however expressed) in this Act to a relative shall be construed accordingly.

NOTES

[0] As amended by the Law Reform (Parent and Child) (Scotland) Act 1986, Sched. 2.

[1] Includes capital transfer tax: see the Capital Transfer Tax Act 1984, Sched. 6, para. 1.

[2] Added by the Law Reform (Parent and Child) (Scotland) Act 1986, Sched. 1, para. 7 (2), with effect from December 8, 1986.

Exclusion of certain matters from operation of Act

37.—[1] (1) Save as otherwise expressly provided, nothing in this Act or (as respects paragraph (*a*) of this subsection) in the Children Act 1975 or the Adoption (Scotland) Act 1978 shall—

(*a*) apply to any title, coat of arms, honour or dignity transmissible on the death of the holder thereof or affect the succession thereto or the devolution thereof;

(*b*) [Repealed by the Law Reform (Miscellaneous Provisions) (Scotland) Act 1968, Sched. 3 (estate of any person dying after the commencement of that Act)];

(*c*) affect any right on the part of a surviving spouse to claim from the representatives of his or her deceased spouse payment of aliment out of the estate of that spouse;

[2] (*d*) affect the administration, winding up or distribution of or the making up of title to any part of the estate of any person who died before the commencement of this Act or the rights of succession to such an estate or any claim for legal rights or terce or courtesy or any rights arising under the Intestate Husband's Estate (Scotland) Acts 1911 to 1959, out of such an estate or the right to take any legal proceedings with respect to any such matters;

(*e*) affect any claim for legal rights arising out of an action of divorce commenced before the commencement of this Act;

and in relation to the matters aforesaid the law in force immediately before the commencement of this Act shall continue to have effect as if this Act had not passed.

(2) Nothing in this Act shall be construed as affecting the operation of any rule of law applicable immediately before the commencement of this Act to the choice of the system of law governing the administration, winding up or distribution of the estate, or any part of the estate, of any deceased person.

NOTES

[1] As amended by the Children Act 1975, Sched. 2, para. 5, and the Adoption Act 1978, Sched. 3, para. 5.

[2] Saved by the Law Reform (Miscellaneous Provisions) (Scotland) Act 1980, s. 6.

Citation, extent and commencement

38.—(1) This Act may be cited as the Succession (Scotland) Act 1964.

(2) This Act shall extend to Scotland only.

(3) This Act shall come into operation on the expiration of the period of three months beginning with the date on which it is passed.

SCHEDULES

Section 15

SCHEDULE 1

FORM OF DOCKET

I, AB, being by virtue of the within confirmation [*or certificate of confirmation*] the executor on the estate of the deceased CD so far as specified in the confirmation [*or certificate or inventory attached hereto*] hereby nominate EF [*designed*] as the person entitled—

(*a*) in [part] satisfaction of his claim to prior rights, as a surviving spouse, on the death of the deceased,
(*b*) in [part] satisfaction of his claim to legal rights on the death of the deceased,
(*c*) in [part] satisfaction of his share in the said estate,
(*d*) in [part] implement of a trust disposition and settlement, [*or will, or as the case may be*] of the deceased dated and registered in the Books of Council and Session ,

to the following item of estate, that it to say, [*short description*] being number of the items of the estate specified in the said confirmation [*or certificate or inventory*].

[*Signature of AB*]

[*To be attested by two witnesses*]

Section 34 SCHEDULE 2

MODIFICATION OF ENACTMENTS

General modifications

[1] 1. Subject to the specific modifications made by the following provisions of this Schedule, references in any enactment to the heir-at-law of a deceased person in relation to any heritable property shall be construed as references to the persons who by virtue of this Act are entitled to succeed to such property on intestacy.

NOTE
[1] As amended by the Law Reform (Miscellaneous Provisions) (Scotland) Act 1968, Sched. 3 (estate of any person dying after the commencement of that Act).

---

2. Subject as aforesaid references in general terms in any enactment to the heirs of a deceased person shall include—
(*a*) the persons entitled by virtue of this Act to succeed on intestacy to any part of the estate of the deceased; and
(*b*) so far as is necessary for the purposes of Part III of this Act, the executor of the deceased.

3. References in any enactment relating to the confirmation of executors or the administration of the moveable estates of deceased persons to the moveable or personal property or estate of a deceased person shall, except where the context otherwise requires, be construed as references to the whole estate of the deceased person.

4. References in any enactment (other than in this Act) to courtesy or terce shall be of no effect.

Specific modifications

See
Registration of Leases (Scotland) Act 1857, ss. 8, 9 and Scheds. (C), (F).
Titles to Land Consolidation (Scotland) Act 1868, s. 20.
Conveyancing (Scotland) Act 1924, ss. 32, 33.

Law Reform (Miscellaneous Provisions) (Scotland) Act 1968

(1968 c. 70)

An Act to amend the law of Scotland relating to succession to the property of deceased persons in cases of illegitimacy; to confer on illegitimate persons in Scotland the right to legitim out of their deceased parents' estates; to amend the law of Scotland with respect to the construction of certain provisions made by deed or otherwise; to extend the provisions of the Succession (Scotland) Act 1964 to tenancies of crofts; to amend the law of evidence in civil proceedings in Scotland; to re-enact, with amendments, the provisions of certain enactments relating to the duration of liferents in Scotland; to amend section 15 (1) of the Succession (Scotland) Act 1964; further to amend the law of Scotland relating to prorogation of the jurisdiction of the sheriff court; to remove a restriction on the extent of land in Scotland which a trade union may purchase or take upon lease and otherwise deal with; and for purposes connected with the matters aforesaid. [25th October 1968]

PART I

SUCCESSION, CONSTRUCTION OF DEEDS, ETC., IN CASES OF ILLEGITIMACY

Rights in estates of deceased persons in cases of illegitimacy

1–6. [Repealed by the Law Reform (Parent and Child) (Scotland) Act 1986, Sched. 2, with effect from December 8, 1986.]

Protection of trustees and executors

Protection of trustees and executors

[1] **7.** A trustee or an executor may distribute any property vested in him as such trustee or executor, or may make any payment out of any such property, without having ascertained—

(*a*) that no illegitimate person exists who is or may be entitled to an interest in that property or payment in consequence of any of the said provisions, and

(*b*) that no illegitimate person exists or has existed, the fact of whose existence is, in consequence of any of the said provisions, relevant to the ascertainment of the persons entitled to an interest in that property or payment, and (*c*) that no paternal relative of an illegitimate person exists who is or may be entitled to an interest in that property or payment,

and such trustee or executor shall not be personally liable to any person so entitled of whose claim he has not had notice at the time of the distribution or payment; but (without prejudice to section 17 of the Act of 1964) nothing in this section shall affect any right of any person so entitled to recover the property, or any property representing it, or the payment, from any person who may have received that property or payment.

NOTE

[1] As amended by the Law Reform (Parent and Child) (Scotland) Act 1986, Sched. 1, para. 10 and Sched. 2, with effect from December 8, 1986.

. . . . . .

Presumption of Death (Scotland) Act 1977

(1977 c. 27)

An Act to make fresh provision in the law of Scotland in relation to the presumed death of missing persons; and for connected purposes. [22nd July 1977]

Action of declarator

1.—(1) Where a person who is missing is thought to have died or has not been known to be alive for a period of at least seven years, any person having an interest may raise an action of declarator of the death of that person (hereafter in this Act referred to as the "missing person") in the Court of Session or the sheriff court in accordance with the provisions of this section.

(2) An action such as is mentioned in subsection (1) above is, in this Act, referred to as an "action of declarator".

(3) The Court of Session shall have jurisdiction to entertain an action of declarator if and only if—

(*a*) the missing person was domiciled in Scotland on the date on which he was last known to be alive or had been habitually resident there throughout the period of one year ending with that date; or

(*b*) the pursuer in the action—

(i) is the spouse of the missing person, and

(ii) is domiciled in Scotland at the date of raising the action or was habitually resident there throughout the period of one year ending with that date.

(4) The sheriff court shall have jurisdiction to entertain an action of declarator if and only if—

(*a*) the provisions of subsection (3) (*a*) above are satisfied and the missing person's last known place of residence in Scotland was in the sheriffdom; or

(*b*) the provisions of subsection (3) (*b*) above are satisfied and the pursuer was resident in the sheriffdom for a period of not less than forty days ending with the date of raising the action.

(5) Any person having an interest may, in an action of declarator, lodge a minute seeking the making by the court under section 2 of this Act of any determination or appointment not sought by the pursuer.

(6) At any stage of the proceedings the sheriff may, of his own accord or on the application of any party to the action, and shall, if so directed by the Court of Session (which direction may be given on the application of any party to the action), remit to the Court of Session an action of declarator raised in the sheriff court where he or, as the case may be, the Court of Session considers such remit desirable because of the importance or complexity of the matters at issue.

Decree in action of declarator and determination of incidental questions in other proceedings

2.—(1) In an action of declarator, the court, having heard proof and being satisfied on a balance of probabilities that the missing person—

(*a*) has died, shall grant decree accordingly and shall include in the decree a finding as to the date and time of death:

Provided that where it is uncertain when, within any period of time, the missing person died, the court shall find that he died at the end of that period;

(*b*) has not been known to be alive for a period of at least seven years, shall find that the missing person died at the end of the day occurring seven years after the date on which he was last known to be alive and shall grant decree accordingly.

(2) The court, in granting decree under subsection (1) above, shall have power to—

(*a*) determine the domicile of the missing person at the date of his death;

(*b*) determine any question relating to any interest in property which arises as a consequence of the death of the missing person;

(*c*) appoint a judicial factor on the estate of the missing person notwithstanding (in relation to such an appointment by the sheriff) what the value of the estate may be.

(3) Where, for the purpose of deciding any issue before it, a court or statutory tribunal has to determine any incidental question as to the death of a person, the court or tribunal may, if it thinks fit, determine that question (but for the purpose only of deciding that issue); and in the determination of that question the court or tribunal shall apply the criteria set out in subsection (1) above.

Effect of decree

3.—(1) Subject to the provisions of this section and sections 4 and 5 of this Act, where no appeal is made against decree in an action of declarator within the time allowed for appeal, or where an appeal against such a decree has been made and refused or withdrawn, the decree shall be conclusive of the matters contained in the decree and shall, without any special form of words, be effective against any person and for all purposes including the dissolution of a marriage to which the missing person is a party and the acquisition of rights to or in property belonging to any person.

(2) A decree under section 2 (1) (*b*) of this Act or a determination as mentioned in section 2 (3) of this Act shall not determine a substantive question which is properly referable to a foreign law otherwise than in accordance with that law.

(3) Where a marriage to which the missing person is a party has been dissolved by virtue of decree in an action of declarator, the dissolution of the marrige shall not be invalidated by the circumstance that the missing person was in fact alive at the date specified in the decree as the date of death.

(4) Where the missing person or any other person has committed any crime or offence, the responsibility of that person therefor shall not be affected by the circumstance that decree in an action of declarator has been granted if the missing person was in fact alive at the date specified in the decree as the date of death.

Recall or variation of decree

4.—(1) Decree in an action of declarator may, on application made at any time by any person having an interest, be varied or recalled by an order of the court which granted the decree or, in a case to which subsection (4) below applies, by an order of the Court of Session.

An order of the court pronounced under this subsection is hereafter in this Act referred to as a "variation order".

(2) By a variation order the court may make any determination or appointment referred to in section 2 of this Act.

(3) Any person having an interest may, in an application for a variation order, lodge a minute seeking the making by the court of any determination or appointment referred to in section 2 of this Act, which has not been sought by the person making the application for the variation order.

(4) At any stage of the proceedings the sheriff may, of his own accord or on the application of any party to the proceedings, and shall, if so directed by the Court of Session (which direction may be given on the application of any party to the proceedings), remit to the Court of Session an application made in the sheriff court for a variation order where he or, as the case may be, the Court of Session considers such remit desirable because of the importance or complexity of the matters at issue.

(5) Nothing in this section shall operate so as to revive a marriage of the missing person dissolved by virtue of decree in an action of declarator.

Effect on property rights of recall or variation of decree

5.—(1) Subject to the following provisions of this section, a variation order shall have no effect on rights to or in any property acquired as a result of a decree under section 2 of this Act.

(2) Notwithstanding the generality of subsection (1) above, where a decree under section 2 of this Act has been varied or recalled by a variation order, the court shall make such further order, if any, in relation to any rights to or in any property acquired as a result of that decree as it considers fair and reasonable in all the circumstances of the case; but no such further order shall affect any income accruing between the date of that decree and the date of the variation order.

(3) In considering what order shall be made under subsection (2) above, the court shall, so far as practicable in the circumstances, have regard to the following considerations, namely:—

(*a*) that, in the case of any property which is being or has been administered under a trust, any person who on account of the variation order would, apart from subsection (1) above, have been entitled to rights to or in any such property, or any person deriving right from him, shall be entitled to have made over to him by the trustee in full satisfaction of these rights only—

(i) the said rights to or in any such property or other property for the time being representing it which is still in the hands of the trustee at the date of the variation order, and

(ii) the value, as at the date of distribution, of the said rights to or in any such property which has been distributed;

(*b*) that any capital sum paid by an insurer as a result of the said decree (other than a capital sum which has been distributed by way of an annuity or other periodical payment) or any part of such sum should be repaid to the insurer if the facts in respect of which the variation order was pronounced justify such repayment.

(4) The court shall not make an order under subsection (2) above unless application for the variation order has been made to the court within the period of five years beginning with the date of the decree under section 2 of this Act.

(5) Where any person who had acquired rights to or in any property as a result of a decree under section 2 of this Act, or any person deriving right from him, enters into a transaction with another person whereby that other person acquires in good faith and for value any right to or in that property or any part of it, the transaction and any title acquired under it by that other person shall not be challengeable on the ground that an order under subsection (2) above has been made in relation to that property.

(6) A trustee shall be liable to any person having entitlement by virtue of an order under subsection (2) above for any loss suffered by that person on account of any breach of trust by the trustee in the administration or distribution of the whole or any part of the property, except in so far as the liability of the trustee may be restricted under any enactment or by any provision in any deed regulating the administration of the trust.

(7) Nothing in this section shall apply to estate duty or capital transfer tax which falls to be repaid as a result of a variation order having been pronounced.

Insurance against claims

6.—(1) Where decree has been granted under section 2 of this Act then, unless the court otherwise directs, the trustee, if any, shall as soon as may be effect a policy of insurance in respect of any claim which may arise by virtue of an order under section 5 (2) of this Act.

(2) Any premium payable by the trustee in respect of a policy of insurance effected under subsection (1) above shall be a proper charge on the estate being administered by the trustee.

(3) Where decree has been granted under section 2 of this Act, an insurer may, before making payment of any capital sum (other than in respect of an annuity or other periodical payment) to any person as a result of that decree, require that person to effect in his own name for the benefit of that insurer a policy of insurance to satisfy any claim which that insurer may establish in the event of a variation order being pronounced.

Value of certain rights may be declared irrecoverable

7. Where decree has been granted under section 2 of the Act, the court may—

(*a*) on the application of—

(i) any person whom the missing person would, at the time of the making of the said application (apart from the said decree), have had a duty (other than a contractual duty) to aliment, or

(ii) the trustee, and

(*b*) subject to such conditions, if any, as it thinks fit,

then or at any time thereafter, make an order directing that the value of any rights to or in any property acquired as a result of the said decree shall not be recoverable by virtue of an order under section 5 (2) of this Act.

Repayment of estate duty

8. Where estate duty or capital transfer tax falls to be repaid as a result of a variation order having been pronounced—

(*a*) the court which pronounced the variation order may order the duty or tax to be repaid to the person entitled to receive repayment;

(*b*) nothing in this Act shall affect the obligation of any person to whom the duty or tax is repaid to account for the amount of the duty or tax to any other person.

Disclosure of information

9.—(1) Any person (including the Secretary of State for Social Services) who possesses information relating to the survival or death of the missing person, and who is aware that an action of declarator has been raised or an application for a variation order has been made, shall have a duty to disclose that information—

(*a*) by means of written communication to the Principal Clerk of Session or, as the case may be, the appropriate sheriff clerk; or

(*b*) in such other manner as may be prescribed by act of sederunt.

(2) Nothing in this section shall impose any duty to disclose information where the person possessing the information would, if cited as a witness or haver, have been entitled to refuse to disclose such information under any rule of law or practice relating to the privilege of witnesses and havers, confidentiality of communications and withholding or non-disclosure of information on the grounds of public interest.

(3) A statement purporting to be an instrument made or issued by or on behalf of any Minister of the Crown and disclosing to the court facts relating to an action of declarator which has been raised or an application for a variation order which has been made in that court shall be sufficient evidence of those facts.

Decree of court furth of Scotland to be sufficient evidence

10. Where a court in any country furth of Scotland in which a person was domiciled or habitually resident on the date on which he was last known to be alive issues a decree or judgment declaring that that person has died or is presumed to have died, or has died or is presumed to have died on a specified date or within a specified period, that decree or judgment shall, in any proceedings in Scotland, be sufficient evidence of the facts so declared.

Appointment or confirmation of executor

11.—(1) Where, in proceedings for the appointment or confirmation of an executor of any person, a document to which subsection (2) below refers is produced, an oath or affirmation that to the best of the deponent's knowledge and belief that person is dead shall, for the purposes of those proceedings, be equivalent to an oath or affirmation that that person has died or died at any place or on any date appearing in such document as the place or date at or on which he died or was presumed to have died or was lost or missing.

(2) This subsection refers to the following documents, that is to say—

(*a*) a duly certified copy of a decree or judgment such as is referred to in section 10 of this Act;

(*b*) a certificate or intimation issued by or on behalf of a competent authority within the United Kingdom that the person—

(i) has died,

(ii) is presumed to have died, or

(iii) is lost or missing in circumstances affording reasonable ground for the belief that he has died as a result of an incident in or in connection with a ship, aircraft, hovercraft or off-shore installation.

(3) Notwithstanding any provision in or under any enactment, it shall not be necessary, in any petition for appointment as executor of any person in regard to whom a duly certified copy of such a decree or judgment as aforesaid or such a certificate or intimation as aforesaid is produced with the petition, to aver that the person died at any specified place or on any specified date, but it shall be sufficient to aver that the duly certified copy of the decree or judgment or (as the case may be) the certificate or intimation is produced and that to the best of the petitioner's knowledge and belief the person is dead.

Particulars of decree or variation order to be intimated to Registrar General

[1] **12.**—(1) Where a decree under section 2 of this Act or a variation order has been granted by any court, the clerk of court shall, where no appeal has been made against such decree or order, on the expiration of the time within which such an appeal may be made, or where an appeal has been made against such a decree or order, on the conclusion of any appellate proceedings, notify the prescribed particulars in connection with such decree or order to the Registrar General of Births, Deaths and Marriages for Scotland, who shall thereupon cause to be made such entry, if any, as appears to him to be appropriate, in a register kept for that purpose.

(2) In this section, "prescribed" means prescribed by regulations made under section 54 of the Registration of Births, Deaths and Marriages (Scotland) Act 1965.

NOTE
[1] See S.I. 1978 No. 160.

Defence to charge of bigamy

13. It shall be a defence against a charge of bigamy for the accused to prove that at no time within the period of seven years immediately preceding the date of the purported marriage forming the substance of the charge had he any reason to believe that his spouse was alive.

Report of proceedings

14. For the avoidance of doubt, it is hereby declared that section 1 (1) (*b*) of the Judicial Proceedings (Regulation of Reports) Act 1926 does not apply to an action of declarator.

Rules of procedure

[1] **15.**—(1) Without prejudice to the generality of the powers conferred on the Court of Session by section 16 of the Administration of Justice (Scotland) Act 1933 and section 32 of the Sheriff Courts (Scotland) Act 1971 to regulate procedure by act of sederunt, the said powers shall include power to make rules of procedure for the purpose of giving effect to the provisions of this Act.

(2) Such rules of procedure shall include provisions—

(*a*) specifying the persons (including the Lord Advocate) upon or to whom service or intimation of the summons or initial writ in an action of declarator or of an application for a variation order is to be made; and

(*b*) relating to the advertisement of the raising of the said action or the making of the said application.

NOTE
[1] See S.I. 1978 Nos. 161 and 162.

Entailed estates

16.—(1) The following provisions of this section shall apply where decree has been granted under section 2 of this Act declaring the death of the missing person who is the heir in possession of an entailed estate.

(2) In the circumstances set out in subsection (1) above, the next heir may apply to the court for authority to disentail the estate and the court may make it a condition of granting such authority that the next heir gives security of such amount and in such manner as the court may direct to meet any contingent interest of the heir if he shall reappear and, within the period of five years beginning with the date of the said decree, application for the relative variation order shall be made.

(3) Where, in the circumstances set out in subsection (1) above—

(*a*) the estate has not been disentailed,

(*b*) the absent heir reappears,

(*c*) application for the relative variation order is made within the period of five years beginning with the date of the said decree, and

(*d*) the relative variation order is pronounced,

then, notwithstanding section 5 of this Act, the absent heir who reappears shall be entitled to resume possesssion of the estate but shall not be entitled to recover the fruits or income of the estate from any following heir in respect of the period of that heir's possession.

(4) In this section, "the court" means the Court of Session.

Interpretation

17. In this Act, unless the context otherwise requires,

"action of declarator" has the meaning assigned to it by section 1 of this Act;

"any person having an interest" includes the Lord Advocate for the public interest;

"the court" means the Court of Session or the sheriff;

"insurer" includes a society registered under the Acts relating to friendly and industrial and provident societies and any person or body which provides for the payment of benefits on the death of another person;

"missing person" has the meaning assigned to it by section 1 (1) of this Act;

"statutory tribunal" means a tribunal established by or under any enactment;

"trust" means—

(*a*) any trust or executry for the administration of property which comes into operation as a result of a decree under section 2 of this Act, or

(*b*) any trust under which property devolves upon or is transmitted to any person by reason of the death of the missing person;

and "trustee" means the trustee, executor, judicial factor or other person administering any such property;

"variation order" has the meaning assigned to it by section 4 (1) of this Act.

Amendment of other enactments

18. The enactments specified in Schedule 1 to this Act shall have effect subject to the amendments specified in that Schedule.

Repeals

19. The enactments specified in Schedule 2 to this Act are hereby repealed to the extent specified in column 3 of that Schedule.

Short title, commencement and extent

20.—(1) This Act may be cited as the Presumption of Death (Scotland) Act 1977.

[1] (2) This Act, except this section, shall come into force on such date as the Lord Advocate may by order made by statutory instrument appoint.

(3) This Act shall extend to Scotland only.

NOTE
[1] The Act came into force on March 1, 1978: see S.I. 1978 No. 159.

. . . .

Forfeiture Act 1982

(1982 c. 34)

An Act to provide for relief for persons guilty of unlawful killing from forfeiture of inheritance and other rights; to enable such persons to apply for financial provision out of the deceased's estate; . . . and for connected purposes. [13th July 1982]

The "forfeiture rule"

1.—(1) In this Act, the "forfeiture rule" means the rule of public policy which in certain circumstances precludes a person who has unlawfully killed another from acquiring a benefit in consequence of the killing.

(2) References in this Act to a person who has unlawfully killed another include a reference to a person who has unlawfully aided, abetted, counselled or procured the death of that other and references in this Act to unlawful killing shall be interpreted accordingly.

Power to modify the rule

2.—(1) Where a court determines that the forfeiture rule has precluded a person (in this section referred to as "the offender") who has unlawfully killed another from acquiring any interest in property mentioned in subsection (4) below, the court may make an order under this section modifying the effect of that rule.

(2) The court shall not make an order under this section modifying the effect of the forfeiture rule in any case unless it is satisfied that, having regard to the conduct of the offender and of the deceased and to such other circumstances as appear to the court to be material, the justice of the case requires the effect of the rule to be so modified in that case.

(3) In any case where a person stands convicted of an offence of which unlawful killing is an element, the court shall not make an order under this section modifying the effect of the forfeiture rule in that case unless proceedings for the purpose are brought before the expiry of the period of three months beginning with his conviction.

(4) The interests in property referred to in subsection (1) above are—

(*a*) any beneficial interest in property which (apart from the forfeiture rule) the offender would have acquired—

(i) under the deceased's will (including, as respects Scotland, any writing having testamentary effect) or the law relating to intestacy or by way of *jus relicti*, *jus relictae* or legitim;

(ii) on the nomination of the deceased in accordance with the provisions of any enactment;

(iii) as a *donatio mortis causa* made by the deceased,; or

(iv) under a special destination (whether relating to heritable or moveable property); or

(*b*) any beneficial interest in property which (apart from the forfeiture rule) the offender would have acquired in consequence of the death of the deceased, being property which, before the death, was held on trust for any person.

(5) An order under this section may modify the effect of the forfeiture rule in respect of any interest in property to which the determination referred to in subsection (1) above relates and may do so in either or both of the following ways, that is—

(*a*) where there is more than one such interest, by excluding the application of the rule in respect of any (but not all) of those interests; and

(*b*) in the case of any such interest in property, by excluding the application of the rule in respect of part of the property.

(6) On the making of an order under this section, the forfeiture rule shall have effect for all purposes (including purposes relating to anything done before the order is made) subject to the modifications made by the order.

(7) The court shall not make an order under this section modifying the effect of the forfeiture rule in respect of any interest in property which, in consequence of the rule, has been acquired before the coming into force of this section by a person other than the offender or a person claiming through him.

(8) In this section—

"property" includes any chose in action or incorporeal moveable property; and

"will" includes codicil.

Application for financial provision not affected by the rule

3.—(1) The forfeiture rule shall not be taken to preclude any person from making any application under a provision mentioned in subsection (2) below or the making of any order on the application.

(2) The provisions referred to in subsection (1) above are—

(*a*) any provision of the Inheritance (Provision for Family and Dependants) Act 1975; and

(*b*) sections 31 (6) (variation etc. of periodical payments orders) and 36 (1) (variation of maintenance agreements) of the Matrimonial Causes Act 1973 and section 5 (4) of the Divorce (Scotland) Act 1976 (variation etc. of periodical allowances).

. . . . . .

Exclusion of murderers

[1] **5.** Nothing in this Act or in any order made under section 2 or referred to in section 3 (1) of this Act or in any decision made under section 4 (1A) of this Act shall affect the application of the forfeiture rule in the case of a person who stands convicted of murder.

NOTE
[1] As amended by the Social Security Act 1986, s. 76 (4).

. . . .

Short title, etc.

7.—(1) This Act may be cited as the Forfeiture Act 1982.

(2) Section 4 of this Act shall come into force on such day as the Secretary of State may appoint by order made by statutory instrument; and sections 1 to 3 and 5 of this Act shall come into force on the expiry of the period of three months beginning with the day on which it is passed.

(3) This Act, except section 6, does not extend to Northern Ireland.

(4) Subject to section 2 (7) of this Act, an order under section 2 of this Act or an order referred to in section 3 (1) of this Act and made in respect of a person who has unlawfully killed another may be made whether the unlawful killing occurred before or after the coming into force of those sections.

INDEX